AMERICAN INDIAN LITERATURE

American Indian Literature
An Anthology

Revised Edition
Edited and with an Introduction by
Alan R. Velie

UNIVERSITY OF OKLAHOMA PRESS
Norman and London

To my father

I would like to thank all those who helped me with this edition, especially Geary Hobson, Maureen Bannon, and Jeannie Rhodes.

Oscar Howe's *Victory Dance* is reproduced on the front cover with the permission of The Philbrook Museum of Art, Tulsa, Oklahoma.

Library of Congress Cataloging-in-Publication Data

American Indian Literature : an anthology / edited and with an introduction by Alan R. Velie. — Rev. ed.
    p.   cm.
    Includes bibliographical references.
    1. Indian literature—United States—Translations into English. 2. English literature—Translations from Indian languages. 3. American literature—Indian authors. I. Velie, Alan R., 1937– .
PM197.E1A4   1991
    897—dc20   90-50700
    ISBN: 0-8061-2331-1 (cloth)
    ISBN: 0-8061-2345-1 (paper)

The paper in this book meets the guidelines for permanence and durability of the Committee on Production Guidelines for Book Longevity of the Council on Library Resources, Inc.

3 4 5 6 7 8 9 10 11 12 13 14 15 16 17 18 19 20 21

CONTENTS

Oratory

Memoirs

Poetry

Fiction

AMERICAN INDIAN LITERATURE

INTRODUCTION

THIS IS AN ANTHOLOGY of Indian literature—that is, literature by Indians on Indian subjects. It does not include writings about Indians like Cooper's *Leatherstocking Tales* or Oliver La Farge's *Laughing Boy*, or selections from books like *Gorky Park*, a novel about Russia by mixed-blood author Martin Cruz Smith.

The collection contains two types of literature: traditional and mainstream. Traditional literature, which includes tales, songs, and oratory, has been composed on this continent for thousands of years. Originally it was composed in tribal languages for a tribal audience. Today the traditional genres remain, but most of the works are composed in English.

Mainstream literature refers to works by Indians written in English in one of the standard American genres—fiction, poetry, biography, history.

Before I say much about Indian literature, I think it is necessary to say a few things about Indians. First, the name: although college departments often prefer the term "Native American," most Indians use "Indian." Second, despite periodic movements urging pan-Indianism, most Indians today identify themselves primarily as members of a particular tribe. Perhaps an apt comparison is with Europeans, who identify themselves first as Portuguese, German, Dutch, or whatever, and only secondarily as Europeans. Similar differences in language, culture, and even physical characteristics, exist among Indians. When Columbus first came to America there were more than two thousand independent tribes, of which more than three hundred survive. They spoke five hundred or more languages from fifty language groups, some of which were as different as English and Chinese.

Physically, the Kiowas and the Osages tend to be large people. Many of the men stand over six feet and weigh more than 250 pounds. On the other hand, the Navajos and Zunis are small; their men often are shorter than five feet six inches, and weigh less than 130.

Culturally, there were—and still are—important differences among Indians. The Cherokees and the Choctaws, for example, two of what were called in Oklahoma the "Five Civilized Tribes," were agricultural peoples with permanent settlements who had developed advanced civilizations in the Southeast. In fact, they were every bit as culturally sophisticated as the white colonists they encountered in the seventeenth and eighteenth centuries, with whom they often intermarried. The Cherokees and the Choctaws had slaves, and fought on the side of the South in the Civil War. In fact, the commanding general of the Arkansas militia was a Cherokee, Stand Watie. Despite the terrible suffering they underwent during their forced removal from the Southeast, the Cherokees and the other Civilized Tribes were able to establish roots in Oklahoma and become integrated into the life of the state.

The Kiowas and Comanches, on the other hand, were nomadic hunters of the prairies who fought the whites until the end of the nineteenth century. The Plains tribes were the losers in the "winning of the West." When defeated, they were forced to take up agriculture, an alien way of life; and until recently they were less able than other so-called Civilized Tribes to adjust to white society.

In short, American Indians include diverse groups of peoples living in very different circumstances: some live among whites in towns and suburbs, some live in urban ghettos, and some live with their tribes on reservations. And the reservations vary immensely too, from the beautiful, lush Flathead Reservation in Montana, to the barren desert reservations of the tribes in southeast California.

Because most tribes were not advanced technologically at the time of their initial contacts with whites, many people today still think of Indians as "primitive." To equate civilizations with technology is a dubious practice, particularly since many of our ideas about what primitive means are questionable. The caveman is our primary symbol of the primitive, and we generally portray cavedwellers as being without morals: in our archetypal depiction, the caveman hits the cavewoman on the head and hauls her back to his lair for sex. In fact, supposedly primitive people often have stronger moral codes than technologically advanced people. Traditionally, Indians had strong laws governing marriage, and premarital or extramarital sex was forbidden. Casual sex is far more common in the singles bars of Los Angeles or Copenhagen than it was on the aboriginal prairies.

Before we consider Indians uncivilized, we might do well to compare their traditional cultures with ours. America has been able to put men on the moon and build hundred-story buildings, but at the foot of those buildings homeless people sleep on subway grates. New York, one of the greatest and most civilized cities in the world, has the wretched slums and hordes of beggars one used to associate with Calcutta. As for the rest of the country, if the turmoil of the sixties is over, the generation gap has closed, and Jimmy Carter's famous malaise has lifted somewhat, America is still a troubled land whose people have become inured to organized crime, a flourishing pornography industry, a serious drug problem, constant political scandals, and the shenanigans of corrupt televangelists.

In contrast, before they encountered the whites, Indian cultures were generally stable, spiritually oriented, and harmonious. They generally endowed tribal members with a sense of worth. There was a great deal of fighting among tribes, but little within them. By and large, Indians had no juvenile delinquency or chemical dependency, and little crime.

Although most tribes were not technologically advanced, they often had a highly sophisticated world view. Hartley Burr Alexander's description of the Oglala Sioux is a good analysis of a supposedly primitive people:

> Every group of human beings has evolved in its life and thought some chart of a world order or mode which is capable of being represented as a philosophy, but in most cases such philosophies represent mainly the bent of mind of a people, to be deduced from the study of ideas not deliberately organized but representing an habitual manner of thought more or less adventiously evolved in tradition. In the case of the Oglala, however, as of other tribes with related ideas, the systemic character of the thinking can hardly be accounted for in this manner; it represents such plan and system as only long deliberation and studied reflection, thoroughly conscious and designed, can explain: it is, in brief, philosophic thought.[1]

However, if it is a mistake to underestimate traditional Indian cultures, it is equally foolish to romanticize them. Most Indian societies were heavily conformist, warlike, chauvinistic, and sexist. Some progressives like to use Indian culture as a stick to beat white America; they portray Indians as sylvan pacifists who longed only to live in peace and harmony with everything and everybody until white invaders despoiled their Eden. Not only is this an inaccurate version of mainstream American history, it is false according to the Indians' own recollections and conceptions of themselves. Vine Deloria writes that

> The Sioux, my own people, have a great tradition of conflict. We were the only nation ever to annihilate the United States Cavalry three times in succession. And when we find no one else to quarrel with, we often fight each other. . . . During one twenty-year period in the last century the Sioux fought over an area from La Crosse, Wisconsin, to Sheridan, Wyoming, against the Crow, Arapaho, Cheyenne,

---

[1] Hartley Burr Alexander, *The World's Rim* (Lincoln: University of Nebraska Press, 1967), p. 164.

Mandan, Arikara, Hidatsa, Ponca, Iowa, Pawnee, Otoe, Omaha, Winnebago, Chippewa, Cree, Assiniboine, Sac and Fox, Potowatomi, Ute, and Gros Ventre.[2]

Even in our time the Indians have kept their military traditions alive. Long after most whites had soured on the Viet Nam War, Indians held parades for returning veterans and inducted them into traditional warrior societies such as the Cheyenne Dog Soldiers.

Misunderstanding and exploitation of Indians is not limited to the bigots in America who dismiss Indians as paupers and alcoholics. As if that were not bad enough, many who profess to be friends of Indians insist on describing them as "people with a plight," ignoring their successes and focussing solely on their problems. Courses in Indian history are remiss if they do not mention massacres carried out by the United States Cavalry and various other atrocities perpetrated on Indians by whites, but it is not fair to the Indians to depict them solely as victims and losers. Not only to foster Indian pride, but also for the sake of historical accuracy, scholars need to stress positive examples and achievements.

Even in Oklahoma, where people are proud to claim Indian ancestry, too many accentuate the negative. Virtually any Oklahoman knows that the Trail of Tears was the forced march from the East on which thousands of Cherokees died, but even native Tulsans are surprised to learn that their city was founded by the Creeks, many of whom became successful oilmen, ranchers, and merchants. It is a curious phenomenon that however prominent a black person becomes he or she is always black, but when Indians become successful, somehow they lose their ethnicity. Almost all Americans have heard of Will Rogers; how many of them know he was Cherokee?

Too much has been made of the "Vanishing American." Indians are alive and well, and many are proud, successful people. Many tribes run large-scale businesses, ranging from catfish farms to ski resorts. Many Americans, recalling the old nursery rhyme about "doctor, lawyer, and Indian chief," assume that Indians only serve in the last of those professions: in fact, Indians are today—and have been for years—in many walks of life, as corporate litigators and endocrinologists as well as tribal politicians. And, of course, Indians are writers, producing some of the best literature written today.

With this background in mind, let us look at Indian literature. Traditional literature was—and still is—primarily oral. Whites have translated and

---

[2]Vine Deloria, Jr., *Custer Died for Your Sins: An Indian Manifesto* (New York, 1969), p. 29.

transcribed songs and tales to transmit them to a broad reading audience, but these works have always been intended to be experienced aurally in the presence of the storyteller or singer. Before contact with whites, Indians did not use writing, and so many Americans assume that either they had no real literature, or that it was not much good. That literature does not need to be written to be great is proved by the *Iliad* and the *Odyssey*, not to mention the Winnebago trickster cycle, the Delaware *Walam Olum*, and many other traditional works.

One characteristic of traditional Indian literature that sets it apart from mainstream American literature—including that written by Indians—is that it was an organic part of everyday life, not something to be enjoyed by an intellectual elite. Saul Bellow, John Updike, and other contemporary novelists are read by only a fraction of the American public, and serious poets like Richard Wilbur and James Merrill by an even smaller fraction. Traditionally, all members of an Indian tribe listened to tales and composed and sang songs. Americans have some universal art forms, of course—television programs, for example—but most people consider them subliterary, if entertaining. Traditionally, Indians did not make a distinction between highbrow and lowbrow art; all their works could have been considered popular culture in the sense that they were intended for the whole tribe.

Furthermore, traditional Indian literature was more functional than ours. Myths and tales were educational tools that taught the young tribal beliefs and values. Songs were sung to cure illnesses, raise morale before battle, increase the fertility of the fields, or win over a recalcitrant lover. For us literature, however highbrow, is almost always purely entertainment—cerebral entertainment perhaps, but entertainment nonetheless. We define art as that which appeals primarily to our aesthetic sense, meaning that it stirs our sense of beauty but has no practical purpose.

The mainstream tradition of American Indian literature consists of works that Indians educated by and with whites produced in standard American genres—novels, short stories, biographies, histories, poems. This tradition extends back at least to Samson Occom, a Mohegan schoolmaster, who wrote a biographical memoir in 1768. The memoir was not published until much later; the first published work by an Indian was Occom's "A Sermon Preached at the Funeral of Moses Paul, American Indian," which appeared in 1772.

Yellow Bird, or John Rollin Ridge, a Cherokee, was the first Indian novelist. His fictional biography of the Hispanic folk hero Joaquín Murieta established the bandit as the Robin Hood of California. Ridge also wrote poetry, most of it highly sentimental. The first Indian novel about Indians is Simon Pokagon's *Queen of the Woods*, which appeared in 1899. Pokagon's highly autobiographical work depicts the destruction of the pastoral life of the Potowatomis by the whites.

In the early years of the twentieth century Charles Eastman, a Sioux, achieved some renown for his autobiography and versions of tribal tales, and Alexander Posey, a Creek, was recognized for political satire and poetry. Will Rogers's humorous books and columns were popular, but although Rogers often spoke of his Cherokee heritage, Americans thought of him as a cowboy rather than an Indian. Essentially, until the 1960s the American reading public was largely unaware of works by Indians in mainstream genres. To some extent the neglect was justified because, with the possible exception of the novels of Flathead writer D'Arcy McNickle (*The Surrounded*, 1936; *Runner in the Sun*, 1954; and *Wind from an Enemy Sky*, 1978), most of the work was pretty pedestrian.[3]

The situation changed dramatically with the publication of Kiowa novelist N. Scott Momaday's *House Made of Dawn* in 1968. When the novel received the Pulitzer Prize in 1969, what is now called the Renaissance in American Indian literature was underway. Momaday's first book is the story of a veteran's disappointing return to the reservation after fighting in World War II.

Momaday published a memoir, *The Way to Rainy Mountain*, in 1969, adapting some of the material he had used in *House Made of Dawn*. An excerpt from that work is included in this anthology, along with a selection of Momaday's poems.

After Momaday, the next Indian writer to come to prominence was James Welch, a Blackfeet–Gros Ventre from Montana. Welch's novels (*Winter in the Blood*, 1974; *The Death of Jim Loney*, 1979; and *Fools Crow*, 1986) do for the Milk River valley and Montana what Faulkner did for Jefferson County and Mississippi—describe the landscape, people, and myths of an area of the country unknown to most Americans, but vital to our history.

The eighties saw the emergence of Gerald Vizenor, Leslie Silko, and Louise Erdrich as major literary figures, successful as both novelists and poets. One interesting difference between Indian writers and their white counterparts is that while few whites are known for both poetry and fiction, most of the successful Indian novelists have published a volume of poetry.

This anthology includes both traditional and mainstream works. From

---

[3] For a detailed discussion of early Indian writers, see La Vonne Brown Ruoff, "Old Traditions and New Forms," in Paula Gunn Allen, ed., *Studies in American Indian Literature: Critical Essays and Course Designs* (New York: Modern Language Association, 1983).

the traditional genres there is a selection of tales, including the Winnebago trickster cycle, a selection of songs, and an epic, the Delaware *Walam Olum*. Mainstream works include fiction by Momaday, Welch, Vizenor, Erdrich, and LeAnne Howe, and poetry by Momaday, Welch, Erdrich, Simon Ortiz, Maurice Kenny, and many younger poets who are just emerging into prominence.

The principle I have used in selecting works from both traditions is literary quality. All selections in this anthology are to be judged as serious literature. They are not presented as quaint relics of a forgotten people or as ethnic curiosities. I urge readers to judge them as they would any other literature, not just for political or sociological relevance. Stereotypes of the mute and stoic Indian are distortions. Indians have always been highly verbal people, and their literature reflects it. It was the first American literature, and much of it ranks with the best any Americans have produced.

TALES

Different Indian tribes had different literary tastes. Alanson Skinner, an early collector of Indian stories, observed that the Sioux preferred war tales; the Ojibways, stories about sex; and the Menominis, tales of the supernatural.[1] Nevertheless, the same tales or variants cropped up among many tribes, and many tribes had similar customs and taboos governing storytelling. In fact, though some stories and rules for telling them seem to be unique to the American Indians, many others are common to peoples around the world. Stories told around campfires in North America were often told in different versions in places as far away as Iceland and Turkey, and American Indian customs of narration also have European and Asian counterparts.

The Indians told their sacred stories—that is, origin myths and tales of culture heroes—on winter nights only. The Kiowas had a fund of stories about a trickster culture hero called Saynday who decreed, "Always tell my stories in the winter, when the outdoors work is finished / Always tell my stories at night, when the day's work is finished." If the teller violated these instructions, Saynday, it was said, would cut off the offender's nose. The Cheyennes were warned that if they told their sacred stories in the daytime the narrators would become hunchbacked. Arapaho grandmothers told "winter stories" or "night stories" about their trickster Spider around tipi fires on winter evenings; at the first sign of spring, when little bugs swam in the puddles after a rain, the storytelling period was over for the year. The Winnebagos told trickster stories only when the snakes were underground.

Indians were not, of course, the only people to tell stories on winter nights. In the old days virtually all folk, that is, the working classes of all

[1] Alanson Skinner, *Folklore of the Menomini Indians*, Anthropological Papers of the American Museum of Natural History, vol. 13, part 3 (New York: American Museum of Natural History, 1915), p. 223.

11

societies, told tales when the day's work was done. In the winter darkness came early, the day's work was done early, there were hours until bedtime, and the weather was too foul for the young to be out courting. So people sitting indoors around a fire with time on their hands would naturally tell tales. In Elizabethan England highly imaginative tales were often called "winter's tales" (hence the name of Shakespeare's dramatic romance). Among the Elizabethans as well as the Arapahos, grandmothers were the favored tellers, as the expression "old wives' tale" attests. Lady Macbeth refers to Macbeth's story of Banquo's ghost as "A woman's story at a winter's fire, / Authoriz'd by her grandam."

One of the most interesting facts about Indian storytelling is that stories were considered private property in many tribes and were owned by a particular person or family. For instance, when Paul Radin went to record the Winnebago trickster cycle, he approached Sam Blowsnake, one of his principal informants, who knew the myth. Blowsnake would not tell it to Radin. Instead, Blowsnake went to a man authorized to tell the story, made the requisite payment, and recorded the story as the man told it.

In many tribes, though by no means all, storytelling was confined to a small number of gifted individuals. Although sacred stories were supposedly always told exactly the same way, the tellers in fact took certain liberties in accordance with their particular interests. What always remained the same was the fundamental plot, themes, and characters. Indeed, these orally transmitted tales are related to drama as well as to narrative fiction. The narrator was an actor who took the part of the characters, mimicking their voices, and his performance played an important part in the hearer's impression of the tale. Just as Hamlet is a far different play with Sir Laurence Olivier in the title role from what it is with Richard Chamberlain, so Indian tales varied from one teller to another. Because they do have a strong element of drama, the transcription on the page is a pale shadow of the story as told at the campfire. If some of the tales seem lifeless at first, imagine the difference between seeing a movie or television show and reading the script. This is not a totally fair comparison, because the tales have a strong narrative element, but it is a valuable corrective to a false impression of simplicity or dullness.

Indian stories fall into several distinct types. Although different tribes made different distinctions, certain patterns emerge throughout. The main distinction is between sacred stories that were of special importance to the tribe and what might be called secular stories, which were treated less seriously. The latter are chiefly anecdotal—stories with a catch to them or embellished accounts of recent events. For instance, the Winnebagos produced two kinds of stories: the waikan and the worak. The waikan, *"what is sacred," deal with an age long passed in which animals talked and spirits were commonly encountered on earth. The* worak, *or "what is recounted," deal with the contemporary world. The* waikan *treat divine or semidivine figures, such as the trickster, and end happily. They could be told only in the winter. The* worak *deal with humans, end tragically, and could be told at any time.[2] The Arapahos differentiated between the* haetaedau, *or "ancient story," which dealt with legendary characters such as the trickster Spider, and the* haucitau, *a story based on recent events. Jokes or catch stories were called* baebaeyat. *Other tribes were basically the same; although they made different distinctions, the most important were between the sacred tales of a bygone age and secular tales based on incidents occurring in daily life.*

---

[2] Paul Radin, *The Trickster* (New York: Philosophical Library, 1969), p. 118.

THE ORIGIN MYTH OF ACOMA

Myths of origin are common to all peoples. They attempt to answer the most nagging human questions: Where did we come from? Where did evil come from, and what caused it? And they answer lesser questions, such as how the elephant got its trunk, why the coyote slinks, and why man's penis is so short.

Indian origin myths differ substantially one from another, but most share certain characteristics. One universal feature is that a god (or gods) and spirits precede humans on earth. It should be noted here that most Indians were monotheistic in the sense that Christians and Jews are—that is, they believed in a single, all-powerful, uncreated God. The minor deities and spirits that appear in their legends are roughly analogous to the angels of the Old Testament: they are superhuman, immortal beings created by and subordinate to God.[1]

Another common feature of the Indian origin myths is that the universe comprises several worlds, often arranged in vertically stacked layers. What exists on this earth is a poor copy of things existing in a better world above this one—a notion similar to Plato's cosmology. Finally, most myths take place in a bygone age in which animals talked and gods and culture heroes walked the earth.

The Acomas are a Pueblo tribe of Keresan linguistic stock. The village of Acoma, in western New Mexico, is purportedly the oldest inhabited settlement in the United States. The Acoma myth has several interesting features. For instance, the first human beings were two sisters, Nautsiti and Iatiku. The tutelary deity, Tsichtinako, is also female. All Keresan Pueblo myths begin with the birth of the two sisters, although in most other Indian origin myths, as in the mythologies of most other peoples, the first human being is male. Another interesting feature is the impregnation of Nautsiti, which seems to combine elements of virgin birth and original sin. Tempted by an evil spirit in the shape of a serpent, Nautsiti lies on her back and "receives" rain, which makes her pregnant. This incident is treated as sin in the Acoma account—the original sin, in fact—but it seems reminiscent not only of Jove's taking Danae in a shower of gold but also of Luke's account of the impregnation of Mary: "The Holy Ghost shall come upon thee, and the power of the Highest shall overshadow thee."

[1] Peter Farb, *Man's Rise to Civilization* (New York: Avon Books, 1969), p. 140.

"The Origin Myth of Acoma" is reprinted from Matthew W. Stirling, *Origin Myth of Acoma and Other Records*, Bureau of American Ethnology Bulletin 135 (Washington, D.C.: U.S. Government Printing Office, 1942).

Matthew W. Stirling obtained the myth in 1928 from a group of Acomas visiting Washington.

In the beginning two female human beings were born. These two children were born underground at a place called *Shipapu*. As they grew up, they began to be aware of each other. There was no light and they could only feel each other. Being in the dark they grew slowly.

After they had grown considerably, a Spirit whom they afterward called *Tsichtinako* spoke to them, and they found that it would give them nourishment. After they had grown large enough to think for themselves, they spoke to the Spirit when it had come to them one day and asked it to make itself known to them and to say whether it was male or female, but it replied only that it was not allowed to meet with them. They then asked why they were living in the dark without knowing each other by name, but the Spirit answered that they were *nuk'timi* (under the earth); but they were to be patient in waiting until everything was ready for them to go up into the light. So they waited a long time, and as they grew they learned their language from Tsichtinako.

When all was ready, they found a present from Tsichtinako, two baskets of seeds and little images of all the different animals [there were to be] in the world. The Spirit said they were sent by their father. They asked who was meant by their father, and Tsichtinako replied that his name was *Ŭch'tsiti*, and that he wished them to take their baskets out into the light, when the time came. Tsichtinako instructed them, "You will find the seeds of four kinds of pine trees, *lă'khok*, *gēi'etsu* . . . , *wanūka*, and *lă'nye* in your baskets. You are to plant these seeds and will use the trees to get up into the light." They could not see the things in their baskets but feeling each object in turn they asked, "Is this it?," until the seeds were found. They then planted the seeds as Tsichtinako instructed. All of the four seeds sprouted, but in the darkness the trees grew very slowly, and the two sisters became very anxious to reach the light as they waited this long time. They slept for many years as they had no use for eyes. Each time they awoke they would feel the trees to see how they were growing. The tree *lanye* grew faster than the others and after a very long time pushed a hole through the earth for them and let in a very little light. The others stopped growing, at various heights, when this happened.

The hole that the tree *lanye* made was not large enough for them to pass through, so Tsichtinako advised them to look again in their baskets where they would find the image of an animal called *dyu-p* (badger) and tell it to become alive. They told it to live, and it did so as they spoke, exclaiming, "*A'uha!* Why have you given me life?" They told it not to be afraid nor to worry about coming to life. "We have brought you to life because you are to be useful." Tsichtinako spoke to them again, instructing them to tell Badger to climb the pine tree, to bore a hole large enough for them to crawl up, cautioning him not to go out into the light, but to return when the hole was finished. Badger climbed the tree and, after he had dug a hole large enough, returned saying that he had done his work. They thanked him and said, "As a reward you will come up with us to the light and thereafter you will live happily. You will always know how to dig and your home will be in the ground where you will be neither too hot nor too cold."

Tsichtinako now spoke again, telling them to look in the basket for *Tāwāi'nū* (Locust), giving it life and asking it to smooth the hole by plastering. It, too, was to be cautioned to return. This they did and Locust smoothed the hole but, having finished, went out into the light. When it returned reporting that it had done its work, they asked it if it had gone out. Locust said no, and every time he was asked he replied no, until the fourth time when he admitted that he had gone out. They asked Locust what it was like outside. Locust replied that it was just *tsī'ītī* (laid out flat). They said, "From now on you will be known as *Tsi-k'ă*. You will also come up with us, but you will be punished for disobedience by being allowed out only a short time. Your home will be in the ground and you will have to return when the weather is bad. You will soon die but you will be reborn each season."

The hole now let light into the place where the two sisters were, and Tsichtinako spoke to them, "Now is the time you are to go out. You are able to take your baskets with you. In them you will find pollen and sacred corn meal. When you reach the top, you will wait for the sun to come up and that direction will be called *ha'nami* (east). With the pollen and the sacred corn meal you will pray to the Sun. You will thank the Sun for bringing you to light, ask for a long life and happiness, and for success in the purpose for which you were created." Tsichtinako then taught them the prayers and the creation song, which they were to sing. This took a long while, but finally the sisters, followed by Badger and Locust, went out into the light, climbing the pine tree. Badger was very strong and skillful and helped them. On reaching the earth, they set down their baskets and saw for the first time what they had. The earth was soft and spongy under their feet as they walked, and they said, "This is not ripe." They stood waiting for the sun, not knowing where it would appear. Gradually it grew lighter and finally the sun came up. Before they began to pray, Tsichtinako told them they were facing east and that their right side, the side their best aim was on, would be known as *kū'ă'mē* (south) and the left *ti dyami* (north) while behind at their backs was the direction *pūna'me* (west) where the sun would go down. They had already learned while underground the direction *nŭk'ŭm'* (down) and later, when they asked where their father was, they were told *tyunami* (four skies above).

And as they waited to pray to the Sun, the girl on the right moved her best hand and was named *Iatiku,* which meant "bringing to life." Tsichtinako then told her to name her sister, but it took a long time. Finally Tsichtinako noticed that the other had more in her basket, so Tsichtinako told Iatiku to name her thus, and Iatiku called her *Nautsiti* which meant "more of everything in the basket."

They now prayed to the Sun as they had been taught by Tsichtinako, and sang the creation song. Their eyes hurt for they were not accustomed to the strong light. For the first time they asked Tsichtinako why they were on earth and why they were created. Tsichtinako replied, "I did not make you. Your father, Uchtsiti, made you, and it is he who has made the world, the sun which you have seen, the sky, and many other things which you will see. But Uchtsiti says the world is not yet completed, not yet satisfactory, as he wants it. This is the reason he has made you. You will rule and bring to life the rest of the things he has given you in the baskets." The sisters then asked how they themselves had come into being. Tsichtinako answered saying, "Uchtsiti first made the world. He threw a clot of his own blood into space and by his power it grew and grew until it became the earth. Then Uchtsiti planted you in this and by it you were nourished as you developed. Now that you have emerged from within the earth, you will have to provide nourishment for yourselves. I will instruct you in this." They then asked where their father lived and Tsichtinako replied, "You will never see your father, he lives four skies above, and has made you to live in this world. He has made you in the image of himself." So they asked why Tsichtinako did not become visible to them, but Tsichtinako replied, "I don't know how to live like a human being. I have been asked by Uchtsiti to look after you and to teach you. I will always guide you." And they asked again how they were to live, whether they could go down once more under the ground, for they were afraid of the winds and rains and their eyes were hurt by the light. Tsichtinako replied that Uchtsiti would take care of that and would furnish them means to keep warm and change the atmosphere so that they would get used to it.

At the end of the first day, when it became dark they were much frightened, for they had not understood that the sun would set and thought that Tsichtinako had betrayed them. "Tsichtinako! Tsichtinako! You told us we were to come into the light," they cried, "Why, then, is it dark?" So Tsichtinako explained, "This is the way it will always be. The sun will go down and the next day come up anew in the east. When it is dark you are to rest and sleep as you slept when all was dark." So they were satisfied and slept. They rose to meet the sun, praying to it as they had been told, and were happy when it came up again, for they were warm and their faith in Tsichtinako was restored.

Tsichtinako next said to them, "Now that you have your names, you will pray with your names and your clan names so that the Sun will know you and recognize you." Tsichtinako asked Nautsiti which clan she wished to belong to. Nautsiti answered, "I wish to see the sun, that is the clan I will be." The spirit told Nautsiti to ask Iatiku what clan she wanted. Iatiku thought for a long time but finally she noticed that she had the seed from which sacred meal was made in her basket and no other kind of seeds. She thought, "With this name I shall be very proud, for it has been chosen for nourishment and it is sacred." So she said, "I will be Corn clan." They then waited for the sun to come up. When it appeared, Tsichtinako once more advised them to sing the first song and to pray, not forgetting their name and their clan name in starting their prayer. After the prayer they were to sing the second song.

When the sun appeared it was too bright for Iatiku and it hurt her eyes. She wondered if Nautsiti's eyes hurt her too, so she put her head down and sideways, letting her hair fall, and looked at Nautsiti. By doing this the light did not strike her squarely in the face and her hair cast a shade. Tsichtinako said, "Iatiku, the sun has not appeared for you. Look at Nautsiti, see how strongly the light is striking her. Notice how white she looks." And although Iatiku turned to the sun, it did not make her as white as Nautsiti, and Iatiku's mind was slowed up while Nautsiti's mind was made fast. But both of them remembered everything and did everything as they were taught.

When they had completed their prayers to the sun, Tsichtinako said, "You have done everything well and now you are both to take up your baskets and you must look to the north, west, south, and east, for you are now to pray to the Earth to accept the things in the basket and to give them life. First you must pray to the north, at the same time lift up your baskets in that direction. You will then do the same to the west, then to the south and east." They did as they were told and did it well. And Tsichtinako said to them, "From now on you will rule in every direction, north, west, south, and east."

They now questioned Tsichtinako again so that they would understand more clearly why they were given the baskets and their contents, and Tsichtinako replied, "Everything in the baskets is to be created by your word, for you are made in the image of Uchtsiti and your word will be as powerful as his word. He has created you to help him complete the world.

You are to plant the seeds of the different plants to be used when anything is needed. I shall always be ready to point out to you the various plants and animals."

The sisters did not realize that they were not taking food and did not understand when Tsichtinako told them they were to plant seeds to give them nourishment. But they were always ready to do as Tsichtinako asked, and she told them to plant first that which would maintain life, grains of corn. "When this plant grows," said Tsichtinako, "it will produce a part which I will point out to you. This will be taken as food." Everything in the basket was in pairs and the sisters planted two of each kind of corn.

The corn grew very slowly so Tsichtinako told them to plant *ĭsthĕ* [the earliest plant to come up in the spring; gray with a small white flower; dies quickly] and to transmit its power of early ripening to the corn.

They were very interested in the corn and watched it every day as it grew. Tsichtinako showed them where the pollen came out. "That you will call *kū'ăch'tĭmu*," she said, "there the pollen will appear. When the pollen is plentiful, you will gather it, and with it and corn meal you will pray to the rising sun each morning." This they did always, but Nautsiti was sometimes a little lazy.

After some time the corn ripened. Tsichtinako told them to look at it and to gather some. They saw that the corn was hard and they picked four ears. Iatiku took two ears carefully without hurting the plant; but Nautsiti jerked hers off roughly. Iatiku noticed this and cautioned her sister not to ruin the plants. They took the ears of corn to Tsichtinako saying, "We have brought the corn, it is ripe." Tsichtinako agreed and explained that the corn ears when cooked would be their food. They did not understand this and asked what they would cook with. Tsichtinako then told them that Uchtsiti would give them fire. That night as they sat around they saw a red light drop from the sky. After they had seen it, Tsichtinako told them it was fire, and that they were to go over and get some of it. They asked with what, and she told them to get it with a flat rock because it was very hot and they could not take it in their hands. After getting it with a rock, they asked what they were to do with it, and were told they were to make a fire, to go to the pine tree they had planted, to break off some of the branches and put them in the fire. They went to the tree and broke some of the twigs from it. When they got back to the fire, they were told to throw the twigs down. They did so and a large pile of wood appeared there. Tsichtinako told them this wood would last many years till there was time for trees to grow, and showed them how to build a fire. She told them that with the flames from the fire they would keep warm and would cook their food.

Tsichtinako next taught them how to roast the corn. "When it is cooked," she explained, "you are to eat it. This will be the first time you have eaten, for you have been fasting for a long time and Uchtsiti has been nourishing you. You will find salt in your baskets; with this you will season the corn." They began to look for this and Tsichtinako pointed it out to them. As soon as they were told this, Nautsiti grabbed some corn and salt. She was the first to taste them and exclaimed that they were very good, but Iatiku was slower. After Nautsiti had eaten part, she gave it to Iatiku to taste. When both had eaten, Tsichtinako told them that this was the way they were going to live and be nourished. They were very thankful, saying, "You have treated us well." They asked if this would be their only food. Tsichtinako said, "No, you have many other things in your baskets; many seeds and images of animals, all in pairs. Some will be eaten and taken for nourishment by you." After they had used the salt, they were asked by Tsichtinako to give life to this salt by praying to the Earth, first in the North direction, then in the West, then in the South, and then in the East. And when they did so, salt appeared in each of these directions. Tsichtinako then instructed them to take always the husks from the corn carefully and to dry them. They were then instructed to plant *hǎ'mi* (tobacco). When the plant matured, they were taught how to roll the leaves in corn husks and to smoke it. (Even now in ceremonies the corn husks must be torn with the fingers and tied in the center with a little strip of corn husk. It may not be cut by artificial means. You smoke in order to make your prayers merge into the minds of the gods to whom prayer is addressed. This will also compel obedience. If a man smokes when a request is made of him, he must obey that request.) They were then told to place the tobacco with the pollen and the corn meal and to remember that these three were always to be together, and to be used in making prayers.

Now they were told that they were to give life to an animal whose flesh they were going to use for food. Tsichtinako named this animal as *Ba'shya* (kangaroo mouse) and also taught them the first song to be sung to animals. She told them to sing this song in order to make the images alive, and pointed out the images to them in the basket. They did everything as they were taught. They sang the song to the image and with the word, "Come to life, Bashya," it came to life. As it did so it asked, "Why have I come to life?" Tsichtinako told it not to ask any questions because, "It is you that is going to give life to other life." After this was done, Nautsiti and Iatiku told this animal that it was going to live on the ground and said to it, "Go now and increase." After the animal increased, Tsichtinako told the sisters to kill one of the animals. "Now eat the two together, the corn and the field mouse, and also the salt to see how it tastes." She had already told them never to let out the fire which had been given to them.

They acted according to Tsichtinako's instructions. They roasted their corn and roasted the flesh of the field mouse with some salt on it. After it was cooked, Tsichtinako told them to pray with the food, not with all of it, but with little pieces from each—corn, flesh, and salt. Each sister did this and prayed to Uchtsiti, the creator of the world, who lives up in the fourth sky. Tsichtinako told them they were to do this always before eating. After this they ate the food. There was not very much of the meat, but it was good. They did not know that there were to be bones but these were not hard and they broke them with their teeth. They liked the flesh so well that they asked Tsichtinako if they might have something larger that would yield more flesh. Tsichtinako answered that they would find other things in their baskets. They went tack to them, and Tsichtinako said they would find *Tsū'na* (rat) and another animal *Katsa* (mole) and also *Nīt* (prairie dog). "Go, make these images alive," said Tsichtinako, pointing them out according to their names. They were to do this in the same way as with Bashya. Tsichtinako also told them that these animals were to be used as food and that they must tell each of these animals to live in the ground because as yet there was no shade on earth to live in. "But before you give life to them," said Tsichtinako, "it is necessary that you plant seeds of grass which will be the food for them." Tsichtinako pointed out the seeds they were to plant, and they took the seeds of the grasses and scattered them first to the North, next to the West, then some to the South, and then to the East. And immediately grass covered the ground. They then took the images and prayed to the cardinal points, and, according to the instructions of Tsichtinako, gave life to all of these animals, giving them names as they came to life. Each one as it came to life asked why it had come to life but Tsichtinako told them not to ask questions, that they would give life to other life. As before, the sisters told the animals to increase. After all of this was done, they proceeded to eat the new animals after praying with them, doing just as they did before. The two sisters were now very happy, they had plenty and some to spare. "It is not yet time for the larger animals to be given life," said Tsichtinako, "first the world must have sufficient plants and small animals to feed them."

After a long time, Tsichtinako spoke to them, "What we are going to do now concerns the earth. We are going to make the mountains." She told them to remember the words she was going to say. They were to say, "*Kaweshtima kōt* (North Mountain), appear in the north, and we will always know you to be in that direction." Tsichtinako also pointed out an article in the basket that she named *ya'ōni* (stone) and instructed them to throw the stone to the North direction as they spoke the words. When they did so, a big mountain appeared in the North. After they had done this, Tsichtinako instructed them to do the same thing in the West, but to name this mountain *Tsipīna kot'*, and in the South, naming it *Da'ōtyuma kot'*, and in the East, naming it *G'ūchana lot'*.

After all this was done, Tsichtinako spoke again and told them, "Now that you have all the mountains around you with plains, mesas, and canyons, you must make the growing things of these places." Tsichtinako told them to go back to the trees which they had planted underground, *lakhok, geietsu, wanuka,* and *lanye*. She told them to take the seeds from these trees, and they did so. Following her instructions they spread some to each of the four directions, naming the mountains in each direction, and saying, "Grow in North Mountain, grow in West Mountain, etc." Tsichtinako said to them, "These are going to be tall trees; from them you will get logs. Later you will build houses and will use these." They asked if that was all that was going to grow on the mountains, and Tsichtinako said, "No, there are many other seeds left in your baskets. You have seeds of trees which are going to yield food. You will find *dyai'its* (piñon tree), *sē'isha* (kind of cedar), *hapani* (oak, acorn) and *maka'yawi* (walnut)." She again instructed them what to do and taught them the prayer to use, which was: "From now on, grow in this mountain and yield fruit which will be used as food. Your places are to be in the mountains. You will grow and be useful." When everything had been done well, Tsichtinako told [them] that there were many smaller seeds left in the baskets and she gave a name to each, telling them to fill the rest of the land. These seeds were planted on every one of the four mountains and in the rest of the world. Tsichtinako spoke to the sisters again and told them, "You still have seeds in your baskets which you will know as *scuts'ō'bewi* (wild fruits). These trees you will grow around you and care for." But they mistook the instructions and instead of instructing them to grow nearby, they named the mountains, and that is where they grew. But there were also some that grew close around. It is not known how long they had to wait for these things to happen, but it was a very long time. They noticed that the wild plants grew very fast and produced much fruit, but Tsichtinako had not told them whether or not to eat these, so they left them alone.

They saw that there were still seeds and images in their baskets and asked Tsichtinako how many more kinds there were. Tsichtinako said there were yet many other seeds which would also be important food. They would grow quickly and easily and she named them squash and beans. They were instructed to act with them as with the other seeds, and these also grew into plants. After a time, when they were ripe, Tsichtinako pointed out the parts of the plants which they were to use as food.

Iatiku later asked Tsichtinako, "What remains in my basket?" and she was answered, "You have still many animals; these will be multiplied to populate the mountains." And as the two grew larger, they required more food. Tsichtinako saw this and told them that they were now to bring to life larger animals. She said they would find in their baskets cottontails, jack rabbits, antelope, and water deer. They were told to give life to these animals and to send them into the open plains. Everything was done as before, and when they killed the animals for food they were always careful to pray to their father as before. As they again asked Tsichtinako what remained in their baskets, Tsichtinako said, "You have images of the still bigger game. You will find deer, elk, mountain sheep, and bison." Iatiku asked where these animals were to be told to live and Tsichtinako told them that the elk and deer were to live in the lower mountains and the mountain sheep higher and in the rougher places. The bison, however, were to live on the plains. They followed the instructions and gave life to these animals and told them to go to these places to live and multiply. They again tried all these different animals for food. Their flesh was very good and always they prayed to Uchtsiti before tasting them.

In Nautsiti's basket there were many more things left than in Iatiku's. Nautsiti was selfish and hoarded her images, but Iatiku was ready to let her seeds and images be used. She was more interested in seeing things grow. They again asked what remained, and Tsichtinako replied, "You will find lion, wolf, wildcat and bear. These are strong beasts; they are going to use as food the same game that you also use. There is now game enough for them." When all these had been selected they were brought to life in the same manner as before.

The sisters again asked what was in their baskets, and they were told, "You will find birds which will fly in the air. These birds will also use small game for their food. You will find in the basket the eagles and the hawks (shpi-ya, ga-wa, i-tsa)." Tsichtinako pointed these out to them and they brought them to life. The birds flew up into the high mountains and over the plains. The sisters told the birds to use small game for food, and again Iatiku asked what was in the basket. Tsichtinako pointed out smaller birds which would populate the country, each living in a different kind of region. They were then given life, as the animals before them. The birds were of many and bright colors, some were blue. The wild turkey was among them and they were instructed to tell it not to fly easily like the others. They were told to tell these birds that their food was to be the different seeds on the mountains and the plains. And all these animals were sampled for food after they had been given life. Again Iatiku asked what remained in the baskets, because she found things there that were thorny. Tsichtinako told them their names. They were the various cacti and were said to be very good for food. But Tsichtinako explained that most were intended for animals to eat. All these were planted as before and tried for food, and they found that some tasted good. . . . After they asked again what was left, Tsichtinako pointed out to them that there were still fish, water snakes, and turtles, of which there were many kinds of each. They gave life to them as before and told them all to live in the water as instructed. Tsichtinako pointed out several that were to be used for food. They tried them all for food, and they found that some were good, and others poor, but offered prayers to all and gave thanks to Uchtsiti. So it happened that many animals came alive in the world and they all increased.

Origin of the Evil Spirit

When Tsichtinako was instructing Iatiku and Nautsiti, Tsichtinako cautioned them to be always very careful in handling their baskets. They were very careful for a while but they soon became too anxious to give life to what was still in their baskets and they became careless. When Iatiku and Nautsiti were giving life to the snakes and fishes, in their eagerness they dropped an image from a basket to the ground. They did not know this had happened, nor did Tsichtinako. The image came to life itself, and with power of its own. It came to life in the form of a serpent, like the rest of the snakes. The two sisters noticed a strange snake among the ones to which they had given life, but they only stopped long enough to ask each other, "Did we give life to that snake?," and paid no more attention to it, as it looked like the others. This was the snake that was to tempt Nautsiti.

Now Nautsiti spoke to Iatiku, who had used more of the seeds and images from her basket, and said she wanted a chance to give life to more of her images. Iatiku replied, "I am the older, you are younger than I," but Nautsiti said, "We should both give equally because we were created equally. Is it true that you are the older? Let us try each other! Tomorrow, when the sun rises, let us see who is going to have the sun rise for her first." But Iatiku was afraid that her sister was going to get the better of her in some way. She knew a white bird that was named *shō'ēka* (magpie). She went to it and asked it to go on ahead into the east, where the sun was to rise, without resting or eating. There it was to shade the sun with its wings from Nautsiti. The bird went as instructed, for it was very strong and skillful. But, while on its way, it got hungry, and it passed a place where a puma had killed a deer. Here, although it had been instructed not to stop, it stopped and found a hole in the side of the deer where the intestines were exposed. The bird put its head into the gash to eat, and as it did so it got blood on its back and wings and tail, and it flew on not noticing that it was stained from the blood. Finally, after a long time, the bird reached the east where the sun was ready to rise, and it spread its wings on the left of the sun, making a shade in the direction of Nautsiti. So the sun struck Iatiku first and she straightway claimed to be the older. And Nautsiti was very angry for she had hoped to win. Iatiku, who did not want her sister to know anything about the trick she had used, whispered to the bird when it returned from the east, telling it not to say anything, and she also punished the bird for disobeying her. She had told it not to stop to eat on the way to the rising sun, but she knew that the bird had stopped for it was all dirty with blood. So she said to it, "For stopping and eating you will not know from now on how to kill your own meat. You will not be a hunter, you will eat what others have killed and left, and most of the time you will eat what is spoiled. Your color also will be spotted from now on, you will not be white as you were at first."

The two sisters were now thinking selfish thoughts. Nautsiti schemed to get the better of her sister. She often wandered off, making plans to outdo Iatiku, but Iatiku watched her and noticed everything. She saw that Nautsiti was falling away from her and was not happy as she used to be. Iatiku also noticed that Nautsiti was becoming solitary and that she would wander off alone. Iatiku tried to comfort her and asked her why she had changed.

A long time before this Tsichtinako has told them that Uchtsiti forbade them to think of having children. In due time other humans made in their likeness would be born to them. But one day Pishuni, the snake that had come to life of itself, met Nautsiti and said to her, "Why are you lonely and unhappy? If you want what will make you happy, I can tell you what to do. You are the only one on earth that is lonely. You and your sister do not like each other. If you bore someone like yourself, you would no longer be lonely. Tsichtinako wants to hold back this happiness from you. Unless you do as I tell you, you will have to wait a long time." Nautsiti asked Pishuni how she could do this, and the serpent replied, "Go to the rainbow. He will meet you and show you what to do." Nautsiti thought it would be well to do what Pishuni said. Soon after she was sitting alone on a rock when it rained. It was very hot and the rain steamed on the hot ground. Nautsiti lay on her back to receive the rain, and the dripping water entered her. This was the work of Rainbow, and she conceived without knowing what had happened. Some time after, Iatiku noticed that Nautsiti was pregnant. After a time she bore twin sons. Iatiku helped her sister to take care of them. Tsichtinako came back to them and asked, "Why have you done this without my instructing you? Uchtsiti had forbidden you this." Tsichtinako left them angrily, saying, "From now on, you will do as you see fit. I will not help you any more because you disobeyed your father." But instead of being sorry, the two sisters felt happier. It happened that Nautsiti disliked one of the children. So Iatiku took this one and cared for it.

Because they had committed a sin, their father called Tsichtinako away from them. But they lived happily, and the children grew up. After a long time Nautsiti said to Iatiku, "We are not happy together. Let us share what we have in our baskets and separate. I still have many things. These animals in my basket, these sheep and cattle I will share with you, but it is understood that these animals will demand much care." Iatiku answered that it would be too hard a task to care for them and that she did not want her children to have them. Nautsiti also pointed out some seeds and told Iatiku to take some of them. They were seeds of wheat and vegetables. Nautsiti knew also that these were going to be hard to raise, but she wanted to share them with Iatiku. But Iatiku again did not want them for her children. In Nautsiti's basket, too, there were many metals. She offered to share these, but Iatiku did not take any. When Nautsiti had looked this far into her basket she found something written (*ti'thyătra'nī*). Nautsiti also offered this, but Iatiku did not want it. Nautsiti said, "There are still many things that are very good for foods in my basket but I know that all of these things will require much care. Why is it, sister, that you are not thankful, why do you not take some of the things I have offered? I am going to leave you. We both understand that we are to increase our kind, and in a long time to come we shall meet again and then you will be wearing clothes. We shall still be sisters, for we have the same father, but I shall have the better of you again. I am going away into the East." Iatiku did not say where she would go. She thought she would stay where she was. So Nautsiti left her, taking the child she loved with her and leaving the other for Iatiku.

So Nautsiti disappeared into the East, while Iatiku stayed on and became very sad. She said to the boy child who stayed with her, "We shall live here with everything that our father has given us." They lived together for a long time and, when he grew up, he became her husband and she named him *Tia'muni*. Iatiku bore many children and she named the first for the clan of her sister—the Sun clan. Now Iatiku had her own power. She did everything in the way she had been instructed; she took the child the fourth day after birth to pray to the sun, as she herself had been taught when she came into the light, and she put some pollen and some sacred corn meal into the child's hands. She taught this to every child that she bore after this. And the brothers and the sisters all lived together and they all began to increase. Iatiku was the mother and ruled.

THREE MENOMINI TALES

The Menominis were traditionally a sedentary tribe of Algonquian stock, native to northern Wisconsin. Their reservation became a county in Wisconsin in 1961, when federal control was temporarily terminated, but since then it has been restored as a reservation. Today they number four thousand. No tribe can top the Menominis for fascinating stories.

The first story below is "The Man Who Transgressed a Taboo." The word taboo originated in the Tongan language in Polynesia. It applies to acts and objects prohibited for religious reasons, either because they are too sacred for the common folk or because they are impure or unclean. Taboos of various sorts were common among American Indians. In tribes divided into clans, taboos dictated behavior toward the totem animal. Sometimes, as among the Navajos, it was taboo to kill the animal; in other tribes there was a ritual apology to the animal or a prohibition from eating certain parts of it. Most tribes had a taboo against sexual intercourse shortly before going on the warpath. And, as mentioned earlier, there were taboos against telling certain stories out of season. "The Man Who Transgressed a Taboo" tells of a man with a personal, as opposed to a tribal or clan, taboo.

The second tale, "A Warrior's Heart," contains two extraordinary vignettes. The first is the scene in which Napop with his torch in his hair cuts such a comical picture that the men who have come to kill him burst out laughing. The second is the description of Napop burying his shattered leg in the sand so that he can continue to stand and fight. Although the narrative is very short, these two intensely graphic scenes achieve a measure of literary greatness.

The third story, "The Jealous Ghost," is a fascinating tale of supernatural love, jealousy, and revenge. Although the devotion of the husband to his deceased wife is remarkable—even necrophilic—it is a startling comment on the status of Indian women that when the wife is brought back to life, the husband does not embrace her or even greet her; she simply "got up and worked the same as ever."

The Man Who Transgressed a Taboo

There was once an Indian who had a taboo against eating porcupine. He himself had originally been an animal but was transformed into a human

The three Menomini tales are reprinted by permission of the American Museum of Natural History from Alanson Skinner and John Satterlee, *Folklore of the Menomini Indians,* American Museum of Natural History Anthropological Papers, vol. 13, part 3 (New York, 1915).

being and therefore durst not eat the flesh of the porcupine lest he be transformed again. He chose to live among the Indians and had for associates nine young warriors, all of whom knew that he must never eat porcupine flesh, either cooked or raw. Wherever he went he always carried with him his sacred dish to eat from. These young men, not believing that his story was true, planned to trick him into eating some of the forbidden meat, just to see what would happen.

Once when they were hunting together, one night one of the young men went out and killed a porcupine. They hurried and cooked it, and put some of the meat into their friend's sacred dish, saying, "Let us eat out of this dish, and daub it up with porcupine grease, then we will put it back into his pack and he will never know the difference."

When their friend came back that evening, the one that was cooking supper said, "Come on, each bring your dishes, and I'll dish up your food for you." Last of all came the man with the sacred dish and when it was filled he sat down to eat, but the moment he looked at it, he could see the shade of the porcupine meat that had been put in it while he was gone, and he knew that it had been defiled. He sat there a while, and then raised his head and looked about saying to his comrades, "Didn't you know enough not to betray your friend, didn't you know enough to stop each other from putting porcupine meat into my dish? Well now if you really want to know me, you will see."

Then they all ate and shortly afterwards they went to bed, to sleep; but the one that had eaten the porcupine meat, kept getting up to drink water, until his comrades were obliged to go several times to bring big pails full of water to him. At last, he got up and went down to the spring to drink and returned. Still he waxed more thirsty, until at last he lay down by the spring and put his head in the water to drink, and continued to take water without stopping.

Meantime the nine comrades ran back and forth, frightened, and wondering, but they could give him no help, all they could say was, "Pa pinisiwug!" Meanwhile they saw their betrayed comrade rapidly changing into a catfish. This kept on till daylight, when they saw the upper part of their friend's body was that of a fish, and his legs were human. Now he began to wiggle to and fro: the spring became a huge lake, and in the center of it the unfortunate man swam as a gigantic catfish.

"Oh, alas!" cried his friends, "When we go home, let us tell his father that his son ate porcupine by mistake and that we did not know it or do it purposely to him." So they sent one of their number to tell the unfortunate man's parents, and the old people came to the place at night and saw their son as a great catfish. Then the father took his tobacco in sorrow and said to the other Indians that had also come to see the miracle, "Take my tobacco and try to find out the cause of this."

Then one of the men, who was a medium, took the tobacco, and said, "Yes, you who are afflicted. I will try tonight, with my power, to see and learn the cause of this thing and find out if there is any remedy." That night the seer went into a trance and learned that it was impossible to bring the catfish back to human shape, but the betrayed youth said that he would help his father, if his father would come and live on the shore of the lake. The father obeyed the catfish son's instruction, and came there. In the morning it was only necessary for him to peep out or to raise the mat door and there he would see a large buck standing between him and the water's edge, and it was easy for him to get all sorts of game, for the animals came to him. Anything that the catfish thought his father might wish to eat, he would cause to come near the camp. Especially in the autumn would his father come there to stay, and once he even stayed all winter collecting meat. On sunshiny days, when there were no clouds in the sky, the father perceived a great catfish lying on the sandbar on the lake, but on dark days the catfish hid. One fine day in the springtime, when the catfish lay there the father said to his son, "We are now going home with all that you have given us, deer meat and bear." So he left and gave some to all the friends in the village, and the seer who had helped him was there and said, "It is good, as it turned out, and your son said that during your lifetime, you will only have to go to the lake shore during the fall and winter and he will supply all your wants and make you happy."

A Warrior's Heart

Ever since the beginning there has been the tradition that a brave man's heart is very small, and now we all know that it is true, because some of our warriors had an opportunity to investigate the matter and proved the words of our ancestors. This is the way it happened.

When we were still residing at our old home on the Menomini River, there was a very brave man among us, whose name was Napop, or Broth. He was renowned for his achievements on the warpath, and everyone respected him because of his courage. More than that, he was a famous mikäo, or war leader, and always brought his men home safely.

One day he took a companion named Päk'wonapit, or Big-seated-bird and went out to hunt deer by torchlight on the Peshtige River. Just at twilight they ran their canoe ashore and set about cooking supper before they started to hunt. Päk'wonapit lolled on one side of the fire while Napop busied himself preparing the meal. It was dark before he was through. He took the kettle off the fire at last, and since it was dark he lit one of the resinous torches he had brought for the jack-light.

"Bring me your dish," he called to Päk'wonapit. His companion brought it over and tossed it on the ground beside him. Napop tried to serve Päk'wonapit with meat and broth, but he found it very awkward work when he held the torch in his hand. It was too blunt to stick in the ground, so he thrust it into the braids of his scalplock and let it stand upright like a feather. He gave his comrade some meat and then started to pour some broth from the kettle into a dish. There was a rich coating of oil on the surface of the hot liquid and since his hands were both full, and he could not skim it off with a spoon, Napop endeavored to blow it back as he poured. He had thought a moment before that he heard a noise in the bushes, but he had said nothing. This time he cut such a comical appearance blowing in the broth with his blazing headdress, that someone laughed outright in the darkness. "Hai! Päk'wonapit!" he cried, "here is the enemy!," and, even as he said the words, "Pah! Pah! Pah! Pah!" went the rifles. Napop and Päk'wonapit snatched their own weapons and returned the fire, shooting at the flashes of the guns in the dark. They killed several of the enemy, but there were many of them, and they crowded hard on the two warriors. Presently, a shot broke Napop's leg, but he jammed the end of the bone into the sand and continued to stand on it and fight. At last Päk'wonapit ran to the water and escaped in the canoe leaving Napop to face the foe.

When Päk'wonapit arrived at the Menomini village he shouted, "Hai! We are being killed! I escaped with the news! Napop was still alive when I left!" The warriors ran out with their weapons, "Let us all go right away," they said, "He was always brave!" So they ran off into the night to his aid. When they arrived everything was in tumultuous disorder about the camp. Pots and kettles were upset, and signs of a terrible fight were everywhere. At last they found the body of Napop lying in the embers. The enemy had killed him, cut off his head, and carried it away with them. When the warriors found his body they mourned mightily. "We have lost our best warrior who used to protect us," they cried.

Then they took up the body to bury it. "We have always been told that brave men have little hearts," said one, "This man's body is spoiled anyway, since his head is gone, let us examine him and see." So they cut a slit between his upper ribs on the left side and took out his heart. Sure enough, it was a tiny organ, and they were obliged to believe what had formerly been said.

That proves that the hearts of brave men are small, while cowards, who run away when there is fighting to be done, have large, soft, hearts.

The Jealous Ghost

This happened very long ago among the Menomini, and it is the truth.

There was once a man and his wife who had four sons and two daughters. The eldest of the sisters got married and went with her husband and family, but she soon took sick and died. Right in the place where she breathed her last they dressed her in beautiful clothes and buried her, and the rest of the party stayed right there for they did not like to leave her. After a while, the four brothers began to suspect that their brother-in-law was going to leave them because his wife was gone. They liked him so much that they begged him not to go and gave him the other sister in place of his dead wife.

The girl was very young, but he stayed to live with her. One day the old mother took the girl out with her to dig wild potatoes which grew a short distance from their camp. Evening approached, and the old woman said: "Now let's go home," but the daughter continued digging as she was finding more and bigger ones. In the meantime her mother took her pack on her back and started off, saying once more; "Come, let's go home!" But the daughter kept right on digging.

The sun set and it began to get dark. The mother by this time was at home, and the young girl started off to find her. As she was walking along with her load she heard someone behind, saying: "Well, you who are marrying and living with your brother-in-law!" The young wife understood right away that this was her sister who had died so she answered: "Well, it was not my intention to live with him; it is not my fault, my four brothers wanted me to live with him because they had loved our sister so much."

The girl was so frightened that she whooped and screamed for help as she hurried through the dark for her house. Her mother and brothers heard her and made a bigger fire to give her light to make for camp. They made birchbark torches and turned out to meet her. The young wife told her mother that a woman had overtaken her and found fault with her because she was living with her own brother-in-law. When the party went out to meet her and bring her to the wigwam they did not see anything or anybody with her, but just as she was about to enter the wigwam door and one of the brothers lifted the door mat for her to go in, she was pushed from behind with such force that she fell head first into the big fire and was burnt to death in a few moments. The mother and brothers saw nobody, but they knew it was the jealous ghost of her dead sister.

Then the mother became so agitated and crazy with rage she went outside their wigwam for a few steps to where her first daughter was buried and dug up her body and pulled her violently out of the grave and flung her around. She threw her down and stripped her, taking off her fancy clothes that they had put on her to show their love. Then the mother spoke to the corpse saying: "Why don't you come to natural life if you have the power of a god?"

Then the distracted mother quit her abuse and left the body lying on the ground naked, taking the pretty clothes to put on the girl who was burned to death and buried her in the elder daughter's grave. The next morning, when the husband went out and saw the body of his first wife lying there naked, it made him very sad, and he did not like it. The old people said to their sons, "Now let us move away from this place." They asked their brother-in-law to go along with them but he replied, "I will remain here until I bury her."

So the old folks and their sons left him, and the husband went out and dragged his first wife's body into the lodge. He took some of her old clothes and dressed her and placed her in his bed, where she lay as though asleep. He himself rested on the other side of the wigwam opposite her, and every time he cooked for himself he offered some of the victuals to her. "Here is your dish, eat!" he would say.

He did this at every meal time, and once as he did this he thought he saw her hand move. It was her shade which had appeared first, like a shadow on the wall, so he thought that after a while she would come to life. He continued to cook, and made some broth or gruel and put some of it in her mouth with a spoon, very slowly, and as the broth went down, she swallowed it. He kept on with this till she really came to life and got up and worked the same as ever.

They both lived right there and stored away meat of all kinds that the husband had killed in hunting, till it happened that some Indians came to camp in the neighborhood. One day the wife's younger brother, who was still a child, saw his brother-in-law when he was out walking and recognized him. He also saw his sister who he knew had died some time ago. He thought it must be another person just like her, it couldn't be she, but when he looked closer he was sure he could not be mistaken. So he went home and told his mother that he had seen his brother-in-law: "Yes, and I saw my eldest sister, too, she has come to life again!"

When the mother learned this she went over to visit her. She knew her but did not say much to her about what had happened to them both. As she went out her daughter gave her some dried meat. The meat was the muscle of deer's legs, and when she began to eat it the first bite choked her to death, and then her daughter was even with her.

HIGH HORSE'S COURTING

"High Horse's Courting" is a classic short story of the type O. Henry used to write—a good yarn with emphasis on a convoluted plot that keeps the reader hooked until the end. The narrator is the Oglala Sioux medicine man Black Elk (see part 4 for a selection from his memoirs). He is repeating a story told him by his friend Watanye. It is an example of a secular humorous story involving recent events, as opposed to a story of a semidivine culture hero set in ancient times. It employs a prototypic humorous situation that has been popular in comic literature from at least the time of the Roman playwrights Plautus and Terence. In this situation a boy wants a girl but cannot have her because of some obstacle, usually parental disapproval. Finally, after all sorts of involved intrigue, love conquers all, and the lovers are united. Shakespeare and Ben Jonson made use of it in their comedies, and it has been used in our time in countless musical comedies and in sophisticated variations such as the film The Graduate. *Like much great literature, "High Horse's Courting" combines such a familiar plot with an original set of specific circumstances, in this case the way the girl is tied to her bed and High Horse's disguise as an evil spirit, which is the basis of the intrigue.*

You know, in the old days, it was not so very easy to get a girl when you wanted to be married. Sometimes it was hard work for a young man and he had to stand a great deal. Say I am a young man and I have seen a young girl who looks so beautiful to me that I feel all sick when I think about her. I can not just go and tell her about it and then get married if she is willing. I have to be a very sneaky fellow to talk to her at all, and after I have managed to talk to her, that is only the beginning.

Probably for a long time I have been feeling sick about a certain girl because I love her so much, but she will not even look at me, and her parents keep a good watch over her. But I keep feeling worse and worse all the time; so maybe I sneak up to her tepee in the dark and wait until she comes out. Maybe I just wait there all night and don't get any sleep at all and she does not come out. Then I feel sicker than ever about her.

Maybe I hide in the brush by a spring where she sometimes goes to get water, and when she comes by, if nobody is looking, then I jump out and hold her and just make her listen to me. If she likes me too, I can tell that from the way she acts, for she is very bashful and maybe will not say a word or even look at me the first time. So I let her go, and then maybe I sneak around until I can see her father alone, and I tell him how many horses I can give him for his beautiful girl, and by now I am feeling so sick that maybe I would give him all the horses in the world if I had them.

Well, this young man I am telling about was called High Horse, and there was a girl in the village who looked so beautiful to him that he was just sick all over from thinking about her so much and he was getting sicker all the time. The girl was very shy, and her parents thought a great deal of her because they were not young any more and this was the only child they had. So they watched her all day long, and they fixed it so that she would be safe at night too when they were asleep. They thought so much of her that they had made a rawhide bed for her to sleep in, and after they knew that High Horse was sneaking around after her, they took rawhide thongs and tied the girl in bed at night so that nobody could steal her when they were asleep, for they were not sure but that their girl might really want to be stolen.

Well, after High Horse had been sneaking around a good while and hiding and waiting for the girl and getting sicker all the time, he finally caught her alone and made her talk to him. Then he found out that she liked him maybe a little. Of course this did not make him feel well. It made him sicker than ever, but now he felt as brave as a bison bull, and so he went right to her father and said he loved the girl so much that he would give two good horses for her—one of them young and the other one not so very old.

But the old man just waved his hand, meaning for High Horse to go away and quit talking foolishness like that.

High Horse was feeling sicker than ever about it; but there was another young fellow who said he would loan High Horse two ponies and when he got some more horses, why, he could just give them back for the ones he had borrowed.

Then High Horse went back to the old man and said he would give four horses for the girl—two of them young and the other two not hardly old at all. But the old man just waved his hand and would not say anything.

So High Horse sneaked around until he could talk to the girl again, and he asked her to run away with him. He told her he thought he would just fall over and die if she did not. But she said she would not do that; she wanted to be bought like a fine woman. You see she thought a great deal of herself too.

That made High Horse feel so very sick that he could not eat a bite, and he went around with his head hanging down as though he might just fall down and die any time.

Red Deer was another young fellow, and he and High Horse were great comrades, always doing things together. Red Deer saw how High Horse was acting, and he said: "Cousin, what is the matter? Are you sick in the belly? You look as though you were going to die."

Then High Horse told Red Deer how it was, and said he thought he could not stay alive much longer if he could not marry the girl pretty quick.

Red Deer thought awhile about it, and then he said: "Cousin, I have a plan, and if you are man enough to do as I tell you, then everything will be all right. She will not run away with you; her old man will not take four horses; and four horses are all you can get. You must steal her and run away with her. Then afterwhile you can come back and the old man cannot do anything because she will be your woman. Probably she wants you to steal her anyway."

So they planned what High Horse had to do, and he said he loved the girl so much that he was man enough to do anything Red Deer or anybody else could think up.

So this is what they did.

That night late they sneaked up to the girl's tepee and waited until it sounded inside as though the old man and the old woman and the girl were sound asleep. Then High Horse crawled under the tepee with a knife. He had to cut the rawhide thongs first, and then Red Deer, who was pulling up the stakes around that side of the tepee, was going to help drag the girl outside and gag her. After that, High Horse could put her across his pony in front of him and hurry out of there and be happy all the rest of his life.

When High Horse had crawled inside, he felt so nervous that he could hear his heart drumming, and it seemed so loud he felt sure it would 'waken the old folks. But it did not, and afterwhile he began cutting the thongs. Every time he cut one it made a pop and nearly scared him to death. But he was getting along all right and all the thongs were cut down as far as the girl's thighs, when he became so nervous that his knife slipped and stuck the girl. She gave a big, loud yell. Then the old folks jumped up and yelled too. By this time High Horse was outside, and he and Red Deer were running away like antelope. The old man and some other people chased the young men but they got away in the dark and nobody knew who it was.

Well, if you ever wanted a beautiful girl you will know how sick High Horse was now. It was very bad the way he felt, and it looked as though he would starve even if he did not drop over dead sometime.

Red Deer kept thinking about this, and after a few days he went to High Horse and said: "Cousin, take courage! I have another plan, and I am sure, if you are man enough, we can steal her this time." And High Horse said: "I am man enough to do anything anybody can think up, if I can only get that girl."

So that is what they did.

They went away from the village alone, and Red Deer made High Horse strip naked. Then he painted High Horse solid white all over, and after that he painted black stripes all over the white and put black rings around High Horse's eyes. High Horse looked terrible. He looked so terrible that when Red Deer was through painting and took a good look at what he had done, he said it scared even him a little.

"Now," Red Deer said, "if you get caught again, everybody will be so scared they will think you are a bad spirit and will be afraid to chase you."

So when the night was getting old and everybody was sound asleep, they sneaked back to the girl's tepee. High Horse crawled in with his knife, as before, and Red Deer waited outside, ready to drag the girl out and gag her when High Horse had all the thongs cut.

High Horse crept up by the girl's bed and began cutting at the thongs. But he kept thinking, "If they see me they will shoot me because I look so terrible." The girl was restless and kept squirming around in bed, and when a thong was cut, it popped. So High Horse worked very slowly and carefully.

But he must have made some noise, for suddenly the old woman awoke and said to her old man: "Old Man, wake up! There is somebody in this tepee!" But the old man was sleepy and didn't want to be bothered. He said: "Of course there is somebody in this tepee. Go to sleep and don't bother me." Then he snored some more.

But High Horse was so scared by now that he lay very still and as flat to the ground as he could. Now, you see, he had not been sleeping very well for a long time because he was so sick about the girl. And while he was lying there waiting for the old woman to snore, he just forgot everything, even how beautiful the girl was. Red Deer who was lying outside ready to do his part, wondered and wondered what had happened in there, but he did not dare call out to High Horse.

Afterwhile the day began to break and Red Deer had to leave with the two ponies he had staked there for his comrade and girl, or somebody would see him.

So he left.

Now when it was getting light in the tepee, the girl awoke and the first thing she saw was a terrible animal, all white with black stripes on it, lying asleep beside her bed. So she screamed, and then the old woman screamed and the old man yelled. High Horse jumped up, scared almost to death, and he nearly knocked the tepee down getting out of there.

People were coming running from all over the village with guns and bows and axes, and everybody was yelling.

By now High Horse was running so fast that he hardly touched the ground at all, and he looked so terrible that the people fled from him and let him run. Some braves wanted to shoot at him, but the others said he might be some sacred being and it would bring bad trouble to kill him.

High Horse made for the river that was near, and in among the brush he found a hollow tree and dived into it. Afterwhile some braves came there and he could hear them saying that it was some bad spirit that had come out of the water and gone back in again.

That morning the people were ordered to break camp and move away from there. So they did, while High Horse was hiding in his hollow tree.

Now Red Deer had been watching all this from his own tepee and trying to look as though he were as much surprised and scared as all the others. So when the camp moved, he sneaked back to where he had seen his comrade disappear. When he was down there in the brush, he called, and High Horse answered, because he knew his friend's voice. They washed off the paint from High Horse and sat down on the river bank to talk about their troubles.

High Horse said he never would go back to the village as long as he lived and he did not care what happened to him now. He said he was going to go on the war-path all by himself. Red Deer said: "No, cousin, you are not going on the war-path alone, because I am going with you."

So Red Deer got everything ready, and at night they started out on the war-path all alone. After several days they came to a Crow camp just about sundown, and when it was dark they sneaked up to where the Crow horses were grazing, killed the horse guard, who was not thinking about enemies because he thought all the Lakotas were far away, and drove off about a hundred horses.

They got a big start because all the Crow horses stampeded and it was probably morning before the Crow warriors could catch any horses to ride. Red Deer and High Horse fled with their herd three days and nights before they reached the village of their people. Then they drove the whole herd right into the village and up in front of the girl's tepee. The old man was there, and High Horse called out to him and asked if he thought maybe that would be enough horses for his girl. The old man did not wave him away that time. It was not the horses that he wanted. What he wanted was a son who was a real man and good for something.

So High Horse got his girl after all, and I think he deserved her.

AWL AND HER SON'S SON

"Awl and Her Son's Son" is a Chinook tale recorded by Melville Jacobs in Oregon in 1930. In form it resembles a comedy in the European tradition: a girl overcomes obstacles to marry the boy of her dreams. In tone it is closer to European melodrama, where the emphasis is more on violence than humor.

Like "Cinderella," "Puss in Boots," and many other European folk tales the story revolves around a youngest-is-best motif: the youngest of a group of siblings, the most competent and virtuous member of the family, overcomes obstacles to triumph over a villain or adversity to marry and live happily ever after. One difference is that whereas European literature observes the rule of threes (three bears, three pigs, three episodes to stories), the Chinooks have a rule of fives: the heroine is the youngest of five daughters.

The hero is a passive figure; it is the heroine who is dynamic. Meadow Lark Woman is the helper in the story. She obviously bears a strong resemblance to the fairy godmother of European folk tales.

A man lived (alone) there. He hunted all the time. The following day he would go again. That is the way he was. I do not know how long a time he lived there. One day he thought, "I will not go today. I will stay and patch my moccasins." And so he did. He sewed all day long. After a while then he broke his (bone) awl. He thought, "Oh me oh my! my poor awl!" He took it, he threw it underneath his bed-platform. "I wish you would turn into a person!" Now he continued to live there. The next day then he went to hunt again. That is what he did.

I do not know how long after, he got back, his (hearth) fire was burning, he saw footprints of small feet (inside his house). He thought, "Where could a person have come from to me?" The next day then he made a bow (and) arrows, he laid them close by the fire. He thought, "If it is a male, then he will take hold of it" (and I will see that it has been moved).

Now he went away, he hunted. He returned in the evening. Again his fire was burning. Someone had fixed his things nicely indeed for him. The arrows (and) the bow just lay there (untouched). He thought, "Oh it is no male. Apparently it is a female."

So the next day he made a camas root-digger. He stood it in the ground close by the fire. Now he went away again. He got back at night. The root-digger was gone, it was standing far over there. He thought, "Indeed that must be a female." And again that was how she had covered (put away) nicely all his things.

So again the next day he went. And he went along, he hunted. He got back in the evening. Now she had swept his house quite clean, his fire was burning. He thought, "Maybe she just went somewhere a short while ago." He went to bed, and then he began to think it over. "Wonder where this person has been coming from? Now tomorrow I shall hide from her."

It became the next day. He finished eating, he got ready, he went outside, he forthwith went around the house. He went up above, he lay on his stomach on the roof, he looked down inside. Pretty soon then someone ran out (from hiding). She said, "Now I guess that my son's son has gone. Suppose I go look." She ran outside. "Oh yes now my son's son has long since gone on." She went inside. "Very well. Now I shall wash and clean up everything." And so she did.

But he himself descended (from the roof) slowly and cautiously now, he went all around the house, he entered, he spoke harshly to her. "Who are you? What people are you from?" She merely sat there. She said absolutely nothing to him. "Why have you come here and disturbed everything?" Now she replied to him, "Yes, but that was what you thought in your heart. You yourself said, I wish that you would turn into a person. That's me here." "Oh oh, I merely said that (unseriously) to you."

Now they lived there, he and his father's mother. She would say to him, "Son's son!" And so they lived on there. He served food to her, and then she said, "No! my son's son! Had you not broken me (the point at the tip of the bone awl), then I would be able to eat. But because you broke me, I cannot eat now." She did not ever eat. He would bring a deer, she would merely assist him. They would smoke-dry it.

Now it became summertime, and some blackberries became ripe. He had gotten there (to a blackberry patch), he got back, he told his father's mother, "Father's mother! Perhaps you can pick berries. Some are commencing to ripen now." "Yes. I shall go tomorrow." He showed her the place where. And to be sure the following day then she went, she went to pick berries. She picked both green ones and red ones, with their stems on. She brought them back. He returned in the evening. She placed it (the basket of berries) before him. "Indeed," he said to her. "You found it (the berry patch)." "Yes," she replied to him. He selected ripe ones, he ate them.

Now they (people at a nearby village) were gossiping, they were dis-

cussing Awl and her son's son. "They live luxuriously." At once one un-
married girl said, "I am going to go tomorrow (to them)." So the next day
the girl got ready (she dressed in her finest and carried all her valuables
with her), she went away, she sought them. She went along, she reached a
spring. She thought, "I shall wash my face right here." She sat, and she
washed her face, she combed her hair, she put on her face paint. All done.
Then she proceeded.

Presently while she was going along, she now reached the (patch of)
blackberries. "Oh dear me, they are mixed red and black now (they are
already ripening)." So then she picked them. Pretty soon now it became
dark (because Awl made a storm with her spirit-power). She (the girl)
thought, "Oh too bad! It will rain, I shall get wet."

Shortly after that then she heard someone hallooing, "Whoooo went
through my patch? they have been pulled unripe! they have been trampled! Hm!" she sounded (angry). She (Awl) commenced stabbing at the
woods. At the place where she (the girl) was hiding (to escape the stabs of
the awl), right close by there she stabbed at her (in order to frighten, not
to kill her). She (the girl) said to her, "Hey! old woman! You nearly picked
at (stabbed) me." "Indeed. Is that you? my son's son's wife?" Now she (the
girl) began to help her, they picked blackberries. She (Awl) said to her,
"Don't pick the ones that are too black (overripe), pick all kinds." "All
right." They filled her (Awl's) berry basket. Then they went home, she
took her with her. They went along.

She (Awl) said to her, "Sit here. This is the bed of my son's son." She
served her food, she ate, she finished eating all of it. Then she said to her,
"Wash your head, son's son's wife. (Then) I shall look and see how you
are." So then she washed her head. When all done she said to her, "Comb
your hair. Stand over there. Let your hair down (over your eyes)." So that
is what she did. Now Awl stood there, she said,

> "I am going to stab you, son's son's wife!
> Put your hair down! son's son's wife!
> I am going to stab you.
> Put your hair down! son's son's wife!"

Now she pierced her right to her heart. Her heart burst, she fell, and then
she died. Now she dragged her to the rear of the house, she laid her
down, she piled things on top of her.

Pretty soon afterward then he returned. He went inside. His father's
mother (Awl) just sat there. "So you are sitting here!" "Yes indeed! son's
son!" Whereupon she set food before him, he ate it. Then she set black-

berries in front of him, he ate them. He said to her, "Oh dear me! father's
mother! You are learning now." "Yes," she said to him. She thought, "I
said to her, Do not pick the ones that are too black."

Then another one (the second oldest of the five girls) also said, "Our
older sister perhaps found them. I shall go also." She got ready, and she
went. She was going along, she got to a spring. She saw her (older sister's)
tracks. Face paint was scattered around (on the ground). "Indeed," she
thought. "Right here is where she must have been." She sat there too
(and prepared herself as the older girl had done. The second girl's experience duplicates the first in almost identical words. A third girl then jour-
neys, and the act is again the same, except that in the woods the girl almost weeps because of a premonition of danger. The day after her murder
the fourth girl departs, and in the woods she weeps profusely in her an-
ticipation of an unknown peril—she knows that her involuntary tears are
a bad omen. The fifth and last girl's experience after the murders of her
four older sisters, and the remainder of the myth, are in the following
words).

Over yonder now there was only one (girl remaining). She thought, "I
shall go too." She said to their (the five girls') parents, "I am going to go
too. I am going to try to find where my older sisters went." "Very well."
She got ready, and then she went away. As she was going along she wept
(involuntarily). She thought, "Why am I doing like that?" She quit doing
it. She kept on, she got to a spring. She saw their footprints where her
older sisters had sat. She wept. In vain did she stop it. Now she wept still
more. She thought, "Why am I weeping like that?" She did not wash her
face, she did not comb her hair. Now she went on.

Presently as she was going along, now she heard, "Ouch ouch ouch
ouch ouch my leg! and that is not my name, (nor) have I been killing your
older sisters. You broke my leg." "Really," she said to her (to the injured
Meadow Lark Woman). "Indeed tell me the truth. I am carrying along
everything (that I possess that is valuable and I shall give you these valuables in return for information)." She took her valuables. She wrapped
her (Lark's broken) leg, she chewed up a money-dentalium, she chewed
it, she spit it over her (Lark's) leg. All done (the leg was repaired and the
payment made).

Now she (Lark) gave her the information. She said to her, "To be sure,
when the first of your older sisters came, she got to the place where Awl's
berry patch is. At that place she (your older sister) assisted her. They filled
up her berry basket. She (Awl) took her along with her to her house. She
said to her, Wash your head! Comb your hair! Stand over there! That is
what she (your older sister) did. She said (chanted) to her,

Undo your hair! son's son's wife!
I am going to stab you! son's son's wife!

She pierced her. Her heart burst. She killed her. She dragged her around to the rear of the house. She did like that to all (four) of them. Your older sisters are lying behind the house."

She (Lark) said to her, "Let us go together. Take me with you. Let us go together. When we get to where her berry patch is, she will come to us at that place. You will help her. You will pick blackberries. You should fill it (the berry basket). Then she will say to you, Let us go now. I shall take you to my son's son's and my house. You will say to her, Yes. Go along. She will take you to there, she will give you food. All done (eating), and then she will say to you, Wash your head! Comb your hair! She will say to you, Stand over there! Put your hair down over your face. You will stand there. Then when she says to you (and chants),

Put your hair down over your face!

Then turn and move your hair, look (peering through it) at her. Then when she says to you,

I am going to stab you!

Watch out! Then she might pierce you. Turn and move (aside)! She will miss you, and then you will kill her. Let us be going! Take me along with you!"

They went along, and she placed her upon her shoulder. As they were going along, they got to blackberries. Now she (Lark) said to her, "This place is where she picks berries." Soon now it became dark (because of Awl's spirit-power to make it so). She (Lark) told her, "She is coming now. She is coming now. It will not rain, it is merely her doing that." Soon then they heard someone hallooing. She said, "Whooo has gone through my berry patch? They are being picked there! It is being trampled there!" She (Lark) said to her, "That is her now." Then she started to stab at the woods. She nearly stabbed them. She (Lark) said to her, "Speak to her!" When she (Lark) sat there (on the girl's shoulder), whatever she might have to say to her, she would nudge her, she would pinch her (with her beak).

She (the girl) stood, she said to her (to Awl), "Hey! old woman! You almost pierced me." "Indeed! son's son's wife! is that actually you?" "Yes," she replied to her. She assisted her (picking blackberries). They picked blackberries. They filled her berry basket. She (Awl) said to her, "Let us go now. I shall take you along to my son's son's and my house."

So they went, they got there, she (Awl) served food to her. She (Awl) did not eat. She got through (eating). She (Awl) said to her, "Wash your head now." She finished doing it. "Comb your hair! Stand over there! Put your hair down!" She went, she stood there. She did the very way that she (Awl) told her. The old woman did (chanted),

> "Put down your hair! son's son's wife!
> I am going to stab you!"

She saw her, she moved and looked at her, she (Awl) stabbed at her. She missed her. She pierced the house (wall). There (stuck in the wall and howling in pain) "Ouch ouch ouch! ouch ouch ouch! ouch ouch ouch!"

Meadow Lark came out from there (because she had hid somewhere), she said to her, "You have killed her now. Now I shall take you to where your older sisters are." They went outside, they went around the house, they opened (uncovered) them where they were lying. She sat there, she wept and wept. She (Lark) said to her, "The man will get back pretty soon."

Presently he himself, while he was hunting, now he broke his bow. He thought, "Oh dear! my poor poor father's mother! Something (bad) had happened to my father's mother!" He went back, he saw his house, smoke was rising (as always) from it. He went on, he entered, he saw the (young) woman seated there. He said nothing. No father's mother (was present). He sat down.

She told him, "Probably what is missing in your heart (is your grandmother), (but the fact is that) I killed your father's mother. Look over there!" He turned and looked, he saw his awl stuck there (in the wall). "Oh," he thought, "Indeed now," he said to her.

She told him, "The first of my older sisters came, another one of them came, all four of them. Then I myself came here too. I found all of them dead. She had killed them. Had I not found her here (my Lark helper), she would have killed me too." "Yes," he replied to her. Then they went, they uncovered them. They were becoming black now. "Indeed," he said to her.

(He proceeded to explain,) "To be sure, she was not actually my father's mother. I was merely sewing my moccasins. I broke my awl. I liked it. I threw it under my bed. Then it became this person (Awl) here." "Indeed."

The next day then they buried them. They worked all day long, they buried them. They wrapped them up in everything (of monetary value which) he had. And as for her she put her very own valuables on her older sisters (too).

Story story.

THE WINNEBAGO TRICKSTER CYCLE

The trickster is one of the oldest and most widespread of mythological and literary figures. He is found almost universally among American Indian tribes, and he appears in European, Asian, and African folklore as well. As the name implies, the trickster is, on one level—probably the most important—an amoral practical joker who wanders about playing pranks on unsuspecting victims. But he is far more complex than that. The same figure, in the same set of tales, appears to be alternately an evil spirit and a benevolent deity, a mortal and a god, a creator and a destroyer, a culture hero and a villain. At times he is an ideal citizen, a model to tribal members; at others he is a totally amoral being who flouts the most sacred taboos with impunity. With all the fluctuation, certain things about the trickster are predictable: he is always a wanderer, always hungry, and usually oversexed.

Tricksters abound in folktales: to name just a few, the modern Greek Nasreddin Hodja; the Grimms' Brave Little Tailor; Jack, the hero of the "Jack tales" of the Carolina mountains; the Medieval French Reynard the Fox; and the black American Br'er Rabbit. Tricksters in more formal literature include Homer's Odysseus, the clever slave of Plautus and Terence's New Comedy, Spanish novelist Diego Hurtado de Mendoza's picaro Lazarillo de Tormes, Thackeray's Becky Sharp, and Thomas Mann's Felix Krull. And the trickster is as popular today as he has ever been: Ratso Rizzo of Midnight Cowboy *and Randle Patrick McMurphy of Ken Kesey's* One Flew Over the Cuckoo's Nest *are examples.*

Gods with trickster characteristics include Hermes, the messenger of the Greek gods, who among other things was the god of cunning and theft; Priapus, the lecherous Greek god of fertility; and the Hindu thunder god Indra, who stole heavenly liquor by disguising himself as a quail. Karl Kerenyi, the classical scholar, in his introduction to Paul Radin's The Trickster, *argues that the brothers Prometheus and Epimetheus act as a composite trickster: Prometheus tricks the gods and acts as a benefactor to humanity in stealing fire; Epimetheus acts to human detriment by being Hermes' dupe and allowing the evils in Pandora's box to escape into the world.*[1]

Among the Indians the trickster figure could change form at will. He took a human appearance among the Kiowas, who called him Saynday;

[1] Karl Kerenyi, in Paul Radin, *The Trickster* (New York: Philosophical Library, 1969), p. 181.

the Blackfeet, who called him Old Man; the Poncas, who called him Ishtinike; and the Arapahos, who called him Wiho, or White Man. Animal tricksters include the Ojibways' Hare, the Pawnees' Coyote, and the Raven of the tribes of the Northwest.

The tales presented below are about Wakdjunkaga, the Winnebago trickster. The Winnebagos are a Siouan people of Wisconsin. Their trickster tales differ somewhat from the unstructured tales of other tribes. They arranged them in a sequence based on definite structural principles. The result is a Siouan literary cycle, the most elaborate expression of the form in Indian North America.

The Wakdjunkaga cycle, like a Homeric epic, starts in medias res. Wakdjunkaga, a chief (whom we later find out is the trickster), is preparing to go on the warpath. This seems to be a routine-enough beginning for an Indian story, but in light of Winnebago culture the audience would have found it highly unusual—startling, in fact. Winnebago chiefs were forbidden to go on the warpath: the chief's role was that of intercessor who acted to "succor the needy and plead for clemency in all cases of infractions of tribal law and custom, even in the case of murder."[2] When the Winnebagos heard the first line, they knew that they were hearing some sort of parody of Winnebago custom. It is as if an American story about Viet Nam started, "The troops of Company A were about to move out on patrol, when President Nixon picked up a rifle and decided to join them."

Before going on the warpath, the Trickster decides to have a feast and invites a large group of guests. After eating, the Trickster suddenly disappears, a breach of etiquette in itself, and after a search the guests find him having intercourse with a woman. Having sex before battle was taboo among the Winnebagos, as it was among most Indian tribes. Even after he sets out on the warpath the Trickster continues his outrageous behavior, smashing his canoe and quiver and destroying the war bundle, the collection of sacred objects. Why does he do these things? It appears that the Trickster represents the spirit of anarchy and disorder—or perhaps, since he breaks the most important Winnebago taboos not only with impunity but also with the sympathy, and to the amusement, of the Winnebago audience, he represents the spirit of saturnalia, or licensed anarchy. The Saturnalia was a Roman harvest holiday marked by unrestrained revelry and license in which slaves became temporarily the equals of their masters. In medieval Europe the Feast of Fools was a Christian saturnalian festival. Deacons and other lower church officers mocked Christian rituals by burning old shoes at the altar for incense,

---

[2] Radin, *The Trickster*, pp. 114–15.

singing filthy songs as part of the liturgy, eating blood pudding in mockery of the Eucharist, and throwing bishops in the river. In the American South, before the civil rights movement brought a measure of equality to the races, one day a year was designated as "nigger day," when blacks were temporarily relieved of their burden of toil and deference. Saturnalian holidays remaining in America today include Mardi Gras (the last blowout before Lent) and perhaps the annual office party.

Underlying saturnalia in any culture is the fear that, unless there is a periodic release from societal restrictions, people will rebel, even to the point of turning on their rulers and killing them. Although the ruling powers may not plan it consciously, they know that allowing slaves and subdeacons to commit outrages once a year in a controlled situation is preferable to being deposed or murdered.

Wakdjunkaga's outrageous behavior finally alientates all his fellow tribesmen, and he is left alone, cast out from society. From this point the Trickster begins a pattern of education and socialization in which he becomes progressively more responsible and more valuable to the community.

In the first stage he is like an infant. One possible interpretation of the stories, in which his left and right arm have a knife fight, and in which he burns his anus as punishment for not protecting his dinner, is that like an infant he is learning to distinguish where he ends and the rest of the world begins.[3]

The second stage in his development is sexual. In episode 15 the trickster discovers his penis, and in the next episode he makes use of it with the chief's daughter. An old lady, playing the role of duenna, saves the chief's daughter by extricating the Trickster's penis. The Trickster is unrepentant, of course, but he has been shown that sexual conduct has prescribed limits; he cannot simply penetrate anyone he desires.

In episode 22 of the 49 episodes the Trickster reaches the next stage of socialization. Abruptly he says: "It's about time that I went back to the woman to whom I am really married. Kunu [the trickster's son] must be a pretty big boy by this time." This is the first we hear of a wife and children, and it shows that the trickster has now reached the stage where he will shoulder the responsibility of a family. We are told little about his domestic life, however, and before long he is back on the move again, breaking rules, playing tricks, and falling victim to the tricks of others. Episode 45, however, resumes the theme of development of responsibility as Trickster returns to his native village and becomes an ideal Winnebago citizen, a model to young men who look up to him.

[3] Ibid., p. 135.

In his final stage of development the Trickster becomes a culture hero. He finally remembers in episode 47 why Earthmaker sent him to earth:

He knew that the river [Mississippi] would be inhabited by the Indians and that is why he travelled down it. Whatever he thought might be a hindrance to the Indians he changed. He suddenly recollected the purpose for which he had been sent to the Earth by Earthmaker. That is why he removed all these obstacles along the river.

As he went along he killed and ate all those beings that were molesting the people.

This done, he has his last supper, a short distance from the present location of Saint Louis, Missouri, and departs for the heavens, where he assumes charge of the world just below that of Earthmaker.

1

Once upon a time there was a village in which lived a chief who was just preparing to go on the warpath. The men who were to obtain the material with which to build the fire, that is, to prepare for the feast, were summoned. To them the chief said, 'You who are to obtain the wherewithal for the fire, bring me four large deer.' These were soon secured and brought to him and then those who had brought them, his nephews, immediately put them on the fire.

The people who had been invited to the feast now began to arrive. Was not the chief, himself, going on the warpath? And so, as many as were capable of fighting decided to join him.

When they had finished their feast, the chief suddenly arose and left them and proceeded towards his own lodge. The guests remained there waiting for him to return. When, after a while, he did not reappear, some of them went over to his lodge to see what had happened. There, to their chagrin and horror, they found him cohabiting with a woman. So they returned to the feasting-place and informed the others, whereupon everyone dispersed.

Shortly afterward it was again rumoured that the chief was going on the warpath. Again, someone was dispatched to find the firebuilders. When they were brought to the chief, he told them to bring him two large deer and two large bears. Soon his nephews came back bringing these animals with them. They killed the precise animals he had asked for, two large deer and two large bears. Then the nephews immediately put them on the fire. However, as the animals were being eaten, the chief, the one for whom the feast was being prepared, left them. Even as the guests were eating, indeed before those honoured with invitations to the feast had finished, the chief left them. They waited for some time but he did not return. Since, however, he had not said anything about dispersing, one of the guests went to look for him while the others waited. As before, so again, he found him at home cohabiting with a woman. 'All the people are waiting for you,' the messenger said, addressing him. 'Is that so? Why, what else is there to be done? When the food has been consumed, one is done,' he replied. Thereupon the messenger returned and reported to those waiting what he had witnessed, and all the guests went to their separate homes for, truly, there was nothing further to be accomplished.

After a while it was again rumoured that the chief wished a feast to be prepared for him because he was going on the warpath. When he was asked what kind of animals he wanted, he said, 'Four of the largest kind of male bears.' Only such, he commanded, were to be obtained. As on the former occasions, the nephews went out to hunt them. Soon, they brought the animals that had been asked for and then put them on the fire to cook. Those invited to take part in the feast now began to arrive. Then the feast started. Shortly after it had been designated what people were to be given heads to eat, the leader arose and went out. He did not return. So, after a while, those he had invited to the feast sent one of their number to look for him. There, in his home, they found him again cohabiting with a woman. When this was reported, all the guests departed. They had expected to go on the warpath!

Shortly after, for the fourth time, it was rumoured that the chief was going on the warpath. By this time, because of what had happened before, all those invited realized that this was all mere talk. There would be a feast to which they would all go. But they also knew that the chief had no intention of going on the warpath. As on the three former occasions, so now, the chief commanded his nephews to bring four animals, this time four large female bears. Soon they returned with them and, immediately, the kettles were put on to cook. They all sat down for the feast. There, among them, sat the chief with those who had been invited and, surprisingly enough, he was still there when the feast was over.

2

Now just as the feast was over, the chief arose and, taking his warbundle and his arrowbundle, exclaimed, 'It is I, I, who am going on the warpath!' Then he descended until he came to where there was a boat. Into this boat he stepped immediately. All those who had been at the feast accompanied him and all those capable of fighting got into their boats also. As a matter of fact all the able-bodied men went along because it was the chief who was going on the warpath. Then they pushed out from the shore. It was a large body of water they were descending. As they paddled along the leader unexpectedly turned the boat back toward the shore again. As he landed, he exclaimed loudly, 'It is I who am going on the warpath to fight, I!' Turning to his boat, he shouted, 'You cannot fight! Why should you come along?' Thereupon he pulled it up on land and smashed it to pieces.

Then those who had before thought he was a wicked person were convinced and returned home. Some, however, remained and accompanied him on foot.

3

After a while they crossed a swamp where they saw masses of grass protruding above the ground. There he stopped and exclaimed again, 'It is I who am going on the warpath, I! I am capable of fighting, that is why I am going. I can move about easily. But you, warbundle, cannot do this, you can do nothing of value. It is only when I carry you on my back that you can move. You, cannot, of yourself, move about, nor can you move anything. How, therefore, can you go on the warpath? You are simply a nuisance; that's all.' Thus he shouted. Thereupon he stamped his warbundle into the ground. A part of those still accompanying him turned back at this point.

Again he started out. Suddenly he threw his arrowbundle away exclaiming, 'You are unable to go on the warpath! It is only I who can do that. It is I who can fight, not you, and that is why I am going on the warpath!' Now, the last few people who still remained with him turned back because they saw that he was indeed a wicked person.

From there on he continued alone. He ambled along calling all the objects in the world younger brothers when speaking to them. He and all objects in the world understood one another, understood, indeed, one another's language.

4

As he, Trickster, walked along, suddenly, he came in sight of a knoll. As he approached it, he saw, to his surprise, an old buffalo near it. 'My, my, what a pity! If I only hadn't thrown away that arrowbundle, I would now be able to kill and eat this animal,' he exclaimed. Thereupon he took a knife, cut down the hay and fashioned it into figures of men. These he placed in a circle, leaving an opening at one end. The place was very muddy. Having constructed this enclosure, he went back to where he had seen the buffalo and shouted, 'Oho! My younger brother, here he is! Here he is indeed eating without having anything to worry about. Indeed let nothing prey on his mind! I will keep watch for him against intruders.' Thus he spoke to the buffalo who was feeding to his heart's content. Then he continued, 'Listen, younger brother, this place is completely surrounded by people! Over there, however, is an opening through which you might escape.' Just then the buffalo raised his head unsuspiciously and, to his surprise, he seemed really to be completely surrounded by people. Only at the place Trickster had designated did an opening appear. In that direction, therefore, the buffalo ran. Soon he sank in the mire and Trickster was immediately upon him with his knife and killed him. Then he dragged him over to a cluster of wood and skinned him. Throughout all these operations he used his right arm only.

5

In the midst of these operations suddenly his left arm grabbed the buffalo. 'Give that back to me, it is mine! Stop that or I will use my knife on you!' So spoke the right arm. 'I will cut you to pieces, that is what I will do to you,' continued the right arm. Thereupon the left arm released its hold. But, shortly after, the left arm again grabbed hold of the right arm. This time it grabbed hold of his wrist just at the moment that the right arm had commenced to skin the buffalo. Again and again this was repeated. In this manner did Trickster make both his arms quarrel. That quarrel soon turned into a vicious fight and the left arm was badly cut up. 'Oh, oh! Why did I do this? Why have I done this? I have made myself suffer!' The left arm was indeed bleeding profusely.

Then he dressed the buffalo. When he was finished he started off again. As he walked along the birds would exclaim, 'Look, look! There is Trickster!' Thus they would cry and fly away. 'Ah, you naughty little birds! I wonder what they are saying?' This continued right along. Every bird he met would call out, 'Look, look! There is Trickster! There he is walking about!'

6

As he walked along, he came unexpectedly to a place where he saw a man with a club. 'Hoho!' said Trickster, 'my younger brother, he, too, is walking about! Younger brother, what are you doing?' But he received no answer. Suddenly this man spoke, 'O, my poor children! They must be very hungry.' Trickster plied him with many questions. Indeed he made quite a nuisance of himself with his questions. Yet not once did he receive an answer. Trickster now saw the man do as follows. It so happened that he was near a knoll. He took his club, struck the knoll and, to Trickster's surprise, killed a large, old bear. After this he built a fire and singed the hair off the bear's body. Then he took a pail which he was carrying along with him and boiled the bear in it. As soon as it was cooked he served the meat and spoke again, 'Hurry, children, hurry for you must indeed be very hungry!' Thereupon he took a wooden bowl, put some soup in it and cooled it. Finally he untied a bladder which he had attached to his belt. In it there were four tiny little children. To these it was that he had been speaking so lovingly.

Then Trickster said, 'My, my, younger brother, what fine little children you have!' Thus spoke Trickster. The father of the children let them eat but he was careful not to let them eat very much. When they finished, he put them back again into the bladder and attached it to his belt. After this he broke off some branches, dished out the remaining contents of the kettle and, sitting down, began to eat himself. He ate all in the bowl. Then he drank all the soup that he had cooled in the pail.

Finally, when he was all through, and only then, did he speak to Trickster, 'I was busy before, that is why I did not speak to you.' Thereupon Trickster replied, 'Truly, you have beautiful children, younger brother. Would you not care to entrust two of them to me?' 'No, indeed, you would certainly kill them.' 'No, indeed, younger brother, that is not so,' said Trickster, 'you exaggerate. I wish merely to have the children as companions. That is why I am asking you to let me have them. I will take care of them in the same manner you have been doing.' Thus he continued and finally persuaded the man to let him have two of the children. The father gave him a club, a pail, a bowl and the bear he had killed. Then he took the bladder that was suspended from his belt and put two of the little children in it. 'Now, Trickster, remember, if you kill any of these children you will die. Remember if you kill these little children, no matter where you may be, I will pursue and kill you. Keep what I am giving you and feed these children once a month. Do not change this rule. If you change it in any respect, you will kill them. You have seen what I have done and do you do the same.' Thus he spoke and Trickster replied, 'My younger brother, you have spoken and I have heard. Just as you have ordered so I will do.' Then they separated, each one having a bladder suspended from his belt.

7

Not long after they had separated, as Trickster was walking along, he suddenly exclaimed to himself, 'My, my! My dear little children must be

hungry by now. But why waste time talking about it? I will let them have
something to eat immediately.' He was quite near a knoll, so he took his
club, struck it and in this manner killed a large old bear. Then he hurriedly built a fire and singed the hair off the bear. The body he cut up and
boiled. As soon as it had begun to boil a little, he dished the meat out,
cooled it and when it was cool opened the bladder and said, 'My dear
little children, I miss them a great deal!' Then he uncovered them and fed
them. He filled the wooden bowl high and gave it to them. In spite of all
that the man had told him he did many things strictly forbidden to him.
After he had done all these prohibited things, he put the children back in
the bladder and attached it dangling to his belt.

He had been gathering together pieces of broken wood as he walked
along and now he was ready to sit down for his meal. He ate up everything
that remained and drank all the soup that was in the pail. Then he proceeded on his journey. All the animals in the world mocked him and
called out, 'Trickster!'

After a little while he himself got hungry. 'The little children were to
eat once a month I was told,' he thought to himself. But now he himself
was hungry. So again he said, 'My, my! It is about time for my dear little
children to be hungry again. I must get something for them to eat.' He
immediately searched for a knoll, struck it and killed a bear of enormous
size. He then built a fire, singed the hairs off the bear; cut it up and put it
on to boil. As soon as it was boiled he dished it out and cooled it quickly.
When it was cooled off he took the bladder attached to his belt and
opened it. To his surprise the children were dead. 'The dear little children! How unfortunate that they have died!'

8

Just as he said this the father of the children appeared and said, 'Well,
Trickster, you will die for this! I will kill you, as I said I would if you killed
my children.' As he approached him, Trickster exclaimed appealingly, 'O
my younger brother!' However the man rushed at him so menacingly that
Trickster drew back at once and fled from him. He ran with all his speed
with the other behind him throwing objects at him which barely missed
him. There seemed to be no escape. Only by making sudden and unexpected turns did Trickster escape being struck.

Thus did the man pursue Trickster. In desperation he thought of seeking refuge up in the sky or under the ground, yet he felt that there, too,
he would be followed. 'Trickster, nowhere, no matter where you flee, will
you be able to save your life,' shouted the man. 'No matter where you go,

I will pursue and kill you. So you might as well give up now and be done with it. You are exhausted already as you see. You have nowhere to go. Indeed, you will not be able to find a refuge-place anywhere.' Thus spoke the man.

He pursued Trickster everywhere. It was only by adroit dodging that he escaped being hit by objects thrown at him. Then, suddenly, Trickster got frightened. By this time he had run over the whole earth and he was now approaching the place where the sun rises, the end of the world. Toward a pointed piece of land that projected, in the form of a steep wall of rock into the ocean, toward this he ran. It was the edge of the ocean. He pressed up against it and finally jumped into the water. Right into the middle of the ocean he fell. 'Ah, Trickster, you have saved yourself! You were indeed destined to die!' Then the man gave up the pursuit. Trickster uttered an exclamation of heartfelt relief and said to himself, 'That such a thing should happen to Trickster, the warrior, I never imagined! Why, I almost came to grief!' . . .

12

As he was walking along suddenly he came to a lake, and there in the lake he saw numerous ducks. Immediately he ran back quietly before they could see him and sought out a spot where there was a swamp. From it he gathered a large quantity of reed-grass and made himself a big pack. This he put on his back and carried it to the lake. He walked along the shore of the lake carrying it ostentatiously. Soon the ducks saw him and said, 'Look, that is Trickster walking over there. I wonder what he is doing? Let us call and ask him.' So they called to him, 'Trickster, what are you carrying?' Thus they shouted at him, but he did not answer. Then, again they called to him. But it was only after the fourth call that he replied and said, 'Well, are you calling me?' 'What are you carrying on your back?' they asked. 'My younger brothers, surely you do not know what it is you are asking. What am I carrying? Why, I am carrying songs. My stomach is full of bad songs. Some of these my stomach could not hold and that is why I am carrying them on my back. It is a long time since I sang any of them. Just now there are a large number in me. I have met no people on my journey who would dance for me and let me sing some for them. And I have, in consequence, not sung any for a long time.' Then the ducks spoke to each other and said, 'Come, what if we ask him to sing? Then we could dance, couldn't we?' So one of them called out, 'Well, let it be so. I enjoy dancing very much and it has been a very long time since I last danced.' So they spoke to Trickster, 'Older brother, yes, if you will sing to us we will dance. We have been yearning to dance for some time but could not do so because we had no songs.' Thus spoke the ducks. 'My younger brothers,' replied Trickster, 'you have spoken well and you shall have your desire granted. First, however, I will erect a dancing-lodge.' In this they helped him and soon they had put up a dancing-lodge, a grass-lodge. Then they made a drum. When this was finished he invited them all to come in and they did so. When he was ready to sing he said, 'My younger brothers, this is the way in which you must act. When I sing, when I have people dance for me, the dancers must, from the very beginning, never open their eyes.' 'Good,' they answered. Then when he began to sing he said, 'Now remember, younger brothers, you are not to open your eyes. If you do they will become red.' So, as soon as he began to sing, the ducks closed their eyes and danced.

After a while one of the ducks was heard to flap his wings as he came back to the entrance of the lodge, and cry, 'Quack!' Again and again this happened. Sometimes it sounded as if the particular duck had somehow tightened its throat. Whenever any of the ducks cried out then Trickster would tell the other ducks to dance faster and faster. Finally a duck whose name was Little-Red-Eyed-Duck secretly opened its eyes, just the least little bit it opened them. To its surprise, Trickster was wringing the necks of his fellow ducks! He would also bite them as he twisted their necks. It was while he was doing this that the noise which sounded like the tightening of the throat was heard. In this fashion Trickster killed as many as he could reach.

Little-Red-Eyed-Duck shouted. 'Alas! He is killing us! Let those who can save themselves.' He himself flew out quickly through the opening above. All the others likewise crowded toward this opening. They struck Trickster with their wings and scratched him with their feet. He went among them with his eyes closed and stuck out his hands to grab them. He grabbed one in each hand and choked them to death. His eyes were closed tightly. Then suddenly all of them escaped except the two he had in his grasp.

When he looked at these, to his annoyance, he was holding in each hand a scabby-mouthed duck. In no way perturbed, however, he shouted, 'Ha, ha, this is the way a man acts! Indeed these ducks will make fine soup to drink!' Then he made a fire and cut some sharp-pointed sticks with which to roast them. Some he roasted in this manner, while others he roasted by covering them with ashes. 'I will wait for them to be cooked,' he said to himself. 'I had, however, better go to sleep now. By the time I awake they will unquestionably be thoroughly done. Now, you, my younger brother, must keep watch for me while I go to sleep. If you notice any people, drive them off.' He was talking to his anus. Then, turning his anus toward the fire, he went to sleep.

13

When he was sleeping some small foxes approached and, as they ran along, they scented something that seemed like fire. 'Well, there must be something around here,' they said. So they turned their noses toward the wind and looked and, after a while, truly enough, they saw the smoke of a fire. So they peered around carefully and soon noticed many sharp-pointed sticks arranged around a fire with meat on them. Stealthily they approached nearer and nearer and, scrutinizing everything carefully, they noticed someone asleep there. 'It is Trickster and he is asleep! Let us eat this meat. But we must be very careful not to wake him up. Come, let us eat,' they said to one another. When they came close, much to their surprise, however, gas was expelled from somewhere. 'Pooh!' such was the sound made. 'Be careful! He must be awake.' So they ran back. After a while one of them said, 'Well, I guess he is asleep now. That was only a bluff. He is always up to some tricks.' So again they approached the fire. Again gas was expelled and again they ran back. Three times this happened. When they approached the fourth time gas was again expelled. However, they did not run away. So Trickster's anus, in rapid succession, began to expel more and more gas. Still they did not run away. Once, twice, three times, it expelled gas in rapid succession. 'Pooh! Pooh!' Such was the sound it made. Yet they did not run away. Then louder, still louder, was the sound of the gas expelled. 'Pooh! Pooh! Pooh!' Yet they did not run away. On the contrary, they now began to eat the roasted pieces of duck. As they were eating, the Trickster's anus continued its 'Pooh' incessantly. There the foxes stayed until they had eaten up all the pieces of duck roasted on sticks. Then they came to those pieces that were being roasted under ashes and, in spite of the fact that the anus was expelling gas, 'Pooh! Pooh! Pooh! Pooh!' continuously, they ate these all up too. Then they replaced the pieces with the meat eaten off, nicely under the ashes. Only after that did they go away.

After a while Trickster awoke, 'My, O my!' he exlcaimed joyfully, 'the things I had put on to roast must be cooked crisp by now.' So he went over, felt around, and pulled out a leg. To his dismay it was but a bare bone, completely devoid of meat. 'How terrible! But this is the way they generally are when they are cooked too much!' So he felt around again and pulled out another one. But this leg also had nothing on it, 'How terrible! These, likewise, must have been roasted too much! However, I told my younger brother, anus, to watch the meat roasting. He is a good cook indeed!' He pulled out one piece after the other. They were all the same. Finally he sat up and looked around. To his astonishment, the pieces of meat on the roasting sticks were gone! 'Ah, ha, now I understand! It must have been those covetous friends of mine who have done me this injury!' he exclaimed. Then he poked around the fire again and again but found only bones. 'Alas! Alas! They have caused my appetite to be disappointed, those covetous fellows! And you, too, you despicable object, what about your behaviour? Did I not tell you to watch this fire? You shall remember this! As a punishment for your remissness, I will burn your mouth so that you will not be able to use it!'

Thereupon he took a burning piece of wood and burnt the mouth of his anus. He was, of course, burning himself and, as he applied the fire, he exclaimed, 'Ouch! Ouch! This is too much! I have made my skin smart. Is it not for such things that they call me Trickster? They have indeed talked me into doing this just as if I had been doing something wrong!'

Trickster had burnt his anus. He had applied a burning piece of wood to it. Then he went away.

As he walked along the road he felt certain that someone must have passed along it before for he was on what appeared to be a trail. Indeed, suddenly, he came upon a piece of fat that must have come from someone's body. 'Someone has been packing an animal he had killed,' he thought to himself. Then he picked up a piece of fat and ate it. It had a delicious taste. 'My, my, how delicious it is to eat this!' As he proceeded however, much to his surprise, he discovered that it was a part of himself, part of his own intestines, that he was eating. After burning his anus, his intestines had contracted and fallen off, piece by piece, and these pieces were the things he was picking up. 'My, my! Correctly, indeed, am I named Foolish One, Trickster! By their calling me thus, they have at last actually turned me into a Foolish One, a Trickster!' Then he tied his intestines together. A large part, however, had been lost. In tying it, he pulled it together so that wrinkles and ridges were formed. That is the reason why the anus of human beings has its present shape.

15

On Trickster proceeded. As he walked along, he came to a lovely piece of land. There he sat down and soon fell asleep. After a while he woke up and found himself lying on his back without a blanket. He looked up above him and saw to his astonishment something floating there. 'Aha, aha! The chiefs have unfurled their banner! The people must be having a great feast for this is always the case when the chief's banner is unfurled.' With this he sat up and then first realized that his blanket was gone. It was his blanket he saw floating above. His penis had become stiff and the blanket had been forced up. 'That's always happening to me,' he said. 'My younger brother, you will lose the blanket, so bring it back.' Thus he spoke to his penis. Then he took hold of it and, as he handled it, it got softer and the blanket finally fell down. Then he coiled up his penis and put it in a box. And only when he came to the end of his penis did he find his blanket. The box with the penis he carried on his back.

16

After that he walked down a slope and finally came to a lake. On the opposite side he saw a number of women swimming, the chief's daughter and her friends. 'Now,' exclaimed Trickster, 'is the opportune time: now I am going to have intercourse.' Thereupon he took his penis out of the box and addressed it, 'My younger brother, you are going after the chief's daughter. Pass her friends, but see that you lodge squarely in her, the chief's daughter.' Thus speaking he dispatched it. It went sliding on the surface of the water. 'Younger brother, come back, come back! You will scare them away if you approach in that manner!' So he pulled the penis back, tied a stone around its neck, and sent it out again. This time it dropped to the bottom of the lake. Again he pulled it back, took another stone, smaller in size, and attached it to its neck. Soon he sent it forth again. It slid along the water, creating waves as it passed along. 'Brother, come back, come back! You will drive the women away if you create waves like that!' So he tried a fourth time. This time he got a stone, just the right size and just the right weight, and attached it to its neck. When he dispatched it, this time it went directly towards the designated place. It passed and just barely touched the friends of the chief's daughter. They saw it and cried out, 'Come out of the water, quick!' The chief's daughter was the last one on the bank and could not get away, so the penis lodged squarely in her. Her friends came back and tried to pull it out, but all to no avail. They could do absolutely nothing. Then the men who had the reputation for being strong were called and tried it but they, too, could not move it. Finally they all gave up. Then one of them said, 'There is an old woman around here who knows many things. Let us go and get her.' So they went and got her and brought her to the place where this was happening. When she came there she recognized immediately what was taking place. 'Why, this is First-born, Trickster. The chief's daughter is having intercourse and you are all just annoying her.' Thereupon she went out, got an awl and straddling the penis, worked the awl into it a number of times, singing as she did so:

'First-born, if it is you, pull it out! Pull it out!'

Thus she sang. Suddenly in the midst of her singing, the penis was jerked out and the old woman was thrown a great distance. As she stood there bewildered, Trickster, from across the lake, laughed loudly at her. 'That old naughty woman! Why is she doing this when I am trying to have intercourse? Now, she has spoiled all the pleasure.' . . .

19

As he continued his aimless wandering unexpectedly, much to his surprise, he met a little fox. 'Well, my younger brother, here you are! You are travelling, aren't you?' 'Yes, yes, here I am!' answered the little fox. 'The world is going to be a difficult place to live in and I am trying to find some clean place in which to dwell. That is what I am looking for.' 'Oh, oh, my younger brother, what you have said is very true. I, too, was thinking of the very same thing. I have always wanted to have a companion, so let us live together.' Trickster consented, and so they went on to look for a place in which to dwell.

As they ran along they encountered a jay. 'Well, well, my younger brother, what are you doing?' asked Trickster. 'Older brother, I am looking for a place to live in because the world is soon going to be a difficult place in which to dwell.'

'We are looking for the very same thing. When I heard my younger brother speaking of this I envied him very much. So let us live together, for we also are hunting for such a place.' Thus spoke Trickster.

Then they went on together and soon they came across a *hetcgeniga* (nit). 'Well, well, my younger brother, what are you doing?' they asked. 'Older brothers, I am looking for a pleasant place to live in,' the bird answered. 'Younger brother, we are travelling about looking for the same thing. When I heard these others saying that they wanted to live together as companions I liked it. Let us, therefore, live together,' said Trickster.

They were all agreed and soon they came to a place where the river forked and where there was a lovely piece of land with red oaks growing upon it. It was indeed a beautiful place. This, they agreed, was a delightful place to live in, and so they stopped there and built themselves a lodge.

In the fall, when everything was ripe, they had, of course, all they

wanted to eat. However, winter soon approached and not long after it began, a deep snow fell. The situation of the four now became indeed very
difficult. They had nothing to eat and they were getting quite hungry.
Then Trickster spoke, 'Younger brothers, it is going to be very difficult.
However, if we do the thing I am about to suggest, it will be good. So, at
least, I think.' 'All right, if it is indeed something good that our older
brother means we certainly will do it, for otherwise some of us will starve
to death. What is it that we should do that is good and by which we can
get something to eat?' 'Listen. There is a village yonder, where they are
enjoying great blessings. The chief has a son who is killing many animals.
He is not married yet but is thinking of it. Let us go over there. I will
disguise myself as a woman and marry him. Thus we can live in peace
until spring comes.' 'Good!' they ejaculated. All were willing and delighted to participate.

20

Trickster now took an elk's liver and made a vulva from it. Then he took
some elk's kidneys and made breasts from them. Finally he put on a
woman's dress. In this dress his friends enclosed him very firmly. The
dresses he was using were those that the women who had taken him for a
racoon had given him. He now stood there transformed into a very pretty
woman indeed. Then he let the fox have intercourse with him and make
him pregnant, then the jaybird and, finally, the nit. After that he proceeded toward the village.

Now, at the end of the village, lived an old woman and she immediately
addressed him, saying, 'My granddaughter, what is your purpose in travelling around like this? Certainly it is with some object in view that you
are travelling!' Then the old woman went outside and shouted, 'Ho! Ho!
There is someone here who has come to court the chief's son.' This, at
least, is what the old woman seemed to be saying. Then the chief said to
his daughters, 'Ho! This clearly is what this woman wants and is the reason for her coming; so, my daughters, go and bring your sister-in-law
here.' Then they went after her. She certainly was a very handsome
woman. The chief's son liked her very much. Immediately they prepared
dried corn for her and they boiled slit bear-ribs. That was why Trickster
was getting married, of course. When this food was ready they put it in a
dish, cooled it, and placed it in front of Trickster. He devoured it at once.
There she (Trickster) remained.

Not long after Trickster became pregnant. The chief's son was very
happy about the fact that he was to become a father. Not long after that

Trickster gave birth to a boy. Then again he became pregnant and gave birth to another boy. Finally for the third time he became pregnant and gave birth to a third boy.

21

The last child cried as soon as it was born and nothing could stop it. The crying became very serious and so it was decided to send for an old woman who had the reputation for being able to pacify children. She came, but she, likewise, could not pacify him. Finally the little child cried out and sang:

'If I only could play with a little piece of white cloud!'

They went in search of a shaman, for it was the chief's son who was asking for this and, consequently, no matter what the cost, it had to be obtained. He had asked for a piece of white cloud, and a piece of white cloud, accordingly, they tried to obtain. But how could they obtain a piece of white cloud? All tried very hard and, finally, they made it snow. Then, when the snow was quite deep, they gave him a piece of snow to play with and he stopped crying.

After a while he again cried out and sang:

'If I could only play with a piece of blue sky!'

Then they tried to obtain a piece of blue sky for him. Very hard they tried, but were not able to obtain any. In the spring of the year, however, they gave him a piece of blue grass and he stopped crying.

After a while he began to cry again. This time he asked for some blue (green) leaves. Then the fourth time he asked for some roasting ears. They gave him green leaves and roasting ears of corn and he stopped crying.

One day later, as they were steaming corn, the chief's wife teased her sister-in-law. She chased her around the pit where they were steaming corn. Finally, the chief's son's wife (Trickster) jumped over the pit and she dropped something very rotten. The people shouted at her, 'It is Trickster!' The men were all ashamed, especially the chief's son. The animals who had been with Trickster, the fox, the jaybird and the nit, all of them now ran away.

22

Trickster also ran away. Suddenly he said to himself, 'Well, why am I doing all this? It is about time that I went back to the woman to whom

I am really married. Kunu must be a pretty big boy by this time.' Thus spoke Trickster. Then he went across the lake to the woman to whom he was really married. When he got here he found, much to his surprise, that the boy that had been born to him was indeed quite grown up. The chief was very happy when Trickster came home. 'My son-in-law has come home,' he ejaculated. He was very happy indeed. Trickster hunted game for his child and killed very many animals. There he stayed a long time until his child had become a grown-up man. Then, when he saw that his child was able to take care of himself, he said, 'Well, it is about time for me to start travelling again for my boy is quite grown up now. I will go around the earth and visit people for I am tired of staying here. I used to wander around the world in peace. Here I am just giving myself a lot of trouble.'

23

As he went wandering around aimlessly he suddenly heard someone speaking. He listened very carefully and it seemed to say, 'He who chews me will defecate; he will defecate!' That was what it was saying. 'Well, why is this person talking in this manner?' said Trickster. So he walked in the direction from which he had heard the speaking and again he heard, quite near him, someone saying: 'He who chews me, he will defecate; he will defecate!' This is what was said. 'Well, why does this person talk in such fashion?' said Trickster. Then he walked to the other side. So he continued walking along. Then right at his very side, a voice seemed to say, 'He who chews me, he will defecate; he will defecate!' 'Well, I wonder who it is who is speaking. I know very well that if I chew it, I will not defecate.' But he kept looking around for the speaker and finally discovered, much to his astonishment, that it was a bulb on a bush. The bulb it was that was speaking. So he seized it, put it in his mouth, chewed it, and then swallowed it. He did just this and then went on.

'Well, where is the bulb gone that talked so much? Why, indeed, should I defecate? When I feel like defecating, then I shall defecate, no sooner. How could such an object make me defecate!' Thus spoke Trickster. Even as he spoke, however, he began to break wind. 'Well this, I suppose, is what it meant. Yet the bulb said I would defecate, and I am merely expelling gas. In any case I am a great man even if I do expel a little gas!' Thus he spoke. As he was talking he again broke wind. This time it was really quite strong. 'Well, what a foolish one I am. This is why I am called Foolish One, Trickster.' Now he began to break wind again and again. 'So this is why the bulb spoke as it did, I suppose.' Once more he broke wind. This time it was very loud and his rectum began to smart.

'Well, it surely is a great thing!' Then he broke wind again, this time with so much force, that he was propelled forward. 'Well, well, it may even make me give another push, but it won't make me defecate,' so he exclaimed defiantly. The next time he broke wind, the hind part of his body was raised up by the force of the explosion and he landed on his knees and hands. 'Well, go ahead and do it again! Go ahead and do it again!' Then, again, he broke wind. This time the force of the expulsion sent him far up in the air and he landed on the ground, on his stomach. The next time he broke wind, he had to hang on to a log, so high was he thrown. However, he raised himself up and, after a while, landed on the ground, the log on top of him. He was almost killed by the fall. The next time he broke wind, he had to hold on to a tree that stood near by. It was a poplar and he held on with all his might yet, nevertheless, even then, his feet flopped up in the air. Again, and for the second time, he held on to it when he broke wind and yet he pulled the tree up by the roots. To protect himself, the next time, he went on until he came to a large tree, a large oak tree. Around this he put both his arms. Yet, when he broke wind, he was swung up and his toes struck against the tree. However, he held on.

After that he ran to a place where people were living. When he got there, he shouted, 'Say, hurry up and take your lodge down, for a big war-party is upon you and you will surely be killed! Come let us get away!' He scared them all so much that they quickly took down their lodge, piled it on Trickster, and then got on him themselves. They likewise placed all the little dogs they had on top of Trickster. Just then he began to break wind again and the force of the expulsion scattered the things on top of him in all directions. They fell far apart from one another. Separated, the people were standing about and shouting to one another; and the dogs, scattered here and there, howled at one another. There stood Trickster laughing at them till he ached.

Now he proceeded onward. He seemed to have gotten over his troubles. 'Well, this bulb did a lot of talking,' he said to himself, 'yet it could not make me defecate.' But even as he spoke he began to have the desire to defecate, just a very little. 'Well, I suppose this is what it meant. It certainly bragged a good deal, however.' As he spoke he defecated again. 'Well, what a braggart it was! I suppose this is why it said this.' As he spoke these last words, he began to defecate a good deal. After a while, as he was sitting down, his body would touch the excrement. Thereupon he got on top of a log and sat down there but, even then, he touched the excrement. Finally, he climbed up a log that was leaning against a tree. However, his body still touched the excrement, so he went up higher. Even then, however, he touched it so he climbed still higher up. Higher and higher he had to go. Nor was he able to stop defecating. Now he was on top of the tree. It was small and quite uncomfortable. Moreover, the excrement began to come up to him.

24

Even on the limb on which he was sitting he began to defecate. So he tried a different position. Since the limb, however, was very slippery he fell right down into the excrement. Down he fell, down into the dung. In fact he disappeared in it, and it was only with very great difficulty that he was able to get out of it. His racoon-skin blanket was covered with filth, and he came out dragging it after him. The pack he was carrying on his back was covered with dung, as was also the box containing his penis. The box he emptied and then placed it on his back again.

25

Then, still blinded by the filth, he started to run. He could not see anything. As he ran he knocked against a tree. The old man cried out in pain. He reached out and felt the tree and sang:
'Tree, what kind of a tree are you? Tell me something about yourself!'
And the tree answered, 'What kind of a tree do you think I am? I am an oak tree. I am the forked oak tree that used to stand in the middle of the valley. I am that one,' it said. 'Oh, my, is it possible that there might be some water around here?' Trickster asked. The tree answered, 'Go straight on.' This is what it told him. As he went along he bumped up against another tree. He was knocked backwards by the collision. Again he sang:
'Tree, what kind of a tree are you? Tell me something about yourself!'
'What kind of a tree do you think I am? The red oak tree that used to stand at the edge of the valley, I am that one.' 'Oh, my, is it possible that there is water around here?' asked Trickster. Then the tree answered and said, 'Keep straight on,' and so he went again. Soon he knocked against another tree. He spoke to the tree and sang:
'Tree, what kind of a tree are you? Tell me something about yourself!'
'What kind of a tree do you think I am? The slippery elm tree that used to stand in the midst of the others, I am that one.' Then Trickster asked, 'Oh, my, is it possible that there would be some water near here?' And the tree answered and said, 'Keep right on.' On he went and soon he bumped into another tree and he touched it and sang:
'Tree, what kind of a tree are you? Tell me something about yourself!'
'What kind of a tree do you think I am? I am the basswood tree that

used to stand on the edge of the water. That is the one I am.' 'Oh, my, it is good,' said Trickster. So there in the water he jumped and lay. He washed himself thoroughly.

It is said that the old man almost died that time, for it was only with the greatest difficulty that he found the water. If the trees had not spoken to him he certainly would have died. Finally, after a long time and only after great exertions, did he clean himself, for the dung had been on him a long time and had dried. After he had cleansed himself he washed his racoon-skin blanket and his box.

26

As he was engaged in this cleansing he happened to look in the water and much to his surprise he saw many plums there. He surveyed them very carefully and then he dived down into the water to get some. But only small stones did he bring back in his hands. Again he dived into the water. But this time he knocked himself unconscious against a rock at the bottom. After a while he floated up and gradually came to. He was lying on the water, flat on his back, when he came to and, as he opened his eyes, there on the top of the bank he saw many plums. What he had seen in the water was only the reflection. Then he realized what he had done. 'Oh, my, what a stupid fellow I must be! I should have recognized this. Here I have caused myself a great deal of pain.'

27

Then he went on to the shore and ate as many plums as possible, and putting a belt around his racoon-skin blanket he filled it likewise with plums and proceeded downstream.

Much to his surprise as he travelled along he came upon an oval lodge. He peeped in and saw two women with many children. He took one of the plums and threw it through the top of the lodge. It made a great noise. The women grabbed it. This he repeated and soon one of the women came out and saw, unexpectedly, a man standing there. 'Aha, it is my older brother who is doing this.' She and her companion asked him to come in, and as he entered the lodge he gave a plum apiece to each of the women. Then they asked him, "Where did you pick these, older brother?' 'There are many of these at a particular place, sisters, and if you wish to pick them I will tell you where to go.' 'We would like very much to have some, brother,' they said. 'However, we cannot leave our children alone for they are very disobedient.' 'Sisters, if you wish to go, I will take care of the children for you,' he said. 'You are very good, older brother,' they said. 'You cannot possibly miss the place,' he added, 'for there are so many plums there. You cannot really pick them all for they are too plentiful. If, toward evening, as the sun sets, you see the sky red, you will know that the plums are causing it. Do not turn back for you will surely find it.'

They started out and as soon as they were out of sight, he killed the children, singed them, and then boiled them. They were racoons. 'Well, now, for once I am going to have a good meal,' he said. There he ate a good deal; he ate a good deal of singed racoon meat. When he was finished, he cut off the head of one of the children, put a stick through its neck and placed it at the door as though the child were peeping out and laughing. After that he went to a hill that was not far off. . . .

34

One day he met a hawk flying about. He was looking for something dead or decaying. 'You ugly, good-for-nothing fellow, you once played a trick on me and I should like to return that compliment.' This is what was in Trickster's mind. So he lay down at the edge of the water where the waves come up and took on the form of a large dead buck-deer, one who had died but whose body had not yet decayed. The crows were already there longing for the carcass yet nowhere could they find a place at which to attack it for the hide was still tough owing to the fact that putrefaction had not yet set in. Then the hawk came and the crows shouted at him. They said to one another, 'He alone generally has a sharp knife.' They had to call for him repeatedly before he came. He was energetic and went all around the animal looking for a place at which to attack it. Finally he came to the hind part and began working his head into the rectum. He hurt Trickster so much in pecking at him that Trickster almost jumped up. Finally, however, he got his head into the rectum so that he could bite at some pieces inside. As soon as hawk's head was far in, Trickster closed his rectum tightly and arose. 'Aha, Mr. Hawk, you once hurt me a good deal and I thought to myself that some day I would get even with you." Then he went on. The hawk tried to get free but all to no avail. He could not free himself. At first he kept his wings flapping all the time but, after a while, he only flapped them intermittently.

35

Then Trickster walked on. Soon he came upon a bear and the bear said to him, 'O, Kunu, how that tail becomes you!' Trickster made no answer but kept on. 'O, Kunu, how that tail becomes you! If only I were that way!' Then, after a while, the bear again spoke, 'O, Kunu, how that tail becomes you! I wish I could have one too!' Then Trickster answered and said, 'You are always talking in that way. What is the difficulty of obtaining one? Why don't you make one for yourself? When I saw one, a little time ago, I liked it and I had one made for me. Anyone who wishes to can get one.' 'All right, Kunu, since you think you can make me one, why I wish you would.' 'Good, that I will do for you. Now, look at the tail carefully and if anyone asks you to give him one like it, do the following.' Thereupon he addressed the hawk, 'Go, get out, for another tail is desired.' So he loosened his hold and there was an odour of foul air. The hawk got up and walked away. All his feathers were gone.

Trickster now turned to the bear, and said, 'Well, let me now first prepare you properly for the tail so that when the hawk comes back I can put him in your rectum.' Then he took a knife and cut out the bear's rectum and, pulling out his intestines, killed him. He built a fire and singed the hair off the bear. 'My, how long it has been since I have had the food that I like best! Now I surely will get my fill.' When he got through preparing the meat he put it on to boil.

36

Suddenly, however, he saw a mink at the edge of the water coming toward him. 'Ah, my little brother, I see you are walking about. Come over here, my younger brother, for I am about to eat. Let us eat together.' Thus he spoke. Then the mink came and he again spoke to him. 'My younger brother, a thought just occurred to me. Let us run a race and let the one who wins be the chief. The one who loses will then dish out the food.' In imagination he was already thinking of how mink would dish out the food for him, for he felt positive he would unquestionably defeat him. He thought that if mink dished it out he would get his fill.

After a while he spoke to mink again, saying, 'Well, little brother, since the ground around here is not suitable for a race, let us run on the ice.' The river at that time was frozen. Both, accordingly, started off for a place in the river from which to start the race. The pot with the food in it was to be the goal and the one who would touch the food first was to be declared the winner. Both agreed to all these things. Thereupon they started the race. Soon Trickster was left far behind. He, however, continued on until he came to a crack in the ice. There he stopped suddenly and spoke to the mink, 'My little brother, what is it you said when you came to the crack in the ice and walked on?' The mink replied, 'I said, "Crack in the ice, become large!" and then I jumped over it.' So Trickster said the same, 'Crack in the ice, become large!' Then he jumped over it. But the crack in the ice became quite large and he fell into the water. Immediately the edges of the crack joined again and Trickster was left under the ice. This is exactly what happened. With Trickster under the ice mink dished out the food for himself and ate it. He ate his fill of it.

Trickster, in the meantime, kept going under the ice until he got alongside of mink and said, 'My little brother, as you have eaten up the food alone, place a little piece in your mouth for me, a good piece.' He was speaking from under the crack in the ice. Then he put a piece in his mouth for Trickster. Then Trickster asked him to do it again and again he did it. The fourth time he asked him he put the last piece in his mouth. Then when the meat was entirely gone he drank up the soup and dropped a piece of bear's dung into Trickster's mouth. 'My, what a bad fellow he is! He even abuses me! You will die for this!' Outraged, he broke through the ice, came out and chased the mink, but the latter finally got under the ice and escaped.

'It is a shame that he played such a trick on me, that despicable fellow! Some day I will get my revenge. He will have no place to which to escape.' Thus he spoke.

37

Soon he came to a human habitation and went to the village where he had previously married. He thought he would then be able to wreak his vengeance on the mink there. He borrowed a very good hunting dog and immediately started off in pursuit. But the mink would not come out from under the ice and there was thus no way in which he could get at him. Trickster did not care how he did it but he certainly wanted to revenge himself on the mink.

38

Then he continued his wandering. Suddenly he heard something singing:

'Trickster, what is it you are packing? Your penis it is you are packing!'

'My, what an awful thing he is saying, that contemptible person! He seems really to know what I am carrying.' On he went. Shortly after this, and from a definite direction, he again heard singing. It was as if it was just at his side:

'Trickster, what is it you are carrying? Your testicles, these you are carrying.'

'My, who is this that is mentioning these things? He must indeed, have been watching me. Well, now I will carry these things correctly.' Thereupon he emptied his box and threw everything out. Then he placed his testicles underneath next to his back. As he was doing this again, suddenly, he heard someone singing right at his side:

'Trickster, what is it you are packing? What is it you are packing? Your testicles underneath, your testicles underneath!'

'My, what a contemptible person it is who is thus teasing me! He must have been watching my pack.' So again he rearranged his pack. He now put the head of his penis on top. Then he went on but soon, unexpectedly, he heard the singing at his side again:

'Trickster, what is it you are packing? Your penis you are packing! The head of your penis you have placed on top, the head of your penis you have placed on top!'

'My, what an evil one it is who is saying this,' and he jumped towards him. But the one who had been singing ran away, exclaiming, 'Tigi! Tigi! Tigi!' It ran into a hollow tree. It was a chipmunk. 'I will kill you for this, you contemptible thing,' said Trickster. Thereupon he spoke to his penis. 'Now then, my younger brother, you may go after him for he has been annoying you for a long time.'

So he took out his penis and probed the hollow tree with it. He could not, however, reach the end of the hole. So he took some more of his penis and probed again, but again he was unable to reach the end of the hole. So he unwound more and more of his penis and probed still deeper, yet all to no avail. Finally he took what still remained, emptying the entire box, and probed and probed but still he could not reach the end of the hole. At last he sat up on a log and probed as far as he could, but still he was unable to reach the end. 'Ho!' said he impatiently, and suddenly withdrew his penis. Much to his horror, only a small piece of it was left. 'My, what a great injury he has done to me! You contemptible thing I will repay you for this!'

39

Then he kicked the log to pieces. There he found the chipmunk and flattened him out, and there, too, to his horror he discovered his penis all gnawed up. 'Oh, my, of what a wonderful organ he has deprived me! But why do I speak thus? I will make objects out of the pieces for human beings to use.' Then he took the end of his penis, the part that has no foreskin, and declared, 'This is what human beings will call the lily-of-the-lake.' This he threw in a lake near by. Then he took the other pieces declaring in turn: 'This the people will call potatoes; this the people will call turnips; this the people will call artichokes; this the people will call ground-beans; this the people will call dog-teeth; this the people will call sharp-claws; this the people will call rice.' All these pieces he threw into the water. Finally he took the end of his penis and declared, 'This the people will call the pond-lily.' He was referring to the square part of the end of his penis.

What was left of his penis was not very long. When, at last, he started off again, he left behind him the box in which he had until then kept his penis coiled up.

And this is the reason our penis has its present shape. It is because of these happenings that the penis is short. Had the chipmunk not gnawed off Trickster's penis our penis would have the appearance that Trickster's had first had. It was so large that he had to carry it on his back. Now it would not have been good had our penis remained like that and the chipmunk was created for the precise purpose of performing this particular act. Thus it is said. . . .

45

One day Trickster said, 'Well, I think it is about time that we went back to the village. Perhaps they are lonesome for us, especially for the children.' 'Well, let us do that. I was thinking of it myself,' said his wife. When they were ready to go back, they packed their possessions and began to carry them away. It required many trips. Trickster would go for a short distance. The children helped but there were so many packs that they did not get very far in a day. After a while they got near their home and all the people in the village came out to greet and help him with the packs. The people of the village were delighted. 'Kunu is back,' they shouted. The chief lived in the middle of the village and alongside of him they built a long lodge for Trickster. The young men would gather there at night and he would entertain them, for he was a very good-natured fellow. The young men always liked to gather around him and, when they were out courting women, he would go along just for the fun of it.

One day a traveller came to the village. The Trickster knew who he was. The other young men tried to get the stranger to go out courting the girls but he would not do it. However, Trickster said to him, 'Say, the chief's daughter is in love with you. That is what the old woman told me she had told her.' 'Well,' said the stranger, 'it is on account of the other young men that I don't go out courting although I am perfectly willing to do so. However, don't say anything about it. I will try it tonight.' Then Trickster took some fish-oil and some artichoke roots, pounded them together and gave them to the young man to eat. He did this purposely in order to play a trick on him. That night he went courting with the stranger and, when they got to the place where the chief's daughter was accustomed to sleep, he showed the place to him. Then the young man went inside and stayed there all night. Trickster watched him all that time. About daybreak something terrible happened! The young man was just about to go away when the oil that he had eaten caused him to have a passage. He did not know, however, that it was Trickster's doing. He soiled the chief's daughter. Then Trickster shouted, 'The traveller has soiled the chief's daughter!' He went through the entire village announcing it. The traveller was very much ashamed for he was no other than the mink and that is why Trickster played this trick on him. He was just going to marry the chief's daughter when this happened to him. Mink then went into the brush and did not return. Trickster laughed heartily at him. 'What a funny fellow! When you escaped from me I just ached to get hold of you and now you have come right here!' Thus he spoke.

46

In the village in which they were staying the people owned two horses. The coyote had married into the village. Trickster was very desirous of revenging himself on him and coyote, on his side, had the desire of playing a trick on Trickster. However, Trickster discovered what coyote intended to do and did not like it. 'Many times he has done me wrong and I let it pass, but this time I am not going to overlook it. This time I intend to play a trick on him,' said Trickster.

Then he went into the wilderness, to the place where the horses belonging to the village generally stayed. He found one of them and put it to sleep. When he was quite certain that the horse was asleep he went after mouse and said, 'Say, there is an animal dead here. Go to coyote and tell him, "My grandson, there is an animal dead over there and I was unable to move him. It is over there near the village. Pull it to one side and then we will be able to have it to ourselves."' Mouse was quite willing and ran over to coyote and said, 'Grandson, I know you are very strong and therefore I wish to tell you that there is an animal over there near the village, lying dead. If you will push it aside, it will be good. I wanted to do it myself but I was unable to pull it and that is why I have come over here to tell you, for I have compassion upon you.' Coyote was very much delighted and went to the place. Trickster, at the same moment ran back to the village and waited for them. The mouse and the coyote soon arrived and the mouse tied the horse's tail to the coyote. Tightly she tied the two together. Then the coyote said, 'I am very strong and I know that I can pull this animal. The animal that I am about to pull is called an elk or a deer.' 'Well, everything is ready, you may pull it now,' said the mouse. 'All right,' said the coyote and tried to pull it. He woke the horse up and it got scared. Up it jumped and finding an animal tied to its tail it got even more frightened and began racing at full speed. Coyote was pulled along looking as through he were a branch being dragged. The horse ran to the village and Trickster shouted at the top of his voice, 'Just look at him, our son-in-law, coyote! He is doing something very disgraceful. Look at him!' Then all the people ran out and there, unexpectedly, they saw coyote tied to the horse's tail bouncing up and down. The horse finally went to its master and there it was caught. They untied the coyote and his mouth just twitched as he sat up. He was very much ashamed. He did not even go back to his lodge. He left the village and was not more seen. He had a wife and many children but those too he left. From that time on he has not lived among people. If a person sees him anywhre he is ashamed of himself and when one gets very close to him his mouth twitches. He is still ashamed of what happened to him long ago.

47

Trickster stayed at that village for a long time and raised many children. One day he said, 'Well, this is about as long as I will stay here. I have been here a long time. Now I am going to go around the earth again and visit different people for my children are all grown up. I was not created for what I am doing here.'

Then he went around the earth. He started at the end of the Mississippi river and went down to the stream. The Mississippi is a spirit-village and the river is its main road. He knew that the river was going to be inhabited by Indians and that is why he travelled down it. Whatever he thought might be a hindrance to the Indians he changed. He suddenly recollected the purpose for which he had been sent to the earth by Earthmaker. That is why he removed all these obstacles along the river.

As he went along he killed and ate all those beings that were molesting the people. The waterspirits had their roads only at a short distance below the surface of the earth so he pushed these farther in. These waterspirit-roads are holes in the rivers. Many rivers have eddies which it would be impossible for a boat to pass through and these he pushed farther down into the ground.

48

He went all over the earth, and one day he came to a place where he found a large waterfall. It was very high. Then he said to the waterfall, 'Remove yourself to some other location for the people are going to inhabit this place and you will annoy them.' Then the waterfall said, 'I will not go away. I chose this place and I am going to stay here.' 'I tell you, you are going to some other place,' said Trickster. The waterfall, however, refused to do it. 'I am telling you that the earth was made for man to live on and you will annoy him if you stay here. I came to this earth to rearrange it. If you don't do what I tell you, I will not use you very gently.' Then the waterfall said, 'I told you when I first spoke to you that I would not move and I am not going to.' Then Trickster cut a stick for himself and shot it into the falls and pushed the falls on to the land.

49

Finally he made a stone kettle and said, 'Now for the last time I will eat a meal on earth. There he boiled his food and when it was cooked he put it in a big dish. He had made a stone dish for himself. There he sat and ate. He sat on top of a rock and his seat is visible to the present day. There, too, can be seen the kettle and the dish and even the imprint of his buttocks. Even the imprint of his testicles can be seen there. This meal he ate at a short distance from the place where the Missouri enters the Mississippi. Then he left and went first into the ocean and then up to the heavens.

Under the world where Earthmaker lives, there is another world just like it and of this world, he, Trickster, is in charge. Turtle is in charge of the third world and Hare is in charge of the world in which we live.

SONGS

Indian songs are usually printed in anthologies as poems, with no indication that they were originally musical compositions. This is unavoidable in many cases because much of the music is lost, but it gives a distorted idea of the pieces. They were, after all, songs and, as such, were not read to a silent audience as literary creations but sung to the accompaniment of instruments such as the drum, rattle, and flute. I have printed the music for the first song to serve as an example. The score reminds us that these are musical compositions and that the words are only half the work. The songs for which the music is lost still merit consideration solely as poetry.

Since Whitman and Pound—not to mention contemporary poets like Ginsberg, Koch, and Ashbery—the once-clear distinction between English prose and poetry has blurred. It is therefore a good idea to make clear the difference between Indian poetry—which comes to us in the form of songs—and prose. Frederick Webb Hodge made the following distinction: "Prose rituals are always intoned, and the delivery brings out the rhythmic character of the composition. Rituals that are sung differ from those that are intoned in that the words, in order to conform to the music, are drawn out by vowel prolongations . . . the musical phrase will determine the length of the line, and the number of musical phrases the number of lines to the stanza."[1]

The heavy use of symbolism in Indian poetry makes it difficult to understand for outsiders to the tribal culture. Natalie Curtis compares the Indian use of poetic symbolism to their use of graphic symbols:

Indian poetry, like Indian art, is expressed in symbol. The cloud form in Indian design is no copy of a cloud, but a conventionalized image that is a symbol mean-

[1] Frederick Webb Hodge, *Handbook of American Indians North of Mexico* (New York: Pageant Books, 1959), vol. 2, p. 271.

73

ing cloud, as a wavy line means water or a cross stands for a star. Even so in poetry. One word may be the symbol of a complete idea that, in English, would
need a whole sentence for its expression. Even those who know the language may
not understand the songs unless they know what meaning lies behind the symbolic words.[2]

*For instance, Geronimo's "Medicine Song" reads in Apache, "Awbizhaye /
Shichl hadahiyago niniya / Tsago degi naleya" (I have taken out the
meaningless vocables put in for rhythmical purposes). Natalie Curtis
translates the song:*

> Through the air
> I fly upon a cloud
> Towards the sky, far, far, far,
> There to find the holy place,
> Ah, now the change comes o'er me![3]

*Naleya—"changing while going thru the air"—is one of the words
Curtis describes as "a symbol for a complete idea that, in English, would
need a whole sentence for its expression."*

*Often Indian songs contain allusions to Indian customs and beliefs
which are unfamiliar to whites. In many cases, a song is meaningless or
misleading unless an explanation accompanies it. For example, the Winnebago song, "Mother, let me go to my uncle," is uncomprehensible unless
one is familiar with the situation. Winnebago braves would sit outside on
warm summer evenings playing the flute in hopes of luring the young girls
out of their tipis. On hearing the plaintive notes of the flutes, the young
ladies would think of excuses to go out; for instance, to run errands or, as
in the song cited above, to pay visits.[4]*

*Another reason Indian songs may at first puzzle modern American
readers is that their style differs markedly from most of the corpus of English poetry. Surprisingly, they bear a strong resemblance to Japanese poetry, particularly the Chippewa and Teton Sioux songs. On the printed
page, Chippewa songs resemble haiku, the seventeen-syllable classical
Japanese verse form. Repetitions and meaningless vocables have been
eliminated by the translator in the selections below, but, as Kenneth
Rexroth has pointed out, repetition and vocables are characteristic of
Japanese poetry also.[5]*

[2] Curtis, *The Indian's Book* (New York: Harper and Brothers, 1970), p. xxx.
[3] Ibid., p. 260.
[4] Ibid., p. 261.
[5] Kenneth Rexroth, *Assays* (Norfolk, Conn.: J. Loughlin, 1961), p. 57.

Harold Henderson describes haiku as poems "intended to express and evoke emotion" depending for their effect on the power of suggestion and employing as their chief technique a "clear-cut picture which serves as a starting point for trains of thought and emotion." [6] *For instance:*

> The tower high
> I climb; there, on that fir top,
> sits a butterfly![7]

It is impossible to paraphrase the poem, but the general idea is that the poet has exerted himself in climbing a tower, possibly to get a view of a vast and beautiful expanse of countryside, yet what catches his attention when he arrives at the top is a simple butterfly that he might have viewed on the ground. He is struck with its beauty and is reminded that beauty exists everywhere, not only at special viewing places.

This haiku, like most, is set out of doors and implies a close relationship between human beings and nature. Haiku are traditionally set in a particular ki, *or season, which the reader recognizes by traditional symbols. For instance, cherry blossoms symbolize spring; snow symbolizes winter; and the butterfly, summer.*

The Chippewa poem that follows is similar to traditional haiku in that it is brief yet manages to evoke a range of thoughts and emotions:

> As my eyes search the prairie
> I feel the summer in the spring.

It is dependent on a visual image, although, as in haiku, there is a strong element of synesthesia (in this case, the additional sense is tactile). Finally, it is set outdoors amid natural surroundings and set in a particular season.

One of the charms of Indian songs and poetry is their directness and openness. There are no wasted words, and there is very little of the coyness, rhetorical posing, and use of assumed attitudes common in English and European sonnets. For example, note the complete absence of false modesty in the Chippewa song:

> I can charm the man.
> He is completely fascinated with me.

---

[6] Harold Henderson, *An Introduction to Haiku* (Garden City, N.Y.: Doubleday, 1958), p. 2.

[7] Ibid., p. 3.

Similarly frank and moving is another Chippewa song:

> Is there anyone who
> would weep for me?
> My wife
> would weep for me.

It is perfectly matter-of-fact and yet profoundly moving because it displays feelings which are obviously genuine and powerful. Perhaps the closest comparable poem in English is the anonymous medieval lyric:

> Western wind, when wilt thou blow,
> The small rain down can rain.
> Christ, that my love were in my arms,
> And I in my bed again.

CHIPPEWA SONGS

The Chippewas (or Ojibwas) have traditionally been among the most musical of the Indians. Frances Densmore relates that when a Chippewa visited another reservation, one of the first questions aksed on his return was "What new songs did you learn?" [1]

Among the Chippewas every phase of life provided subjects for songs, particularly, love, war, medicine, and religion. Many songs were composed to celebrate particular events; others arose naturally out of exciting or painful situations. Although no songs were the exclusive property of a family or clan, the Chippewas associated a song with its composer and used to recite its history before singing it on formal occasions.

The relative importance of the elements of Chippewa songs is interesting. Rhythm seems to be the most important element, followed by melody and, least important, words. Rhythm—that is, the pattern of measures of irregular lengths and the subdivisions of these measures—is "as much a matter of composition as the melody, and often expresses the idea of the song." [2] *The words may vary widely in different renditions. Although the melody varies less, it too undergoes changes. The rhythm is the only constant.*

The idea of a song was strongly linked with the melody in the minds of the Chippewas, and the melody changed far less than the words, which were often rewritten. If a song was played successively in several renditions, often the words were sung only once.

Densmore collected the songs that follow on the White Earth, Leech Lake, Bois Fort, and Red Lake reservations in Minnesota between 1907 and 1909.

[1] Frances Densmore, *Chippewa Music* (Washington, D.C.: U.S. Government Printing Office, 1910), p. 1.

[2] *Ibid.*, p. 5.

The Chippewa songs are reprinted from Frances Densmore, *Chippewa Music* (Washington, D.C.: U.S. Government Printing Office, 1910), Bureau of American Ethnology Bulletin 45.

My Love Has Departed

Sung by MRS. MARY ENGLISH

Man-go-dŭg - win   nĭn - dĭ - nĕn-dûm man-go-dŭg-win nĭn - di - nĕn-dûm,

mi-gwe - na-wĭn   nĭn , Ĭ - mu-ce ĕ-ni-wa-wa - sa- bo - ye-zud.

Ba - wi - tĭñ   gi - nĭ - ma-dja   nĭn-ĭ-mu-ce a - ni - ma-dja

ka - wĭn - i - na-wa nĭn-da-wa-ba-ma - si   Si   Man-go-dûg - win

nĭn - dĭ - nĕn-dum   man - go-dûg - win   nĭn - dĭ - nĕn-dum,

mi-gwe - na-wĭn ka - wĭn - i-mu-ce,   ĕ-ni-wa-wa - sa - bo - ye-zud

WORDS

Part 1

Mangodŭg′win	A loon
Nĭn′dĭnen′dûm	I thought it was
Mi′gwenawĭn′	But it was
Nin′ĭmuce′	My love's
Ĕni′wawasa′boyezud′	Splashing oar

Part 2

Ba′witĭng′	To Sault Ste. Marie
Gi′nĭma′dja	He has departed
Nin′ĭmuce′	My love
A′nima′dja	Has gone on before me
Kawĭn′inawa′	Never again
Nĭndawa′bama′si	Can I see him

I Can Charm the Man

I can charm the man.
He is completely fascinated by me.

This song is a charm song intended to bewitch the victim into loving the singer. Densmore heard it from a woman in her sixties who remembered it from her salad days.

Why Should I Be Jealous?

Why should
I, even I,
be jealous
because of that bad boy?

If I Am Beaten

I will go home,
if I am beaten,
after more articles
to wager.

This is a moccasin-game song. In the moccasin game, which was the Chippewas' principal form of gambling at the time, one player hides four bullets or balls under four moccasins. One of the bullets or balls is marked, and the object for the other players is to find it in the fewest possible tries. Densmore remarks that "a characteristic of the moccasin game songs worthy of special note is the combining of a rapid metric unit of drum with a slow metric unit of voice, strongly indicating the elements of excitement and control which prevail in the game." When a moccasin game is in progress, the whole village can tell by the drum beat.

I Am as Brave as Other Men

Men who are brave and heroic
as you esteem them to be,
like them
I also
consider myself to be.

Come, Let Us Drink

Come,
Let us drink.

This is the song of a lovelorn youth who asks a friend to join him in drowning his misery.

The Man Who Stayed at Home

Although
Jingwa' be
a man
considers himself,
his wife
certainly
takes all his attention.

This song was sung before war parties. The man named once stayed home instead of joining one, and his example was intended to shame all who stayed home when they should have gone.

Scalp Song

I wonder
if she is humiliated,
the Sioux woman,
that I cut off her head.

A Song of Indecision

Part 1
They are talking about me,
saying "come with us."

Part 2
Is there anyone who
would weep for me?
My wife
would weep for me.

This song is sung by a warrior who cannot decide whether to join a war party.

You Desire Vainly

You desire vainly
that I seek you.
The reason is
I come
to see your younger sister.

He Is Gone

I might grieve;
I am sad
that he is gone,
my lover.

Love Song

I will go and talk with
my sweetheart,
the widow
I love,
my sweetheart
the widow.

One Wind

One
wind
I am master of it.

The Noise of the Village

Whenever I pause,
whenever I pause,
whenever I pause,
the noise
of the village
whenever I pause,
whenever I pause.

With Dauntless Courage

On the warpath
I give place to none.
With dauntless courage I live.

TETON SIOUX SONGS

The musical customs of the Sioux are basically similar to those of the Chippewas. Frances Densmore cited the "same reticence concerning old ceremonial and 'medicine' songs, the same acknowledged ownership of personal songs, the same custom of replacing in a war song the name of a half-forgotten hero with that of a new favorite." One difference between the tribes is that where the Chippewas invariably coupled certain rhythms with certain types of songs, the Sioux were freer in that regard.[1]

The Sioux often sang in gatherings around a drum. One man acted as leader. The songs were sung repeatedly until the leader tapped a signal on the drum, after which the song was sung a final time, and the leader began another. Unlike the Chippewas, Sioux women joined the men at the drum during dancing songs. The women sat in a circle in back of the men, singing in a falsetto an octave above them.[2]

The Sioux were more flexible than the Chippewas in their use of songs. According to Densmore, "the songs in honor of a warrior could be sung when begging food before his lodge, as well as at the victory dance and at meetings of societies. The songs of those who went to seek a suitable pole for the sun dance were used also by those who went to look for buffalo or for the enemy." Densmore noted the differences between traditional and modern Sioux songs. One difference is in the choice of subject: traditional songs deal with war, hunting, and sacred ceremonies no longer practiced; modern songs are love songs or songs dealing with other social situations. Modern Sioux music is also more harmonic than the older music and more complex rhythmically, possibly suggesting the influence of the whites.

The first three songs reprinted here are part of the sun-dance ceremony that was the principal religious celebration of the Plains Indians. It was held in midsummer every year. Participants had made vows in times of danger that, if they survived, they would undergo the painful sun-dance rituals. Although the rituals differed from tribe to tribe, the self-torture that Densmore described among the Tetons was common to most tribes:

---

[1] *Teton Sioux Music*, Bureau of American Ethnology Bulletin 61 (Washington, D.C.: U.S. Government Printing Office, 1918), p. 9.

[2] Ibid., p. 10.

The Teton Sioux songs are reprinted from Frances Densmore, *Teton Sioux Music* (Washington, D.C.: U.S. Government Printing Office, 1918), Bureau of American Ethnology Bulletin 61.

A man might take part in the Sun Dance in one of six ways, according to the nature of his vow. The requirement of fasting was the same in every vow. The first way of taking part in the Sun Dance consisted merely in dancing; the second added a laceration of the flesh, and the other four required that a stick be thrust through the flesh and strain placed upon it until the flesh tore or was cut. The Indians stated that the stick, or skewer, was "put through the skin," and probably it pierced into the subcutaneous fascia. The two most common forms of this treatment consisted in the piercing of the flesh over the chest with skewers attached by cords to the crossbar of the sacred pole, and the fastening of buffalo skulls to the flesh of the back and arms. The two more severe and less employed forms were the suspending of the entire body by the flesh of the back, and the fastening of the flesh of both back and chest to four poles at some distance from the body, the poles being placed at the corners of a square.[3]

A great deal of ritual went into the selection and cutting of the sacred pole around which the dance took place. Four braves were entrusted with the task. Before their departure, tribesmen sang war songs because the tree "was regarded as something to be conquered."[4]

Like the Chippewa songs above and the Mandan and Hidatsa songs below, the following selections were collected by Frances Densmore. She did her fieldwork on the Standing Rock Reservation in North and South Dakota between 1911 and 1914.

Opening Prayer of the Sun Dance

Grandfather,
a voice I am going to send.
Hear me.
All over the universe,
a voice I am going to send.
Hear me,
Grandfather.
I will live.
I have said it.

Wakan'tanka Hears Me

Wakan'tanka,
when I pray to him,
hears me.
Whatever is good
he grants me.

[3] Ibid., p. 106.
[4] Ibid., p. 108.

I Have Conquered Them

Well, a war party
which was supposed to come
now is here.
I have obliterated every trace of them.

Song of the Strong Heart Society

Friends,
whoever
runs away
shall not be admitted.

Watch Your Horses

Crow Indian,
you must watch your horses.
A horse thief
often
am I.

You Have No Horses

Well,
when I was courting,
"Horses you have none"
to me was said.
Therefore
over all the land
I roam.

The Earth Only Endures

The old men
say
the earth
only
endures.
You spoke
truly.
You are right.

Song Concerning a Message from Washington

The great grandfather (the President)
has said,
so they report,
"Dakotas,
be citizens,"
he said,
so they report.
But
it will be impossible for me.
The Dakota (ways)
them
I love,
I said.
Therefore
I have helped (to keep the old ways).

MANDAN AND HIDATSA SONGS

The Mandans and the Hidatsas are related Siouan tribes from the northern Missouri Valley. They have lived in close conjunction since the eighteenth century. Although closely related to the Sioux ethnically, they differed from them greatly in their style of living. The Sioux were nomadic hunters who lived in buffalo-hide tipis they carried with them. The Mandans and the Hidatsas were sedentary, agricultural people. Their chief crops were squash and corn, which they preserved by drying on scaffolds. They lived in round earth-covered lodges in permanent villages. Mandan lodges were built around a central "ceremonial space" in which there was an "ark" or "big canoe"—a small wooden structure containing a cedar post representing "One Man, brother of First Man." [1]

Mandan and Hidatsa musical instruments included the drum, rattle, whistle, and flute. Drums were usually small and often made of hide stretched over turtle shells. Two types of rattles were common: pouches filled with pebbles and carved sticks with deer hooves loosely attached. Whistles included war whistles made of goose or other bird wing bones and courting whistles carved from wood. Courting whistles varied in length with the size of the owner. The prescribed length was the distance between the tip of the fingers of the outstretched right arm to the left armpit. Flutes (which were called "singing whistles") were the chief melodic instrument. They were made of box-elder boughs hollowed out with flint. The length of the flute was the distance from the inside of a man's elbow to the end of his middle finger. They had seven holes. [2]

Frances Densmore collected the songs between 1912 and 1918.

The Corn Is My Pleasure

My best friend
what do you like?

You said,
"The corn
is
my pleasure."

---

[1] Frances Densmore, *Mandan and Hidatsa Music* (Washington, D.C.: U.S. Government Printing Office, 1923), p. 5.

[2] Ibid., p. 8.

The Mandan and Hidatsa songs are reprinted from Frances Densmore, *Mandan and Hidatsa Music* (Washington, D.C.: U.S. Government Printing Office, 1923), Bureau of American Ethnology Bulletin 80.

He Stared at Me

My dear friend,
your husband
at me
how he stared!
Will you throw him away?

Take Me to the Sioux

The Hunkpapa Sioux
are to be feared.
Take me to them.

I Will Go

If that is the enemy
I will go.
Here
I am.

Comrades, Sleep On

My comrades
sleep on.
I precede you as scout.

Densmore related this incident in connection with the following song:
"Some Sioux warriors, pursued by the Mandan, covered themselves with
buffalo robes and walked single file, pretending to be buffalos. When out
of sight they threw away the buffalo robes. The Mandan found the robes
and saw the trick of the Sioux. Renewing the chase, they overtook the
Sioux and killed them all."

Disguised as a Buffalo

O Yankton Sioux,
"I
am a man,"
you said,
"a man."

Why
are you disguised as a buffalo?
You discredit
yourselves.

We Made Fire

Comrade,
in the daytime when we made fire
it was pleasant.
I understand women.

KIOWA "49" SONGS

The Kiowas were originally a mountain people. They moved onto the prairies in the late seventeenth century, acquired horses, and soon became, with the Comanches, the dominant warriors of the southern plains. Their whole existence revolved around the buffalo, which provided them food, clothing, and the hides from which they built their tipis. When the whites virtually exterminated the buffalo, the Kiowas' traditional way of life collapsed, and they were forced to capitulate to white rule and turn to farming. Today there are 9,900 Kiowas on the tribal rolls, most of whom live in western Oklahoma.[1]

"49" songs are sung at powwows and other social gatherings, usually late in the evening after other types of dances and songs are completed. The songs were originally called war-journey songs and were sung by women when their men were leaving for war. After the Kiowas stopped making war, the women continued the practice of singing, although the subject of the songs changed.

The name "49" can be traced to an incident that occurred at the Caddo County Fair in the 1920s. A barker luring crowds to a burlesque show featuring a California Gold Rush theme called out repeatedly, "See the girls of '49, see the '49 girls." One night a group of Kiowa women were singing war-journey songs, dancing with their arms interlocked, when a wag called out, "See the '49 girls." The remark was widely repeated, and the name stuck. The practicing of "singing 49" has spread from the Kiowas to other tribes, and it has become particularly an activity of the young.

In singing "49" songs the singers chant a nonverbal refrain to an accompanying drumbeat. After an extended period of chanting, they sing the short lyric once, either in Kiowa or in English. Although some war-journey songs are still sung, many other topics—particularly marital infidelity—are also touched on.

The following songs were collected by Raymond Tahbone, a Kiowa from Anadarko, Oklahoma, at a workshop at Oklahoma College of Liberal Arts, Chickasha. Contributors of songs to this collection include Ernest Toppah, Evalu Russell, Georgia Chrisman, Bernice Nestell, and Marjorie Tahbone.

---

[1] Marian Wolf, "The Kiowa" (Washington, D.C.: U.S. Department of the Interior, 1973).

To heck with your ole wife [*or* ole man].
Come up and see me sometime.

You are the *only* one
That I could ever love,
You are the *only* one.

You are the *only* one
That I love so dearly,
You are the *only* one.

You know that I love you, sweetheart, but every time I come around
You always say you got another one.
You know damn good and well that I love you.

I am lonesome for my sweetheart.
He's [*or* she's] in jail.

I got drunk on the western front,
Sobered up in the county jail.

Kiowa boys, take me along with you everywhere,
Through the moonlight shadows.

I don't care if you're married, I'll still get you,
I'll get you yet.

I don't care if you're married sixteen times,
I'll get you yet.

When the dance is over, sweetheart,
I will take you home in my one-eyed Ford.

She said she don't love me anymore because I drink whiskey.
I don't care, I got a *better* one.

You are bringing [*or* presenting] your wife,
And here I am laughing at you.

My thoughts are of you and it hurts
Me to think of you.
But all you do is stay with [*or* love] your boyfriend,
But he really is not worth it.

If you really love me, honey, hey-yah.
If you really love me, honey, hey-yah.
Come back, come back if you really love me, honey.

I'm from Oklahoma, far away from my home,
Down here looking for you.
If you'll be my honey, I will be your sugar pie.

I'm from Carnegie, so far away from my home,
Down here looking for you.
If you'll be my snag, I'll be your snag-a-roo.

The following two songs are older "49" songs:

There is a man I think of a lot.
For a long time I have thought of him,
And still yet I think of him.

I am tired of this lady and I am going to leave her.
I am tired of this lady and I am going to leave her.
Anyone can have her, but you are getting
Her secondhand.

The following lyrics were composed by inmates at the Oklahoma State Prison at McAlester and taught to other Indians in the powwow world:

You must always think of me when you're feeling fine,
Just remember that I'm still doing time.
Don't you ever leave, dear; if you do I'll go
To the electric chair, Baby Doll.

I get the old yearning; I get the old yearning;
Everytime I see my old sweetheart, I get the old yearning.
I must not have any sense.

This "49" song is about an unfaithful man or woman who has been caught by his or her mate:

Do not kill me
For I am pitiful.

This is a war journey song:

I am thinking of my son, I am wondering
Where he is [*or* where he has gone].

These two songs are usually sung in Kiowa:

You will die if you eat turtle.
Sounds like you are chewing on one now.

I don't think your boyfriend will hurt us [*or* kill us];
Look toward my way and smile.

WALAM OLUM

The Walam Olum *is the Bible and* Aeneid *of the Delawares, the story of their creation and the poetic record of their history. The Delawares, or Lenni Lenape, as they called themselves in earlier times, are an Algonquian tribe closely related to the Powhatans and the Mahicans. The Algonquians occupied much of eastern North America in the eighteenth century, and they were consequently among the first Indians encountered by white settlers. (Most of the words that Americans consider Indian are Algonquian; for example, moccasin, powwow, tomahawk, and wampum).*[1] *During the colonial period the Delawares occupied the Delaware River Valley and much of what is now New Jersey. They were eventually forced westward by the whites and the Iroquois and today are principally settled in Kansas and Oklahoma.*

The name Walam Olum *means "painted record." The work has two parts: the narrative and the pictographs. The pictographs, symbolic illustrations largely based on sign language, were usually inscribed on wood or birchbark. The narrative was preserved orally and is the closest thing we know of in Indian literature to the European epic. Long narrative poems are rare in Indian literature. Stories were almost always related in prose; poetry was used primarily in ritual chants or in the brief lyrics that Indians were so fond of singing. I have included the original Delaware text here, because poetry even more than prose depends for its effect on sound as well as sense; no translation can render even a faint idea of the sound of a poetic work. Without knowing a word of Delaware, the reader can discern the rhythm of the original and observe the use of rhyme, alliteration, and rhythmic repetition.*

Unfortunately, what we have is not the Walam Olum *as it was originally composed by the Delawares. As Daniel G. Brinton, one of the most distinguished scholars on the Delawares, wrote: "[The] genuine native production . . . was repeated orally to someone indifferently conversant with the Delaware language, who wrote it down to the best of his ability. In its present form it can lay no claim either to antiquity or to purity of linguistic form."*[2] *Even so, much power and beauty shine through in Brinton's edition, the one we use here. The Indiana Historical Society issued a more reliable text in 1954, but technical factors preclude its use.*

---

[1] A. Grove Day, *The Sky Clears* (Lincoln: University of Nebraska Press, 1961), p. 60.

[2] Daniel G. Brinton, *The Lenape and Their Legends* (Philadelphia: D. G. Brinton, 1885), p. 224.

Reprinted from Daniel G. Brinton, *The Lenape and Their Legends* (Philadelphia, 1885).

The poem primarily does two things: it relates the creation myth of the Delawares, and it gives a record of Delaware history from the earliest times to their contact with the whites. It begins with Manito, "a manito to manitos" (pt. I, v. 9), creating the sun, moon, and stars, and (human beings) and animals. The Snake God, (pt. I, v. 21), created evil beings, monsters, and insects. The Snake God is reminiscent of Satan as he appears in the Garden of Eden, but is a more formidable figure. The Christian Satan's powers are only those that God permits him, and he is never a creator. The Snake God is closer to the Manichaean Satan, who fights on an equal basis with God.

Before the Snake God makes his evil felt, the Delaware world is an Eden. The manitos act as servants to men, fetching them wives and food; "all had cheerful knowledge, all had leisure, all thought in gladness" (pt. I, v. 20). The Snake God puts an end to this by bringing quarreling, bad weather, sickness, and death. The Delawares engage in a bitter struggle with the Snake God and the beings he creates to aid him, until Nanabush, the Delaware culture hero, saves them. Nanabush—or Manabozho, as he was known to the other Algonquians—was a trickster figure like Wakdjunkaga of the Winnebago trickster cycle.

The historical portion of the poem that follows is a record of Delaware leaders, battles, and migrations. Leaders are listed serially in a manner reminiscent of the "begats" in the Old Testament and cryptically described in a single phrase: ". . . Not-Black was chief, who was a straight man. . . . After him, No-Blood was chief, who walked in cleanliness" (pt. IV, vv. 19 and 21). The accounts of Delaware migrations and battles are also cryptic. Brinton speculates that the early historical references to the snowy coastline refer to Labrador and that from there the Delaware moved south and west through New York to Ohio and Indiana before returning east to the Delaware Valley.

Eli Lilly, in an essay in the Indiana Historical Society edition of the Walam Olum, *argues that the Delaware came from Asia, not Labrador, crossed the Bering Strait around 360 B.C., travelled a route approximating that of the present Alaska Highway south through Canada, and then headed east, crossing the Mississippi about the year 1000. The Delawares reached the Alleghenies in the early fourteenth century. Lilly speculates that the ship that the Delawares mention at the end of the epic is that of John Cabot, the British explorer who sailed down the Atlantic coast in 1498.*

If Lilly is correct, the ending of the Walam Olum *is doubly ironic. The naïveté of the Delawares is touching: "They are peaceful; they have great things; who are they?" And, if Cabot did meet the Delawares it was one of the last things he did, since he disappeared without a trace soon after.*

I.

1. Sayewi talli wemiguma wokgetaki,

2. Hackung kwelik owanaku wak yutali
   Kitanitowit-essop.

3. Sayewis hallemiwis nolemiwi elemamik
   Kitanitowit-essop.

4. Sohawalawak kwelik hakik owak[1]
   awasagamak.

5. Sohalawak gishuk nipahum alankwak.

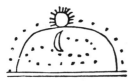

6. Wemi-sohalawak yulikyuchaan.

7. Wich-owagan kshakan moshakwat[2] kwelik
   kshipehelep.

8. Opeleken mani-menak delsin-epit.

9. Lappinup Kitanitowit manito manitoak.

10. Owiniwak angelatawiwak chichankwak
    wemiwak.

[1] Read, *woak*.   [2] Var. *moshakguat*.

I.

1. At first, in that place, at all times, above the earth,

2. On the earth, [was] an extended fog, and there the great Manito was.

3. At first, forever, lost in space, everywhere, the great Manito was.

4. He made the extended land and the sky.

5. He made the sun, the moon, the stars.

6. He made them all to move evenly.

7. Then the wind blew violently, and it cleared, and the water flowed off far and strong.

8. And groups of islands grew newly, and there remained.

9. Anew spoke the great Manito, a manito to manitos,

10. To beings, mortals, souls and all,

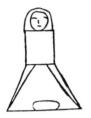

11. Wtenk manito jinwis lennowak mukom.

12. Milap netami gaho owini gaho.

13. Namesik milap, tulpewik milap, awesik milap, cholensak milap.

14. Makimani shak sohalawak makowini nakowak amangamek.

15. Sohalawak uchewak, sohalawak pungusak.

16. Nitisak wemi owini w'delisinewuap.

17. Kiwis, wunand wishimanitoak essopak.

11. And ever after he was a manito to men, and their grandfather.

12. He gave the first mother, the mother of beings.

13. He gave the fish, he gave the turtles, he gave the beasts, he gave the birds.

14. But an evil Manito made evil beings only, monsters,

15. He made the flies, he made the gnats.

16. All beings were then friendly.

17. Truly the manitos were active and kindly

18. Nijini netami lennowak, nigoha netami okwewi, nantinéwak.

19. Gattamin netami mitzi nijini nantiné.

20. Wemi wingi-namenep, wemi ksin-elendamep, wemi wullatemanuwi.

21. Shukand eli-kimi mekenikink wakon powako init'ako.

22. Mattalogas pallalogas maktaton owa-gan payat-chik yutali.

23. Maktapan payat, wihillan payat, mboagan payat.

24. Won wemi wiwunch kamik atak kitahikan netamaki epit.

II.

1. Wulamo maskanako anup lennowak makowini essopak.

18. To those very first men, and to those first mothers; fetched them
   wives,

19. And fetched them food, when first they desired it.

20. All had cheerful knowledge, all had leisure, all thought in gladness.

21. But very secretly an evil being, a mighty magician, came on earth,

22. And with him brought badness, quarreling, unhappiness,

23. Brought bad weather, brought sickness, brought death.

24. All this took place of old on the earth, beyond the great tidewater,
   at the first.

II.

1. Long ago there was a mighty snake and beings evil to men.

2. Maskanako shingalusit nijini essopak
   shawelendamep eken shingalan.

3. Nishawì palliton, nishawi machiton,
   nishawi matta lungundowin.

4. Mattapewi wiki nihanlowit mekwazoan.

5. Maskanako gishi penauwelendamep
   lennowak owini palliton.

6. Nakowa petonep, amangam petonep,
   akopehella petonep.

7. Pehella pehella, pohoka pohoka,
   eshohokesohok, palliton palliton.

8. Tulapit menapit Nanaboush maskaboush
   owinimokom linowimokom.

2. This mighty snake hated those who were there (and) greatly disquieted those whom he hated.

3. They both did harm, they both injured each other, both were not in peace.

4. Driven from their homes they fought with this murderer.

5. The mighty snake firmly resolved to harm the men.

6. He brought three persons, he brought a monster, he brought a rushing water.

7. Between the hills the water rushed and rushed, dashing through and through, destroying much.

8. Nanabush, the Strong White One, grandfather of beings, grandfather of men, was on the Turtle Island.

9. Gishikin-pommixin tulagishatten-
   lohxin.

10. Owini linowi wemoltin,
    Pehella gahani pommixin,
    Nahiwi tatalli tulapin.

11. Amanganek makdopannek alen-
    dyuwek metzipannek.

12. Manito-dasin mokol-wichemap,
    Palpal payat payat wemichemap.

13. Nanaboush Nanaboush
    wemimokom,
    Wimimokom linnimokom
    tulamokom.

14. Linapi-ma tulapi-ma tulapewi tapitawi.

15. Wishanem tulpewi pataman tulpewi
    poniton wuliton.

16. Kshipehelen penkwihilen,
    Kwamipokho sitwalikho,
    Maskan wagan palliwi palliwi.

III.

1. Pehella wtenk lennapewi tulapewini
   psakwiken woliwikgun wittank talli.

9. There he was walking and creating, as he passed by and created the turtle.

10. Beings and men all go forth, they walk in the floods and shallow waters, downstream thither to the Turtle Island.

11. There were many monster fishes, which ate some of them.

12. The Manito daughter, coming, helped with her canoe, helped all, as they came and came.

13. [And also] Nanabush, Nanabush, the grandfather of all, the grandfather of beings, the grandfather of men, the grandfather of the turtle.

14. The men then were together on the turtle, like to turtles.

15. Frightened on the turtle, they prayed on the turtle that what was spoiled should be restored.

16. The water ran off, the earth dried, the lakes were at rest, all was silent, and the mighty snake departed.

III.

1. After the rushing waters (had subsided) the Lenàpe of the turtle were close together, in hollow houses, living together there.

2. Topan-akpinep, wineu-akpinep, kshakan-
akpinep, thupin akpinep.

3. Lowankwamink wulaton wtakan tihill kelik
meshautang sili ewak.

4. Chintanes-sin powalessin peyachik
wikhichik pokwihil.

5. Eluwi-chitanesit eluwi takauwesit, elowi
chiksit, elowichik delsinewo.

6. Lowaniwi, wapaniwi, shawaniwi,
wunkeniwi, elowichik apakachik.

7. Lumowaki, lowanaki tulpenaki elowaki
tulapiwi linapiwi.

8. Wemiako yagawan tendki lak-
kawelendam nakopowa wemi
owenluen atam.

9. Akhokink wapaneu wemoltin palliaal
kitelendam aptelendam.

10. Pechimuin shakowen[1] nungihillan
lusasaki pikikihil pokwihil
akomenaki.

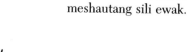

[1]Var. *showoken*.

2. It freezes where they abode, it snows where they abode, it storms where they abode, it is cold where they abode.

3. At this northern place they speak favorably of mild, cool (lands), with many deer and buffaloes.

4. As they journeyed, some being strong, some rich, they separated into house-builders and hunters;

5. The strongest, the most united, the purest, were the hunters.

6. The hunters showed themselves at the north, at the east, at the south, at the west.

7. In that ancient country, in that northern country, in that turtle country, the best of the Lenape were the Turtle men.

8. All the cabin fires of that land were disquieted, and all said to their priest, "Let us go."

9. To the Snake land to the east they went forth, going away, earnestly grieving.

10. Split asunder, weak, trembling, their land burned, they went, torn and broken, to the Snake Island.

11. Nihillapewin komelendam lowaniwi
    wemiten chihillen winiaken.

12. Namesuagipek pokhapockhapek
    guneunga waplanewa ouken wap-
    tumewi ouken.

13. Amokolon nallahemen agunouken
    pawasinep wapasinep akomenep.[2]

14. Wihlamok kicholen luchundi, Wematam
    akomen luchundi.

15. Witehen wemiluen wemaken nihillen.

16. Nguttichin lowaniwi,
    Nguttichin wapaniwi,
    Agamunk topanpek
    Wulliton epannek.

17. Wulelemil w'shakuppek,
    Wemopannek hakhsinipek,
    Kitahikan pokhakhopek.

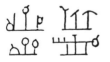

18. Tellenchen kittapakki nillawi,
    Wemoltin gutikuni nillawi,
    Akomen wapanawaki nillawi,
    Ponskan, ponskan, wemiwi olini.

19. Lowanapi, wapanapi, shawanapi,
    Lanewapi, tamakwapi, tumewapi,
    Elowapi, powatapi, wilawapi,
    Okwisapi, danisapi, allumapi,

[2]Var. *menakinep*.

11. Those from the north being free, without care, went forth from the
    land of snow, in different directions.

12. The fathers of the Bald Eagle and the White Wolf remain along the
    sea, rich in fish and mussels.

13. Floating up the streams in their canoes, our fathers were rich, they
    were in the light, when they were at those islands.

14. Head Beaver and Big Bird said,
    "Let us go to Snake Island," they said.

15. All say they will go along to destroy all the land.

16. Those of the north agreed,
    Those of the east agreed.
    Over the water, the frozen sea,
    They went to enjoy it.

17. On the wonderful slippery water,
    On the stone-hard water all went,
    On the great Tidal Sea, the mussle-bearing sea.

18. Ten thousand at night,
    All in one night,
    To the Snake Island, to the east, at night,
    They walk and walk, all of them.

19. The men from the north, the east, the south,
    The Eagle clan, the Beaver clan, the Wolf clan,
    The best men, the rich men, the head men,
    Those with wives, those with daughters, those with dogs,

20. Wemipayat gunéunga shinaking,
    Wunkenapi chanelendam payaking,
    Allowelendam kowiyey tulpaking.

IV.

1. Wulamo linapioken manup shinaking.

2. Wapallanewa sittamaganat yukeepechi
   wemima,

3. Akhomenis michihaki wellaki kun-
   dokanup.

4. Angomelchik elowichik elmusichik
   menalting.

5. Wemilo kolawil sakima lissilma.

6. Akhopayat kihillalend akhopokho as-
   kíwaal.

7. Showihilla akhowemi gandhaton
   mashkipokhing.

8. Wtenkolawil shinaking sakimanep
   wapagokhos.

20. They all come, they tarry at the land of the spruce pines;
    Those from the west come with hesitation,
    Esteeming highly their old home at the Turtle land.

IV.

1. Long ago the fathers of the Lenape were at the land of spruce pines.

2. Hitherto the Bald Eagle band had been the pipe bearer,

3. While they were searching for the Snake Island, that great and fine
    land.

4. They having died, the hunters, about to depart, met together.

5. All say to Beautiful Head, "Be thou chief."

6. "Coming to the Snakes, slaughter at that Snake hill, that they
    leave it."

7. All of the Snake tribe were weak, and hid themselves in the
    Swampy Vales.

8. After Beautiful Head, White Owl was chief at Spruce Pine land.

9. Wtenk nekama sakimanep janotowi
   enolowin.

10. Wtenk nekama sakimanep chilili
    shawaniluen.

11. Wokenapi nitaton wullaton apakchik-
    ton.

12. Shawaniwaen chilili, wapaniwaen tamakwi.

13. Akolaki shawanaki, kitshinaki shabiyaki.

14. Wapanaki namesaki, pemapaki sisilaki.

15. Wtenk chilili sakimanep ayamek
    weminilluk.

16. Chikonapi akhonapi makatapi as-
    sinapi.

9. After him, Keeping-Guard was chief of that people.

10. After him, Snow Bird was chief; he spoke of the south,

11. That our fathers should possess it by scattering abroad.

12. Snow Bird went south, White Beaver went east.

13. The Snake land was at the south, the great Spruce Pine land was
    toward the shore;

14. To the east was the Fish land, toward the lakes was the buffalo land.

15. After Snow Bird, the Seizer was chief, and all were killed,

16. The robbers, the snakes, the evil men, the stone men.

17. Wtenk ayamek tellen sakimak machi tonanup shawapama.

18. Wtenk nellamawa sakimanep lan-gundowi akolaking.

19. Wtenk nekama sakimanep tasukamend shakagapipi.

20. Wtenk nekama sakimanep pemaholend wulitowin.

21. Sagimawtenk matemik, sagimawtenk pilsohalin.

22. Sagimawtenk gunokeni, sagimaw-tenk mangipitak.

23. Sagimawtenk olumapi, leksahowen sohalawak.

24. Sagimawtenk taguachi shawaniwaen minihaking.

25. Sakimawtenk huminiend minigeman sohalgol.

17. After the Seizer there were ten chiefs, and there was much warfare south and east.

18. After them, the Peaceable was chief at Snake land.

19. After him, Not-Black was chief, who was a straight man.

20. After him, Much-Loved was chief, a good man.

21. After him, No-Blood was chief, who walked in cleanliness.

22. After him, Snow-Father was chief, he of the big teeth.

23. After him, Tally-Maker was chief, who made records.

24. After him, Shiverer-with-Cold was chief, who went south to the corn land.

25. After him, Corn-Breaker was chief, who brought about the planting of corn.

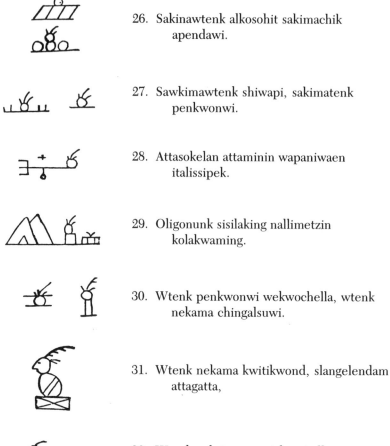

26. Sakinawtenk alkosohit sakimachik apendawi.

27. Sawkimawtenk shiwapi, sakimatenk penkwonwi.

28. Attasokelan attaminin wapaniwaen italissipek.

29. Oligonunk sisilaking nallimetzin kolakwaming.

30. Wtenk penkwonwi wekwochella, wtenk nekama chingalsuwi.

31. Wtenk nekama kwitikwond, slangelendam attagatta,

32. Wundanuksin wapanickam[1] allen-dyachick kimimikwi.

33. Gunehunga wetatamowi wakaholend sakimalanop.

34. Wisawana lappi wittank michi mini madawasim.

26. After him, the Strong-Man was chief, who was useful to the
    chieftains.

27. After him, the Salt-Man was chief; after him the Little-One was
    chief.

28. There was no rain, and no corn, so they moved further seaward.

29. At the place of caves, in the buffalo land, they at last had food, on a
    pleasant plain.

30. After the Little-One (came) the Fatigued; after him, the Stiff-One.

31. After him, the Reprover; disliking him, and unwilling (to remain),

32. Being angry, some went off secretly, moving east.

33. The wise ones who remained made the Loving-One chief.

34. They settled again on the Yellow river, and had much corn on
    stoneless soil.

35. Weminitis tamenend sakimanep
    nekohatami.

36. Eluwiwulit matemenend wemi linapi nitis
    payat.

37. Wtenk wulitma maskansisil sakimanep
    w'tamaganat.

38. Machigokloss sakimanep, wapkicho-
    len sakimanep.

39. Wingenund sakimanep powatanep
    gentikalanep.

40. Lapawin sakimanep, wallama sakimanep.

41. Waptipatit sakimanep, lappi mahuk
    lowashawa.

42. Wewoattan menatting tumaokan
    sakimanep.

43. Nitatonep wemi palliton maskansini
    nihillanep.

35. All being friendly, the Affable was chief, the first of that name.

36. He was very good, this Affable, and came as a friend to all the Lenape.

37. After this good one, Strong-Buffalo was chief and pipe-bearer.

38. Big-Owl was chief; White-Bird was chief.

39. The Willing-One was chief and priest; he made festivals.

40. Rich-Again was chief; the Painted-One was chief.

41. White-Fowl was chief; again there was war, north and south.

42. The Wolf-Wise-in Counsel was chief.

43. He knew how to make war on all; he slew Strong-Stone.

44. Messissuwi sakimanep akowini pallitonep.

45. Chitanwulit sakimanep lowanuski pallitonep.

46. Alokuwi sakimanep towakon pallitonep.

47. Opekasit sakimanep sakhelendam pallitonepit.

48. Wapagishik yuknohokluen makeluhuk wapaneken.

49. Tsehepieken nemassipi[1] nolandowak gunehunga.

50. Yagawanend sakimanep talligewi wapawullaton.

51. Chitanitis sakimanep wapawaki gotatamen.

52. Wapallendi pomisinep talegawil allendhilla.

53. Mayoksuwi wemilowi palliton palliton.

[1] Var. *mixtisipi.*

44. The Always-Ready-One was chief; he fought against the Snakes.

45. The Strong-Good-One was chief; he fought against the northerners.

46. The Lean-One was chief; he fought against the Tawa people.

47. The Opossum-Like was chief; he fought in sadness,

48. And said, "They are many; let us go together to the east, the sunrise."

49. They separated at Fish river; the lazy ones remained there.

50. Cabin-Man was chief; the Talligewi possessed the east.

51. Strong-Friend was chief; he desired the eastern land.

52. Some passed on east; the Talega ruler killed some of them.

53. All say, in unison, "War, war."

54. Talamatan nitilowan payatchik wemiten.

55. Kinehepend sakimanep tamaganat
    sipakgamen.

56. Wulatonwi makelima pallihilla talegawik.

57. Pimokhasuwi sakimanep wsamimas-
    kan talegawik.

58. Tenchekentit sakimanep wemilat
    makelinik.

59. Pagan chichilla sakimanep shawanewak
    wemi talega.

60. Hattan wulaton sakimanep, wingelendam
    wemi lennowak.

61. Shawanipekis gunehungind low-
    anipekis talamatanitis.

62. Attabchinitis gishelendam gunitakan
    sakimanep.

63. Linniwulamen sakimanep pallitonep
    talamatan.

54. The Talamatan, friends from the north, come, and all go together.

55. The Sharp-One was chief; he was the pipe-bearer beyond the river.

56. They rejoiced greatly that they should fight and slay the Talega towns.

57. The Stirrer was chief; the Talega towns were too strong.

58. The Fire-Builder was chief; they all gave to him many towns.

59. The Breaker-in-Pieces was chief; all the Talega go south.

60. He-has-Pleasure was chief; all the people rejoice.

61. They stay south of the lakes; the Talamatan friends north of the lakes.

62. When Long-and-Mild was chief, those who were not his friends conspired.

63. Truthful-Man was chief; the Talamatans made war.

64. Shakagapewi sakimanep nungiwi talamatan.

V.

 1. Wemilangundo wulamo talli talegaking.

2. Tamaganend sakimanep wapalaneng.

 3. Wapushuwi sakimanep kelitgeman.

 4. Wulitshinik sakimanep makdopannik.

5. Lekhihitin sakimanep wallamolumin.

 6. Kolachuisen sakimanep makeliming.

 7. Pematalli sakimanep makelinik.

8. Pepomahenem sakimanep makelaning.

 9. Tankawon sakimanep makeleyachik,

10. Nentegowi shawanowi shawanaking.

11. Kichitamak sakimanep wapahoning.

64. Just-and-True was chief; the Talamatans trembled.

V.

1. All were peaceful, long ago, there at the Talega land.

2. The Pipe-Bearer was chief at the White river.

3. White-Lynx was chief; much corn was planted.

4. Good-and-Strong was chief; the people were many.

5. The Recorder was chief; he painted the records.

6. Pretty-Blue-Bird was chief; there was much fruit.

7. Always-There was chief; the towns were many.

8. Paddler-up-Stream was chief; he was much on the rivers.

9. Little-Cloud was chief; many departed,

10. The Nanticokes and the Shawnees go to the south.

11. Big-Beaver was chief, at the White Salt Lick.

12. Onowutok awolagan wunkenahep.

13. Wunpakitonis wunshawononis wun-
    kiwikwotank.

 14. Pawanami sakimanep taleganah.

15. Lokwelend sakimanep makpalliiton.

16. Lappi towako lappi sinako lappi lowako.

17. Mokolmokom sakimanep mokolako-
    lin.

18. Winelowich sakimanep low-
    ushkakiang.

19. Linkwekinuk sakimanep talegachukang.

 20. Wapalawikwan sakimanep wap-
    talegawing.

21. Amangaki amigaki wapakisinep.

12. The Seer, the praised one, went to the west.

13. He went to the west, to the southwest, to the western villages.

14. The Rich-Down-River-Man was chief, at Talega river.

15. The Walker was chief; there was much war.

16. Again with the Tawa people, again with the Stone people, again with the northern people.

17. Grandfather-of-Boats was chief; he went to lands in boats.

18. Snow-Hunter was chief; he went to the north land.

19. Look-About was chief; he went to the Talega mountains.

20. East-Villager was chief; he was east of Talega.

21. A great land and a wide land was the east land,

22. Mattakohaki mapawaki mawulitenol.

 23. Gikenopalat sakimanep pekochilo-
wan.

 24. Saskwihanang hanaholend sakimanep.

 25. Gattawisi sakimanep winakaking.

 26. Wemi lowichik gishikshawipek lappi
kichipek.

 27. Makhiawip sakimanep lapihaneng.

 28. Wolomenap sakimanep maskekitong.

 29. Wapanand tumewand waplowaan.

 30. Wulitpallat sakimanep piskwilowan.

31. Mahongwi pungelika wemi nungwi.

32. Lappi tamenend sakimanepit wemi
langundit.

22. A land without snakes, a rich land, a pleasant land.

23. Great Fighter was chief, toward the north.

24. At the Straight river, River-Loving was chief.

25. Becoming-Fat was chief at Sassafras land.

26. All the hunters made wampum again at the great sea.

27. Red-Arrow was chief at the stream again.

28. The Painted-Man was chief at the Mighty Water.

29. The Easterners and the Wolves go northeast.

30. Good-Fighter was chief, and went to the north.

31. The Mengwe, the Lynxes, all trembled.

32. Again an Affable was chief, and made peace with all,

33. Wemi nitis wemi takwicken sakima
    kichwon.

 36. Kichitamak sakimanep winakununda.

 37. Wapahakey sakimanep sheyabian.

 38. Elangomel sakimanep makeliwulit.

 39. Pitenumen sakimanep unchihillen.

 40. Wonwihil wapekunchi wapsipayat.

 41. Makelomush sakimanep wulatena-
    men.

 42. Wulakeningus sakimanep shawanipalat.

43. Otaliwako akowetako ashkipalliton.

33. All were friends, all were united, under this great chief.

36. Great-Beaver was chief, remaining in Sassafras land.

37. White-Body was chief on the sea shore.

38. Peace-Maker was chief, friendly to all.

39. He-Makes-Mistakes was chief, hurriedly coming.

40. At this time whites came on the Eastern sea.

41. Much-Honored was chief; he was prosperous.

42. Well-Praised was chief; he fought at the south.

43. He fought in the land of the Talega and Koweta.

44. Wapagamoshki sakimanep lamatanitis.

45. Wapashum sakimanep talegawunkik.

46. Mahiliniki mashawoniki makonowiki.

47. Nitispayat sakimanep kipemapekan,

48. Wemiamik weminitik kiwikhotan.

49. Pakimitzin sakimanep tawanitip.

50. Lowaponskan sakimanep gan-
    showenik.

51. Tashawinso sakimanep shayabing.

52. Nakhagattamen nakhalissin wen-
    chikit,

44. White-Otter was chief; a friend of the Talamatans.

45. White-Horn was chief; he went to the Talega,

46. To the Hilini, to the Shawnees, to the Kanawhas.

47. Coming-as-a-Friend was chief; he went to the Great Lakes,

48. Visiting all his children, all his friends.

49. Cranberry-Eater was chief, friend of the Ottawas.

50. North-Walker was chief; he made festivals.

51. Slow-Gatherer was chief at the shore.

52. As three were desired, three those were who grew forth,

52. *bis.* Unamini minsimini chikimini.

53. Epallahchund sakimanep mahongwipallat.

54. Langomunwi sakimanep
    mahongwichamen.

55. Wangomend sakimanep ikalawit,

 56. Otaliwi wasiotowi shingalusit.

 57. Wapachikis sakimanep sahyabinitis.

 58. Nenachihat sakimanep peklinkwe-
    kin.

 59. Wonwihil lowashawa wapayachik.

 60. Langomuwak kitohatewa ewenikik-
    tit?

52. *bis*. The Unami, the Minsi, the Chikini.

53. Man-Who-Fails was chief; he fought the Mengwe.

54. He-is-Friendly was chief; he scared the Mengwe.

55. Saluted was chief; thither,

56. Over there, on the Scioto, he had foes.

57. White-Crab was chief; a friend of the shore.

58. Watcher was chief; he looked toward the sea.

59. At this time, from north and south, the whites came.

60. They are peaceful; they have great things; who are they?

ORATORY

Oratory played an extremely important part in Indian life. Although tribes varied in their forms of governance and in the amount of power they accorded to their chiefs, the chiefs, in most cases, led by persuasiveness—that is, they led only insofar as they were able to persuade their peers to follow them. What Henri Marrou says of Athens in the fifth century B.C. was equally true of Indians in nineteenth-century America: "The democracy . . . knew only the direct method of government, and consequently it had most respect for the kind of politician who was able to impose his own point of view in the citizens' assembly, or in various councils, as a result of his power of speech."[1] What applied to the councils of Greece also applied to the council fires of North America: the greatest chiefs were often the greatest orators. The Greeks and the Romans were aware that oratory was not only a source of power but also an art. In fact, they considered it the highest art. (Titus Livy, the great Roman historian, said of Rome's great orator Cicero that one should study other authors only insofar as they resembled him.) The Indians possessed similar reverence for oratory and for their great orators, as we can see from the career of the great Seneca chief Red Jacket.

[1] Henri Marrou, *A History of Education in Antiquity*, trans. George Lamb (New York: New American Library, 1956), p. 84.

135

RED JACKET

Red Jacket was born in 1752. His Seneca name was Sa-go-ye-wat-ha, or "He Keeps Them Awake"; his English name derived from the British coat he always wore. He was one of the greatest Indian orators, and he was acutely aware of his own rhetorical prowess. When asked by a white man what military feats he had accomplished for the Senecas, he replied only: "I am an orator! I was born an orator!" He was for years the principal chief of the Senecas and the most important figure in the Six Nations of the Iroquois, despite the fact that he had proven himself several times to be a coward in battle. Although cowardice in battle had to have a devastating effect on the reputation of an ordinary man in a warrior society, Red Jacket's biographer, William L. Stone, estimated that, "Few men have arrived at a greater degree of consideration among [their] own people, or exerted a more commanding influence."[1]

The first of Red Jacket's speeches we have included here is his famous reply to Missionary Cram of the Boston Missionary Society, who had come to seek converts among the Senecas in the summer of 1805. The presumptuousness of the missionary's speech is worth noting, so I will quote it first. It and all the speeches that follow are reprinted from The Life and Times of Sa-Go-Ye-Wat-Ha, *by William L. Stone (New York, 1866).*

Missionary Cram:

My friends, I am thankful for the opportunity afforded us of uniting together at this time. I had a great desire to see you, and inquire into your state and welfare. For this purpose I have travelled a great distance, being sent by your old friends, the Boston Missionary Society. You will recollect they formerly sent missionaries among you, to instruct you in religion, and labor for your good. Although they have not heard from you for a long time, yet they have not forgotten their brothers, the Six Nations, and are still anxious to do you good.

Brothers, I have not come to get your lands or your money, but to enlighten your minds, and to instruct you how to worship the Great Spirit

---

[1]William L. Stone, *The Life and Times of Sa-Go-Ye-Wat-Ha* (Albany: Munsell, 1866), pp. 2–3.

Red Jacket's speeches are reprinted from *The Life and Times of Sa-Go-Ye-Wat-Ha*, by William Stone (New York, 1866).

agreeably to His mind and will, and to preach to you the gospel of His Son, Jesus Christ. There is but one religion, and but one way to serve God, and if you do not embrace the right way you cannot be happy together. You have never worshipped the Great Spirit in a manner acceptable to him; but have all your lives been in great errors and darkness. To endeavor to remove these errors, and open your eyes, so that you might see clearly, is my business with you.

Brothers, I wish to talk with you as one friend talks with another; and if you have any objections to receive the religion which I preach, I wish you to state them; and I will endeavor to satisfy your minds and remove the objections.

Brothers, I want you to speak your minds freely: for I wish to reason with you on the subject, and, if possible, remove all doubts, if there be any on your minds. The subject is an important one, and it is of consequence that you give it an early attention while the offer is made you. Your friends the Boston Missionary Society will continue to send you good and faithful ministers, to instruct and strengthen you in religion, if, on your part, you are willing to receive them.

Brothers, since I have been in this part of the country, I have visited some of your small villages and talked with your people. They appear willing to receive instruction, but as they look up to you as their older brothers in council, they want first to know your opinion on the subject. You have now heard what I have to propose and give me an answer before we part.

Red Jacket answered as follows:

Friend and Brother, it was the will of the Great Spirit that we should meet together this day. He orders all things, and has given us a fine day for our Council. He has taken his garment from before the sun, and caused it to shine with brightness upon us. Our eyes are opened, that we see clearly; our ears are unstopped, that we have been able to hear distinctly the words you have spoken. For all these favors we thank the Great Spirit and Him only.

Brother, this council fire was kindled by you. It was at your request that we came together at this time. We have listened with attention to what you have said. You requested us to speak our minds freely. This gives us great joy; for we now consider that we stand upright before you, and can speak what we think. All have heard your voice, and all speak to you now as one man. Our minds are agreed.

Brother, you say you want an answer to your talk before you leave this place. It is right you should have one; as you are a great distance from home, and we do not wish to detain you. But we will first look back a little, and tell you what our fathers have told us, and what we have heard from the white people.

Brother, listen to what we say. There was a time when our forefathers owned this great island. Their seats extended from the rising to the setting sun. The Great Spirit had made it for the use of Indians. He had created the buffalo, the deer, and other animals for food. He had made the bear and the beaver. Their skins served us for clothing. He had scattered them over the country, and taught us how to take them. He had caused the earth to produce corn for bread. All this He had done for his red children, because he loved them. If we had some disputes about our hunting ground, they were generally settled without the shedding of much blood. But an evil day came upon us. Your forefathers crossed the great water and landed on this island. Their numbers were small. They found friends and not enemies. They told us they had fled from their own country for fear of wicked men, and had come here to enjoy their religion. They asked for a small seat. We took pity on them; granted their request; and they sat down amongst us. We gave them corn and meat; they gave us poison [rum]. in return.

The white people, Brother, had now found our country. Tidings were carried back, and more came amongst us. Yet we did not fear them. We took them to be friends. They called us brothers. We believed them and gave them a larger seat. At length their numbers had greatly increased. They wanted more land; they wanted our country. Our eyes were opened, and our minds became uneasy. Wars took place. Indians were hired to fight against Indians, and many of our people were destroyed. They also brought strong liquor amongst us. It was strong and powerful, and has slain thousands.

Brother, our seats were once large and yours were small. You have now become a great people, and we have scarcely a place left to spread our blankets. You have got our country, but are not satisfied; you want to force your religion upon us.

Brother, continue to listen. You say that you are sent to instruct us how to worship the Great Spirit agreeably to his mind, and, if we do not take hold of the religion which you white people teach, we shall be unhappy hereafter. You say that you are right and we are lost. How do we know this to be true? We understand that your religion is written in a book. If it was intended for us as well as you, why has not the Great Spirit given to us, and not only to us, but why did he not give to our forefathers, the knowledge of that book, with the means of understanding it rightly? We only know what you tell us about it. How shall we know when to believe, being so often deceived by the white people?

Brother, you say there is but one way to worship and serve the Great Spirit. If there is but one religion, why do you white people differ so much about it? Why not all agreed, as you can all read the book?

Brother, we do not understand these things. We are told that your religion was given to your forefathers, and has been handed down from father to son. We also have a religion, which was given to our forefathers, and has been handed down to us their children. We worship in that way. It teaches us to be thankful for all the favors we receive; to love each other, and to be united. We never quarrel about religion.

Brother, the Great Spirit has made us all, but He has made a great difference between his white and red children. He has given us different complexions and different customs. To you He has given the arts. To these He has not opened our eyes. We know these things to be true. Since He has made so great a difference between us in other things, why may we not conclude that he has given us a different religion according to our understanding? The Great Spirit does right. He knows what is best for his children; we are satisfied.

Brother, we do not wish to destroy your religion, or take it from you. We only want to enjoy our own.

Brother, you say you have not come to get our land or our money, but to enlighten our minds. I will now tell you that I have been at your meetings, and saw you collect money from the meeting. I cannot tell what this money was intended for, but suppose that it was for your minister, and if we should conform to your way of thinking, perhaps you may want some from us.

Brother, we are told that you have been preaching to the white people in this place. These people are our neighbors. We are acquainted with them. We will wait a little while, and see what effect your preaching has upon them. If we find it does them good, makes them honest and less disposed to cheat Indians, we will then consider again of what you have said.

Brother, you have now heard our answer to your talk, and this is all we have to say at present. As we are going to part, we will come and take you by the hand, and hope the Great Spirit will protect you on your journey, and return you safe to your friends.

After he had finished speaking, Red Jacket, and a number of other Senecas, walked over to shake hands and say good-bye to Missionary Cram. The missionary refused to shake, however; "there being," he said, "no fellowship between the religion of God and the devil."

Red Jacket made the following speech in May 1811, to a Mr. Rich-ardson of the New York Company who wanted to buy Seneca lands.

Brother, we opened our ears to the talk you lately delivered to us, at our council fire. In doing important business it is best not to tell long stories, but come to it in a few words. We therefore shall not repeat your talk, which is fresh in our minds. We have well considered it and the advantages and disadvantages of your offers. We request your attention to our answer, which is not from the speaker alone, but from all the Sachems and Chiefs now around our Council fire.

Brother, we know that great men as well as great nations having different interests have different minds, and do not see the same subject in the same light—but we hope our answer will be agreeable to you and to your employers.

Brother, your application for the purchase of our lands is to our minds very extraordinary. It has been made in a crooked manner—you have not walked in the straight path pointed out by the great Council of your nation. You have no writings from our great father the President.

Brother, in making up our minds we have looked back and remembered how the Yorkers purchased our lands in former times. They bought them piece after piece for a little money paid to a few men in our nation, and not to all our brethren; our planting and hunting grounds have become very small, and if we sell these we know not where to spread our blankets.

Brother, you tell us your employers have purchased of the Council of Yorkers a right to buy our lands—we do not understand how this can be—the lands do not belong to the Yorkers; they are ours, and were given to us by the Great Spirit.

Brother, we think it strange that you should jump over the lands of our brethren in the East, to come to our Council fire so far off, to get our lands. When we sold our lands in the East to the white people, we determined never to sell those we kept, which are as small as we can live comfortably on.

Brother, you want us to travel with you, and look for other lands. If we should sell our lands and move off into a distant country, towards the setting sun, we should be looked upon in the country to which we go as foreigners, and strangers, and be despised by the red as well as the white men, and we should soon be surrounded by the white man, who will there also kill our game, come upon our lands, and try to get them from us.

Brother, we are determined not to sell our lands, but to continue on them—we like them—they are fruitful and produce us corn in abundance, for the support of our women and children, and grass and herbs for our cattle.

Brother, at the treaties held for the purchase of our lands, the white men with sweet voices and smiling faces told us they loved us, and that they would not cheat us, but that the king's children on the other side of the lake would cheat us. When we go on the other side of the lake the king's children tell us your people will cheat us, but with sweet voices and smiling faces assure us of their love and that they will not cheat us. These things puzzle our heads, and we believe that the Indians must take care of themselves, and not trust either in your people or in the king's children.

Brother, at a late council we requested our agents to tell you that we would not sell our lands, and we think you have not spoken to our agents, or they would have informed you so, and we should not have met you at our Council fire at this time.

Brother, the white people buy and sell false rights to our lands; your employers have, you say, paid a great price for their right; they must have plenty of money, to spend it in buying false rights to lands belonging to Indians; the loss of it will not hurt them, but our lands are of great value to us and we wish you to go back with your talk to your employers, and to tell them and the Yorkers that they have no right to buy and sell false rights to our lands.

Brother, we hope you clearly understand the words we have spoken. This is all we have to say.

The date and occasion of the following speech is not known. In it Red Jacket repeats his desire to keep the Senecas out of the American melting pot. He wanted them to retain their own lands, way of life, and religion. Although many Senecas converted to Christianity, including Red Jacket's wife, the chief remained adamant in adhering to the religion of his forefathers. The split between the Christian and the traditional Senecas became extremely bitter, until finally the Christian Senecas succeeded temporarily in deposing Red Jacket as chief. He was able to win reinstatement shortly before he died.

Brother, I rise to return you the thanks of this nation and to return them back to our ancient friends—if any such we have—for their good wishes toward us in attempting to teach us your religion. Inform them we will look well into this matter. We have well weighed your exertions, and find your success not to answer our expectations. But, instead of producing that happy effect which you so long promised us, its introduction so far has rendered us uncomfortable and miserable. You have taken a number of our young men to your schools. You have educated them and taught them your religion. They have returned to their kindred and color neither white men nor Indians. The arts they have learned are incompatible with the chase, and ill adapted to our customs. They have been taught that which is useless to us. They have been made to feel artificial wants, which never entered the minds of their brothers. They have imbibed, in your great towns, the seeds of vices which were unknown in the forest. They become discouraged and dissipated—despised by the Indians, neglected by the whites, and without value to either—less honest than the former, and *perhaps* more knavish than the latter.

Brother, we were told that the failure of these first attempts was attributable to miscalculation, and we were invited to try again, by sending others of our young men to different schools, to be taught by different instructors. Brother, the result has been invariably the same. We believe it wrong for you to attempt further to promote your religion among us or to introduce your arts, manners, habits, and feelings. We believe that it is wrong for us to encourage you in so doing. We believe that the Great Spirit made the whites and the Indians but for different purposes.

Brother, in attempting to pattern your example, the Great Spirit is angry—for you see he does not bless or crown your exertions. But, Brother, on the other hand we know that the Great Spirit is pleased that we follow the traditions and customs of our forefathers—for in so doing we receive his blessing—we have received strength and vigor for the chase. The Great Spirit has provided abundance—when we are hungry we find the forest filled with game—when thirsty, we slake our thirst in the pure streams and springs that spread around us.

When weary, the leaves of the trees are our bed—we retire with contentment to rest—we rise with gratitude to the Great Preserver. Renovated strength in our limbs, and bounding joy in our hearts, we feel blessed and happy. No luxuries, no vices, no disputed titles, no avaricious desires, shake the foundations of our society, or disturb our peace and happiness. We know the Great Spirit is better pleased with his red children than with his white, when he bestows upon us a hundredfold more blessings than upon you.

Perhaps, Brother, you are right in your religion—it may be peculiarly adapted to your condition. You say that you destroyed the Son of the Great Spirit. Perhaps this is the merited cause of all your troubles and misfortunes. But, Brothers, bear in mind that we had no participation in this murder. We disclaim it—we love the Great Spirit—and as we never had any agency in so unjust, so merciless an outrage, he therefore continues to smile upon us, and to give us peace, joy and plenty.

Brother, we pity you—we wish you to bear to our good friends our best wishes. Inform them that in compassion toward them, we are willing to send them missionaries to teach them our religion, habits and customs. We would be willing they should be as happy as we are, and assure them that if they should follow our example, they would be more, far more happy than they are now. We cannot embrace your religion. It renders us divided and unhappy—but by your embracing ours, we believe that you would be more happy and more acceptable to the Great Spirit. Here [pointing his finger to several whites present who had been captured when children, and been brought up among them], here, Brother [with an animation and exulting triumph which cannot be described], here is the living evidence before you. Those young men have been brought up with us. They are contented and happy. Nothing would be an inducement with them to abandon their enjoyments and adopt yours—for they are too well aware of the blessings of our society, and the evils of yours. But, as you have our good will, we would gladly know that you have relinquished your religion, productive of so much disagreement and inquietude among yourselves, and instead thereof that you should follow ours.

Accept of this advice, Brother, and take it back to your friends as the best pledge of our wishes for your welfare. Perhaps you think we are ignorant and uninformed. Go, then and teach the whites. Select, for example, the people of Buffalo. We will be spectators and remain silent. Improve their morals and refine their habits—make them less disposed to cheat Indians. Make the whites generally less inclined to make Indians drunk, and to take them from their lands. Let us know the tree by the blossoms, and the blossoms by the fruit. When this shall be made clear to our minds we may be more willing to listen to you. But until then we must be allowed to follow the religion of our ancestors.

Brother, Farewell!

Red Jacket delivered the following speech to Governor Ogden of New York in 1822. Ogden was president of the Ogden Land Company, which had been pressuring the Senecas to sell their holdings for years. Despite Red Jacket's pleadings, the Senecas decided to sell their lands, and by 1840 they had signed away their beautiful homeland in New York. Some remained in New York on reservations; others moved to lands provided in Oklahoma.

We first knew you a feeble plant which wanted a little earth whereon to grow. We gave it you—and afterward, when we could have trod you under our feet, we watered and protected you—and now you have grown to be a mighty tree, whose top reaches the clouds, and whose branches overspread the whole land; whilst we, who were then the tall pine of the forest, have become the feeble plant, and need your protection.

When you first came here, you clung around our knee, and called us father. We took you by the hand and called you brothers. You have grown greater than we, so that we no longer can reach up to your hand. But we wish to cling around your knee and be called your children.

Not long ago you raised the war club against him who was once our great Father over the waters. You asked us to go with you to the war. It was not our quarrel. We knew not that you were right. We asked not, we cared not: it was enough for us that you were our brothers. We went with you to the battle. We fought and bled for you: and now [with great feeling, pointing to some Indians who had been wounded in the contest] dare you pretend to us that our Father the President, while he sees our blood running fresh from the wounds received while fighting his battles, has sent you with a message to persuade us to relinquish the poor remains of our once boundless possessions—or sell the birthplace of our children, and the graves of our fathers. No! Sooner than believe that he gave you this message, we will believe that you have stolen your commission and are a cheat and a liar.

You tell us of your claim to our land and that you have purchased it from your State. We know nothing of your claim, and we care nothing for it. Even the whites have a law, by which they cannot sell what they do not own. How, then, has your state, which never owned our land, sold it to you? We have a title to it, and we know that our title is good; for it came direct from the Great Spirit, who gave it to us, his red children. When you can ascend to where He is [pointing toward the skies] and will get His deed, and show it to us, then, and never till then, will we acknowledge your title. You say that you came not to cheat us of our lands, but to buy them. Who told you that we have lands to sell? You never heard it from us.

Did I not tell you, the last time we met, that whilst Red Jacket lived you would get no more lands of the Indians? How then, while you see him alive and strong [striking his hand violently on his breast] do you think to make him a liar?

PONTIAC'S ALLEGORY

Pontiac was born around 1720, probably on the Maumee River in Ohio. He was the principal chief of the Ottawas, who were part of a loose confederation with the Ojibwas and the Pottawatomis. Pontiac was the dominant figure in that group, and in fact, his alliance included most of the tribes northwest of the Ohio River. As his speech reveals, Pontiac was sympathetic to the French and hostile to the English. The British were farmers bent on acquiring land for permanent use. As a result they were in constant conflict with the Indians, who were reluctant to relinquish their ancestral homelands. The French were interested primarily in sending furs back to Europe rather than settling the land. As hunters and trappers like the Indians, they were able to coexist with them. Unfortunately for the Indians, the British defeated the French in the war for control of the northern part of the continent.

In 1763, upon hearing the false rumor that the French were planning a campaign to win back their lost territories, Pontiac planned a massive Indian uprising to help them. The Indians recaptured Sandusky, Fort Wayne, and several other garrisons, but they failed to take Detroit, the objective of Pontiac's band of Ottawas. When the French concluded a peace with the British, Pontiac was forced to abandon his hopes of throwing the British out of his territory, and he made peace in 1765. In 1769 he was killed by a Kaskaskia who had been bribed by a trader with a barrel of whiskey.

The speech below was delivered on April 27, 1763, the eve of Pontiac's uprising against the British. Since visions played an important part in Indian life, the idea of the Great Spirit's supernatural sanction of Pontiac's project would have weighed heavily with his followers.

A Delaware Indian . . . conceived an eager desire to learn wisdom from the Master of Life; but, being ignorant where to find him, he had recourse to fasting, dreaming, and magical incantations. By these means it was revealed to him, that by moving forward in a straight, undeviating course, he would reach the abode of the Great Spirit. He told his purpose to no one, and having provided the equipments of a hunter—gun, powderhorn, ammunition, and a kettle for preparing his food—he set forth on his errand. For some time he journeyed on in high hope and confidence. On the evening of the eighth day, he stopped by the side of a brook at the

Pontiac's allegory is reprinted from Francis Parkman, *The Conspiracy of Pontiac* (Boston, 1903).

edge of a small prairie, where he began to make ready his evening meal, when, looking up, he saw three large openings in the woods on the opposite side of the meadow, and three well-beaten paths which entered them. He was much surprised; but his wonder increased when, after it had grown dark, the three paths were more clearly visible than ever. Remembering the important object of his journey, he could neither rest nor sleep; and, leaving his fire, he crossed the meadow, and entered the largest of the three openings. He had advanced but a short distance into the forest, when a bright flame sprang out of the ground before him, and arrested his steps. In great amazement, he turned back, and entered the second path, where the same wonderful phenomenon again encountered him; and now, in terror and bewilderment, yet still resolved to persevere, he pursued the last of the three paths. On this he journeyed a whole day without interruption, when at length, emerging from the forest, he saw before him a vast mountain of dazzling whiteness. So precipitous was the ascent, that the Indian thought it hopeless to go farther, and looked around him in despair: at that moment, he saw, seated at some distance above, the figure of a beautiful woman arrayed in white, who arose as he looked upon her, and thus accosted him: "How can you hope, encumbered as you are, to succeed in your design? Go down to the foot of the mountain, throw away your gun, your ammunition, your provisions, and your clothing; wash yourself in the stream which flows there, and you will then be prepared to stand before the Master of Life." The Indian obeyed, and again began to ascend among the rocks, while the woman, seeing him still discouraged, laughed at his faintness of heart, and told him that, if he wished for success, he must climb by the aid of one hand and one foot only. After great toil and suffering, he at length found himself at the summit. The woman had disappeared, and he was left alone. A rich and beautiful plain lay before him, and at a little distance he saw three great villages, far superior to the squalid dwellings of the Delawares. As he approached the largest, and stood hesitating whether he should enter, a man gorgeously attired stepped forth, and, taking him by the hand, welcomed him to the celestial abode. He then conducted him into the presence of the Great Spirit, where the Indian stood confounded at the unspeakable splendor which surrounded him. The Great Spirit bade him be seated, and thus addressed him:

"I am the Maker of heaven and earth, the trees, lakes, rivers, and all things else. I am the Maker of mankind; and because I love you, you must do my will. The land on which you live I have made for you, and not for others. Why do you suffer the white men to dwell among you? My children, you have forgotten the customs and traditions of your forefathers. Why do you not clothe yourselves in skins, as they did, and use the bows and arrows, and the stone-pointed lances, which they used? You have bought guns, knives, kettles, and blankets from the white men, until you can no longer do without them; and what is worse, you have drunk the poison firewater, which turns you into fools. Fling all these things away; live as your wise forefathers lived before you. And as for these English—these dogs dressed in red, who have come to rob you of your hunting-grounds, and drive away the game—you must lift the hatchet against them. Wipe them from the face of the earth, and then you will win my favor back again, and once more be happy and prosperous. The children of your great father, the King of France, are not like the English. Never forget that they are your brethren. They are very dear to me, for they love the red men, and understand the true mode of worshipping me."

TECUMSEH'S PLEA TO THE
CHOCTAWS AND THE CHICKASAWS

The great Shawnee chief Tecumseh was born in 1768 near the site of present-day Springfield, Ohio. With his brother Tenskwatawa, the Prophet, he was a strong opponent of the advance of the American settlers. He claimed that the Ohio Valley belonged in common to the different tribes that resided there, and that the United States had no right to purchase lands from any single tribe. During the War of 1812, Tecumseh sided with the British and was made a brigadier general. He commanded a detachment of two thousand Indian warriors from several tribes. He died in 1813 fighting in Ontario against American troops led by William Henry Harrison.

Tecumseh delivered the speech below urging the Choctaws and Chickasaws to fight the Americans in the spring of 1811, when it was apparent that America was headed for war with England. After he had finished speaking, the Choctaw chief Pushmataha spoke and convinced the Choctaws and Chickasaws that the Americans were their friends, and that if they broke their "sacred treaties" with the Americans, the Great Spirit would punish them. The Americans considered friendship less important, and treaties less sacred, with the result that in the early 1830s, the Choctaws and the Chickasaws were forced to leave their homeland and walk the Trail of Tears to Indian Territory.

In view of questions of vast importance, have we met together in solemn council tonight. Nor should we here debate whether we have been wronged and injured, but by what measures we should avenge ourselves; for our merciless oppressors, having long since planned out their proceedings, are not about to make, but have and are still making attacks upon our race who have as yet come to no resolution. Nor are we ignorant by what steps, and by what gradual advances, the whites break in upon our neighbors. Imagining themselves to be still undiscovered, they show themselves the less audacious because you are insensible. The whites are already nearly a match for us all united, and too strong for any one tribe alone to resist; so that unless we support one another with our collective and united forces; unless every tribe unanimously combines to give check

Tecumseh's "Plea to the Choctaws and the Chickasaws" is reprinted from W. C. Vanderwerth, *Indian Oratory* (© copyright 1971, 1972 by University of Oklahoma Press).

to the ambition and avarice of the whites, they will soon conquer us apart and disunited, and we will be driven away from our native country and scattered as autumnal leaves before the wind.

But have we not courage enough remaining to defend our country and maintain our ancient independence? Will we calmly suffer the white intruders and tyrants to enslave us? Shall it be said of our race that we knew not how to extricate ourselves from the three most dreadful calamities— folly, inactivity and cowardice? But what need is there to speak of the past? It speaks for itself and asks, Where today is the Pequod? Where the Narragansetts, the Mohawks, Pocanokets, and many other once powerful tribes of our race? They have vanished before the avarice and oppression of the white men, as snow before a summer sun. In the vain hope of alone defending their ancient possessions, they have fallen in the wars with the white men. Look abroad over their once beautiful country, and what see you now? Naught but the ravages of the pale face destroyers meet our eyes. So it will be with you Choctaws and Chickasaws! Soon your mighty forest trees, under the shade of whose wide spreading branches you have played in infancy, sported in boyhood, and now rest your wearied limbs after the fatigue of the chase, will be cut down to fence in the land which the white intruders dare to call their own. Soon their broad roads will pass over the grave of your fathers, and the place of their rest will be blotted out forever. The annihilation of our race is at hand unless we unite in one common cause against the common foe. Think not, brave Choctaws and Chickasaws, that you can remain passive and indifferent to the common danger, and thus escape the common fate. Your people, too, will soon be as falling leaves and scattering clouds before their blighting breath. You, too, will be driven away from your native land and ancient domains as leaves are driven before the wintry storms.

Sleep not longer, O Choctaws and Chickasaws, in false security and delusive hopes. Our broad domains are fast escaping from our grasp. Every year our white intruders become more greedy, exacting, oppressive and overbearing. Every year contentions spring up between them and our people and when blood is shed we have to make atonement whether right or wrong, at the cost of the lives of our greatest chiefs, and the yielding up of large tracts of our lands. Before the palefaces came among us, we enjoyed the happiness of unbounded freedom, and were acquainted with neither riches, wants nor oppression. How is it now? Wants and oppression are our lot; for are we not controlled in everything, and dare we move without asking, by your leave? Are we not being stripped day by day of the little that remains of our ancient liberty? Do they not even kick and strike us as they do their black-faces? How long will it be before they will tie us to a post and whip us, and make us work for them in their corn fields as they do them? Shall we wait for that moment or shall we die fighting before submitting to such ignominy?

Have we not for years had before our eyes a sample of their designs, and are they not sufficient harbingers of their future determinations? Will we not soon be driven from our respective countries and the graves of our ancestors? Will not the bones of our dead be plowed up, and their graves be turned into fields? Shall we calmly wait until they become so numerous that we will no longer be able to resist oppression? Will we wait to be destroyed in our turn, without making an effort worthy of our race? Shall we give up our homes, our country, bequeathed to us by the Great Spirit, the graves of our dead, and everything that is dear and sacred to us, without a struggle? I know you will cry with me: Never! Never! Then let us by unity of action destroy them all, which we now can do, or drive them back whence they came. War or extermination is now our only choice. Which do you choose? I know your answer. Therefore, I now call on you, brave Choctaws and Chickasaws, to assist in the just cause of liberating our race from the grasp of our faithless invaders and heartless oppressors. The white usurpation in our common country must be stopped, or we, its rightful owners, be forever destroyed and wiped out as a race of people. I am now at the head of many warriors backed by the strong arm of English soldiers. Choctaws and Chickasaws, you have too long borne with grievous usurpation inflicted by the arrogant Americans. Be no longer their dupes. If there be one here tonight who believes that his rights will not sooner or later be taken from him by the avaricious American pale faces, his ignorance ought to excite pity, for he knows little of the character of our common foe.

And if there be one among you mad enough to undervalue the growing power of the white race among us, let him tremble in considering the fearful woes he will bring down upon our entire race, if by his criminal indifference he assists the designs of our common enemy against our common country. Then listen to the voice of duty, of honor, of nature and of your endangered country. Let us form one body, one heart, and defend to the last warrior our country, our homes, our liberty, and the graves of our fathers.

Choctaws and Chickasaws, you are among the few of our race who sit indolently at ease. You have indeed enjoyed the reputation of being brave, but will you be indebted for it more from report than fact? Will you let the whites encroach upon your domains even to your very door before you will assert your rights in resistance? Let no one in this council imagine that I speak more from malice against the pale face Americans than just grounds of complaint. Complaint is just toward friends who have failed in their duty; accusation is against enemies guilty of injustice. And surely, if any people ever had, we have good and just reasons to believe we have ample grounds to accuse the Americans of injustice; especially when such great acts of injustice have been committed by them upon our race, of which they seem to have no manner of regard, or even to reflect. They are a people fond of innovations, quick to contrive and quick to put their schemes into effectual execution no matter how great the wrong and injury to us; while we are content to preserve what we already have. Their designs are to enlarge their possessions by taking yours in turn; and will you, can you longer dally, O Choctaws and Chickasaws?

Do you imagine that that people will not continue longest in the enjoyment of peace who timely prepare to vindicate themselves, and manifest a determined resolution to do themselves right whenever they are wronged? Far otherwise. Then haste to the relief of our common cause, as by consanguinity of blood you are bound; lest the day be not far distant when you will be left single-handed and alone to the cruel mercy of our most inveterate foe.

MEMOIRS

The tales and songs in parts 1 and 2 were composed by Indians for Indians, and, with a couple of exceptions, they were written in an Indian language. The first two memoirs in this section were related by Indians to whites with a white readership in mind. The intention of the narrators was to tell their side of what happened between the "fat takers," as the Sioux called the whites, and the Indians. They are a valuable corrective to our understanding of the history of the West.

Too often in high school and college, students get the impression that, while literature deals with imaginary events, history is what "really happened" in a certain time and place. History, or at any rate the books that record it, is no such thing: it is what people say happened, and individuals always see things from a particular bias. The history of Alabama would be written very differently by George Wallace and Jesse Jackson, even if both tried to be scrupulously honest and fair. And history is usually written by the conquerors rather than the conquered, so that we often get only one side of the story. While the losers brood and lick their wounds, the winners tell us who started it, who committed the atrocities, what "really happened."

In the case of what is often called "the winning of the West," we have heard all too little from the people who lost it. Traditionally, American historians, filled with a sense of manifest destiny, have painted a picture of brave settlers taming a wilderness populated only by bloodthirsty savages. Hollywood has confirmed this image in the popular imagination: mention Indians, and most Americans imagine embattled and outnumbered whites crouched behind their wagons as murderous Comanches circled them emitting blood-chilling whoops. In contrast, the accounts given by Black Elk and Lame Deer show the Indians as brave but vastly outnumbered, trying only to get along as they always had as they were overwhelmed by waves and waves of white settlers who did senseless things such as go crazy over a yellow metal and slaughter buffaloes for the sheer sport of it.

When one is reading an Indian autobiography, it is important to note whether the writer is working alone, as Momaday was in The Way to Rainy Mountain, *or whether the writer has a collaborator, as Black Elk and Lame Deer did.*

Black Elk related his life story in Sioux. His son, Benjamin Black Elk, translated it into English, and a white poet, John Neihardt, prepared the manuscript for publication. Neihardt interviewed Black Elk in 1931, but ended Black Elk's story in 1890 with the Battle of Wounded Knee. In the book Black Elk reiterates that he considered himself primarily a shaman, although he had been a warrior and a hunter as well.

The focus of Black Elk Speaks *is on Black Elk's devotion to the Lakota religion. Lame Deer tells us in his memoir that Black Elk became a Christian and had his daughter sit behind him on his horse reading him the Bible. Neihardt never tells us this, even in the introduction he wrote after Black Elk's death. It is possible that Neihardt was unaware of Black Elk's conversion, but it seems far more likely that Neihardt thought that revealing it would make Black Elk look as if he had sold out, and would lessen the impact of the book, in particular the message of the power and beauty of the Lakota religion. Perhaps some readers may have gotten that impression; nonetheless, Black Elk's conversion is an important fact in his life, and someone trying to understand that life should know about it.*

BLACK ELK SPEAKS

by John G. Neihardt

Black Elk was an Oglala Sioux warrior and medicine man. He was born in 1863, while the Sioux still ruled the northern plains. He grew to manhood in the period after the Civil War ended, when America turned its energies to winning the West, that is, to taking it away from the Indians. As a boy, Black Elk fought at the Little Bighorn when Custer made his last stand. As a man, he was present at Wounded Knee, the last military encounter between whites and Indians in this country (unless one counts the sporadic fighting at Wounded Knee II in 1973). He danced in the Ghost Dance, the Indians' last desperate attempt to keep their country. He rode in Buffalo Bill's Wild West Show as it toured the United States and Europe.

Our selection deals chiefly with what happened at the Little Bighorn. George Armstrong Custer was long considered one of America's greatest heroes. Bruce Rosenberg, an English professor interested in folk heroes, recorded that by the early 1970s there were more than 950 paintings and illustrations of Custer and his last stand, and that Custer has been the subject of 640 biographies, nearly 2,000 works of fiction, and at least 25 television serials. Until recently, Custer's nobility went unquestioned. His death on a hilltop, in a "lonely and desolate land," at the hands of brutal infidels is the stuff of tragedy—reminiscent of the deaths of Roland, Saul, and Gawain.[1]

Today Custer has been reassessed in the light of greater American sympathy for and understanding of the Indian viewpoint. Custer is now often depicted as egotistical, ambitious, and brutal. His last stand is seen as a foolhardy attempt to win a spectacular victory that might propel him into contention in the 1876 presidential election. A Custer series on television, in 1967, ran only nine episodes before pressure from the National Congress of American Indians forced ABC to take it off the air. The NCAI tabbed Custer the "Adolph Eichmann of the 19th Century."[2] Although most Americans would probably find that description harsh, accounts like

---

[1] Bruce Rosenberg, "The Myth of Custer's Last Stand," *Penn State Alumni News*, November 1971, p. 4.

[2] Vine Deloria, Jr., *Custer Died for Your Sins* (New York: Avon Books, 1969), p. 31.

Black Elk's are a valuable corrective to the picture depicted on the walls of Legion halls and barrooms showing the valiant blond Custer standing his ground against a horde of red devils.

Early Boyhood

I am a Lakota of the Ogalala band. My father's name was Black Elk, and his father before him bore the name, and the father of his father, so that I am the fourth to bear it. He was a medicine man and so were several of his brothers. Also, he and the great Crazy Horse's father were cousins, having the same grandfather. My mother's name was White Cow Sees; her father was called Refuse-to-go, and her mother, Plenty Eagle Feathers. I can remember my mother's mother and her father. My father's father was killed by the Pawnees when I was too little to know, and his mother, Red Eagle Woman, died soon after.

I was born in the Moon of the Popping Trees (December) on the Little Powder River in the Winter When the Four Crows Were Killed (1863), and I was three years old when my father's right leg was broken in the Battle of the Hundred Slain. From that wound he limped until the day he died, which was about the time when Big Foot's band was butchered on Wounded Knee (1890). He is buried here in these hills.

I can remember that Winter of the Hundred Slain as a man may remember some bad dream he dreamed when he was little, but I can not tell just how much I heard when I was bigger and how much I understood when I was little. It is like some fearful thing in a fog, for it was a time when everything seemed troubled and afraid.

I had never seen a Wasichu then, and did not know what one looked like; but every one was saying that the Wasichus were coming and that they were going to take our country and rub us all out and that we should all have to die fighting. It was the Wasichus who got rubbed out in that battle, and all the people were talking about it for a long while; but a hundred Wasichus was not much if there were others and others without number where those came from.

I remember once that I asked my grandfather about this. I said: "When the scouts come back from seeing the prairie full of bison somewhere, the people say the Wasichus are coming; and when strange men are coming to kill us all, they say the Wasichus are coming. What does it mean?" And he said, "That they are many."

When I was older, I learned what the fighting was about that winter and the next summer. Up on the Madison Fork the Wasichus had found much of the yellow metal that they worship and that makes them crazy, and they wanted to have a road up through our country to the place where the yellow metal was; but my people did not want the road. It would scare the bison and make them go away, and also it would let the other Wasichus come in like a river. They told us that they wanted only to use a little land, as much as a wagon would take between the wheels; but our people knew better. And when you look about you now, you can see what it was they wanted.

Once we were happy in our own country and we were seldom hungry, for then the two-leggeds and the four-leggeds lived together like relatives, and there was plenty for them and for us. But the Wasichus came, and they have made little islands for us and other little islands for the four-leggeds, and always these islands are becoming smaller, for around them surges the gnawing flood of the Wasichu; and it is dirty with lies and greed.

A long time ago my father told me what his father told him, that there was once a Lakota holy man, called Drinks Water, who dreamed what was to be; and this was long before the coming of the Wasichus. He dreamed that the four-leggeds were going back into the earth and that a strange race had woven a spider's web all around the Lakotas. And he said: "When this happens, you shall live in square gray houses, in a barren land, and beside those square gray houses you shall starve." They say he went back to Mother Earth soon after he saw this vision, and it was sorrow that killed him. You can look about you now and see that he meant these dirt-roofed houses we are living in, and that all the rest was true. Sometimes dreams are wiser than waking. . . .

The Rubbing Out of Longhair

Black Elk Continues:
Crazy Horse whipped Three Stars on the Rosebud that day, and I think he could have rubbed the soldiers out there. He could have called many more warriors from the village and he could have rubbed the soldiers out at daybreak, for they camped there in the dark after the fight.

He whipped the cavalry of Three Stars when they attacked his village on the Powder that cold morning in the Moon of the Snowblind (March). Then he moved farther west to the Rosebud; and when the soldiers came to kill us there, he whipped them and made them go back. Then he moved farther west to the valley of the Greasy Grass. We were in our own country all the time and we only wanted to be let alone. The soldiers came there to kill us, and many got rubbed out. It was our country and we did not want to have trouble.

We camped there in the valley along the south side of the Greasy Grass

before the sun was straight above; and this was, I think, two days before
the battle. It was a very big village and you could hardly count the tepees.
Farthest up the stream toward the south were the Hunkpapas, and
the Ogalalas were next. Then came the Minneconjous, the Sans Arcs, the
Blackfeet, the Shyelas; and last, the farthest toward the north, were the
Santees and Yanktonais. Along the side towards the east was the Greasy
Grass, with some timber along it, and it was running full from the melting
of the snow in the Big Horn Mountains. If you stood on a hill you could
see the mountains off to the south and west. On the other side of the river,
there were bluffs and hills beyond. Some gullies came down through the
bluffs. On the westward side of us were lower hills, and there we grazed
our ponies and guarded them. There were so many they could not be
counted.

There was a man by the name of Rattling Hawk who was shot through the
hip in the fight on the Rosebud, and people thought he could not get well.
But there was a medicine man by the name of Hairy Chin who cured him.

The day before the battle I had greased myself and was going to swim
with some boys, when Hairy Chin called me over to Rattling Hawk's
tepee, and told me he wanted me to help him. There were five other boys
there, and he needed us for bears in the curing ceremony, because he had
his power from a dream of the bear. He painted my body yellow, and my
face too, and put a black stripe on either side of my nose from the eyes
down. Then he tied my hair up to look like bear's ears, and put some eagle
feathers on my head.

While he was doing this, I thought of my vision, and suddenly I
seemed to be lifted clear off the ground; and while I was that way, I knew
more things than I could tell, and I felt sure something terrible was going
to happen in a short time. I was frightened.

The other boys were painted all red and had real bear's ears on their
heads.

Hairy Chin, who wore a real bear skin with the head on it, began to
sing a song that went like this:

"At the doorway the sacred herbs are rejoicing."

And while he sang, two girls came in and stood one on either side of the
wounded man; one had a cup of water and one some kind of a herb. I tried
to see if the cup had all the sky in it, as it was in my vision, but I could not
see it. They gave the cup and the herb to Rattling Hawk while Hairy Chin
was singing. Then they gave him a red cane, and right away he stood up
with it. The girls then started out of the tepee, and the wounded man
followed, learning on the sacred red stick; and we boys, who were the

little bears, had to jump around him and make growling noises toward the man. And when we did this, you could see something like feathers of all colors coming out of our mouths. Then Hairy Chin came out on all fours, and he looked just like a bear to me. Then Rattling Hawk began to walk better. He was not able to fight next day, but he got well in a little while.

After the ceremony, we boys went swimming to wash the paint off, and when we got back the people were dancing and having kill talks all over the village, remembering brave deeds done in the fight with Three Stars on the Rosebud.

When it was about sundown we boys had to bring the ponies in close, and when this was done it was dark and the people were still dancing around fires all over the village. We boys went around from one dance to another, until we got too sleepy to stay up any more.

My father 'woke me at daybreak and told me to go with him to take our horses out to graze, and when we were out there he said: "We must have a long rope on one of them, so that it will be easy to catch; then we can get the others. If anything happens, you must bring the horses back as fast as you can, and keep your eyes on the camp."

Several of us boys watched our horses together until the sun was straight above and it was getting very hot. Then we thought we would go swimming, and my cousin said he would stay with our horses till we got back. When I was greasing myself, I did not feel well; I felt queer. It seemed that something terrible was going to happen. But I went with the boys anyway. Many people were in the water now and many of the women were out west of the village digging turnips. We had been in the water quite a while when my cousin came down there with the horses to give them a drink, for it was very hot now.

Just then we heard the crier shouting in the Hunkpapa camp, which was not very far from us: "The chargers are coming! They are charging! The chargers are coming!" Then the crier of the Ogalalas shouted the same words; and we could hear the cry going from camp to camp northward clear to the Santees and Yanktonais.

Everybody was running now to catch the horses. We were lucky to have ours right there just at that time. My older brother had a sorrel, and he rode away fast toward the Hunkpapas. I had a buckskin. My father came running and said: "Your brother has gone to the Hunkpapas without his gun. Catch him and give it to him. Then come right back to me." He had my six-shooter too—the one my aunt gave me. I took the guns, jumped on my pony and caught my brother. I could see a big dust rising just beyond the Hunkpapa camp and all the Hunkpapas were running around and yelling, and many were running wet from the river. Then out of the dust came the soldiers on their big horses. They looked big and strong and tall and they were all shooting. My brother took his gun and yelled for me to go back. There was brushy timber just on the other side of the Hunkpapas, and some warriors were gathering there. He made for that place, and I followed him. By now women and children were running in a crowd downstream. I looked back and saw them all running and scattering up a hillside down yonder.

When we got into the timber, a good many Hunkpapas were there already and the soldiers were shooting above us so that leaves were falling from the trees where the bullets struck. By now I could not see what was happening in the village below. It was all dust and cries and thunder; for the women and children were running there, and the warriors were coming on their ponies.

Among us there in the brush and out in the Hunkpapa camp a cry went up: "Take courage! Don't be a woman! The helpless are out of breath!" I think this was when Gall stopped the Hunkpapas, who had been running away, and turned them back.

I stayed there in the woods a little while and thought of my vision. It made me feel stronger, and it seemed that my people were all thunder-beings and that the soliders would be rubbed out.

Then another great cry went up out in the dust: "Crazy Horse is coming! Crazy Horse is coming!" Off toward the west and north they were yelling "Hoka hey!" like a big wind roaring, and making the tremolo; and you could hear eagle bone whistles screaming.

The valley went darker with dust and smoke, and there were only shadows and a big noise of many cries and hoofs and guns. On the left of where I was I could hear the shod hoofs of the soldiers' horses going back into the brush and there was shooting everywhere. Then the hoofs came out of the brush, and I came out and was in among men and horses weaving in and out and doing upstream, and everybody was yelling, "Hurry! Hurry!" The soldiers were running upstream and we were all mixed there in the twilight and the great noise. I did not see much; but once I saw a Lakota charge at a soldier who stayed behind and fought and was a very brave man. The Lakota took the soldier's horse by the bridle, but the soldier killed him with a six-shooter. I was small and could not crowd in to where the soldiers were, so I did not kill anybody. There were so many ahead of me, and it was all dark and mixed up.

Soon the soldiers were all crowded into the river, and many Lakotas too; and I was in the water awhile. Men and horses were all mixed up and fighting in the water, and it was like hail falling in the river. Then we were out of the river, and people were stripping dead soldiers and putting the clothes on themselves. There was a soldier on the ground and he was still kicking. A Lakota rode up and said to me: "Boy, get off and scalp him." I got off and started to do it. He had short hair and my knife was not very sharp. He ground his teeth. Then I shot him in the forehead and got his scalp.

Many of our warriors were following the soldiers up a hill on the other side of the river. Everybody else was turning back downstream, and on a hill away down yonder above the Santee camp there was a big dust, and our warriors whirling around in and out of it just like swallows, and many guns were going off.

I thought I would show my mother my scalp, so I rode over toward the hill where there was a crowd of women and children. On the way down there I saw a very pretty young woman among a band of warriors about to go up to the battle on the hill, and she was singing like this:

"Brothers, now your friends have come!
Be brave! Be brave!
Would you see me taken captive?"

When I rode through the Ogalala camp I saw Rattling Hawk sitting up in his tepee with a gun in his hands, and he was all alone there singing a song of regret that went like this:

"Brothers, what are you doing that I can not do?"

When I got to the women on the hill they were all singing and making the tremolo to cheer the men fighting across the river in the dust on the hill. My mother gave a big tremolo just for me when she saw my first scalp.

I stayed there awhile with my mother and watched the big dust whirling on the hill across the river, and horses were coming out of it with empty saddles.

Standing Bear Speaks:

I am a Minneconjou, and our camp was third from the south. We got up late the morning of the fight. The women went out to dig turnips and two of my uncles went hunting. My grandmother, who was very old and feeble, and one of my uncles and I stayed in a tepee. When the sun was overhead, I went down to the river to swim, and when I came back all I had on was a shirt. My grandmother cooked some meat in the ashes and fed us. While we were eating, my uncle said: "When you have eaten, you must go to the horses right away. Something might happen." An older brother of mine and another man were herding the horses in two bunches on Muskrat Creek down stream below the Santee camp.

Before I finished eating, there was an excitement outside. Then I heard our crier saying that the chargers were coming. When we heard this, my uncle said: "I told you before that something might happen. You'd better go right away and help bring in the horses."

I crossed the Greasy Grass, which was breast deep, and got on top of Black Butte to look. On the other side of the Hunkpapas toward the south, I saw soldiers on horseback spreading out as they came down a slope to the river. They crossed and came on at a trot. I started down the butte, but I was barefoot and there was a big bed of cactus there. I had to go slow, picking my way. A dust cloud was rising up yonder; and then I could see that the Hunkpapas were running, and when I looked over onto the hills toward the south and east I saw other soldiers coming there on horseback. I did not go to the horses. I went down through the cactus as fast as I could and into the village. There were voices all over, and everybody was shouting something and running around. After awhile my older brother came driving our horses, and my uncle said: "Hurry up! We shall go forth!" I caught my gray horse and took my six-shooter and hung my bow and arrows over my shoulder. I had killed a red bird a few days before and I fastened this in my hair. I had made a vow that I would make an offering if this would keep me from getting hurt in the next fight; and it did.

We started and went downstream to the mouth of Muskrat Creek beyond the Santee camp. We were going to meet the second band of soldiers. By the time we got there, they must have been fighting on the hill already, because as we rode up east from the mouth of Muskrat Creek we met a Lakota with blood running out of his mouth and down over his horse's shoulders. His name was Long Elk. There were warriors ahead of us, the "fronters," who are the bravest and have had most practice in war. I was sixteen years old and I was in the rear with the less brave, and we had waited for our horses quite awhile.

Part way up we met another Lakota. He was on foot and he was bleeding and dizzy. He would get up and then he would fall down again. When we got farther up the hill, I could see the soldiers. They were off their horses, holding them by the bridles. They were ready for us and were shooting. Our people were all around the hill on every side by this time. I heard some of our men shouting: "They are gone!" And I saw that many of the soldiers' horses had broken loose and were running away. Everywhere our warriors began yelling: "Hoka hey! Hurry! Hurry!" Then we all went up, and it got dark with dust and smoke. I could see warriors flying all around me like shadows, and the noise of all those hoofs and guns and cries was so loud it seemed quiet in there and the voices seemed to be on top of the cloud. It was like a bad dream. All at once I saw a soldier right beside me, and I leaned over and knocked him down with the butt of the six-shooter. I think I had already shot it empty, but I don't remember when. The soldier fell off and was under the hoofs. There were so many of us that I think we did not need guns. Just the hoofs would have been enough.

After this we started down the hillside in formation toward the village, and there were dead men and horses scattered along there too. They were all rubbed out.

We were all crazy, and I will tell you something to show how crazy we were. There was a dead Indian lying there on his face, and someone said: "Scalp that Ree!" A man got off and scalped him; and when they turned the dead man over, it was a Shyela—one of our friends. We were all crazy.

We could see the women coming over now in a swarm and they were all making the tremolo. We waited around there awhile, and then we saw soldiers coming on a hill toward the south and east. Everybody began yelling: "Hurry!" And we started for the soldiers. They ran back toward where they came from. One got killed, and many of us got off and couped him. Then we chased all the soldiers back to the hill where they were before.

They had their pack mules and horses on the inside and they had saddles and other things in front of them to hide themselves from bullets, but we surrounded them, and the hill we were on was higher and we could see them plain. We put our horses down under the hills so that they were safe. We all kept shooting at the soldiers and their horses. It was very hot, and there were some soldiers who started down the hill with kettles to get water from the river. They did not get far, and what was left of them went running back up the hill. I heard that some soldiers did get some water later, but I did not see them. Once a Lakota on the other side charged alone right up to the soldiers to show how brave he was, but they killed him, and we could not get his body.

By now it was nearly sundown. I had not been feeling hungry because there was the smell of blood everywhere; but now I began to feel hungry anyway. The bravest of the braves got together and talked over what we should do that night. They decided that some of us should go home and eat and bring back something for those who stayed to watch the soldiers. We could not get at the soldiers, so we were going to starve and dry them out.

I went back home with the others, and it was sundown then. At first I thought they had broken camp, but they had not. They had only gathered all the camps together in one solid village.

I did not go back to the hill with the others that night. We built fires all over the camp, and everybody was excited. I couldn't sleep because when I shut my eyes I could see all those horrible sights again. I think nobody slept.

Next morning early the crier went around and said: "The remainder of the soldiers shall die today!" So after we had eaten, we all got ready. This time I was dressed and had my moccasins and leggings on. The day before I had only a shirt. This time I had my saddle too. I was prepared to fight.

We all rode over there, and the party that had watched all night went home. We were scattered all around the soldiers, with our horses under the hill; but it was harder to hit the soldiers now, because they had been digging in the night. The day was very hot, and now and then some soldiers would start crawling down toward the river for a drink. We killed some of these, then the others would run back. Maybe some got water. I do not know. We kept shooting at each other. Once I heard some one cry "Hey-hey!" I crawled over there, and a Lakota had been shot above the eyebrow and he was dead.

After a long while we heard that more soldiers were coming. Then everybody started back home, and there the people were saying: "We will leave this and let it go!"

Then we all broke camp and started for the Big Horn Mountains.

If those soldiers had not come, we would have rubbed them all out on the hill.

Iron Hawk Speaks:

I am a Hunkpapa, and, as I told you before, I was fourteen years old. The sun was overhead and more, but I was eating my first meal that day, because I had been sleeping. While I was eating I heard the crier saying: "The chargers are coming." I jumped up and rushed out to our horses. They were grazing close to camp. I roped one, and the others stampeded, but my older brother had caught his horse already and headed the others off. When I got on my horse with the rope hitched around his nose, the soldiers were shooting up there and people were running and men and boys were catching their horses that were scared because of the shooting and yelling. I saw little children running up from the river where they had been swimming; and all the women and children were running down the valley.

Our horses stampeded down toward the Minneconjous, but we rounded them up again and brought them back. By now warriors were running toward the soldiers, and getting on the ponies, and many of the Hunkpapas were gathering in the brush and timber near the place where the soldiers had stopped and got off their horses. I rode past a very old man who was shouting: "Boys, take courage! Would you see these little children taken away from me like dogs?"

I went into our tepee and got dressed for war as fast as I could; but I could hear bullets whizzing outside, and I was so shaky that it took me a long time to braid an eagle feather into my hair. Also, I had to hold my pony's rope all the time, and he kept jerking me and trying to get away. While I was doing this, crowds of warriors on horses were roaring by up stream, yelling: "Hoka hey!" Then I rubbed red paint all over my face and took my bow and arrows and got on my horse. I did not have a gun, only a bow and arrows.

When I was on my horse, the fight up stream seemed to be over, because everybody was starting back downstream and yelling: "It's a good day to die!" Soldiers were coming at the other end of the village, and nobody knew how many there were down there.

A man by the name of Little Bear rode up to me on a pinto horse, and he had a very pretty saddle blanket. He said: "Take courage, boy! The earth is all that lasts!" So I rode fast with him and the others downstream, and many of us Hunkpapas gathered on the east side of the river at the foot of a gulch that led back up the hill where the second soldier band was. There was a very brave Shyela with us, and I heard someone say: "He is going!" I looked, and it was this Shyela. He had on a spotted war bonnet and a spotted robe made of some animal's skin and this was fastened with a spotted belt. He was going up the hill alone and we all followed part way. There were soldiers along the ridge up there and they were on foot holding their horses. The Shyela rode right close to them in a circle several times and all the soldiers shot at him. Then he rode back to where we had stopped at the head of the gulch. He was saying: "Ah, ah!" Someone said: "Shyela friend, what is the matter?" He began undoing his spotted belt, and when he shook it, bullets dropped out. He was very sacred and the soldiers could not hurt him. He was a fine looking man.

We stayed there awhile waiting for something and there was shooting everywhere. Then I heard a voice crying: "Now they are going, they are going!" We looked up and saw the cavalry horses stampeding. These were all gray horses.

I saw Little Bear's horse rear and race up hill toward the soldiers. When he got close, his horse was shot out from under him, and he got up limping because the bullet went through his leg; and he started hobbling back to us with the soldiers shooting at him. His brother-friend, Elk Nation, went up there on his horse and took Little Bear behind him and rode back safe with bullets striking all around him. It was his duty to go to his brother-friend even if he knew he would be killed.

By now a big cry was going up all around the soldiers up there and the warriors were coming from everywhere and it was getting dark with dust and smoke.

We saw soldiers start running down hill right towards us. Nearly all of them were afoot, and I think they were so scared that they didn't know what they were doing. They were making their arms go as though they were running very fast but they were only walking. Some of them shot their guns in the air. We all yelled "Hoka hey!" and charged toward them, riding all around them in the twilight that had fallen on us.

I met a soldier on horseback, and I let him have it. The arrow went through from side to side under his ribs and it stuck out on both sides. He screamed and took hold of his saddle horn and hung on, wobbling, with his head hanging down. I kept along beside him, and I took my heavy bow and struck him across the back of the neck. He fell from his saddle, and I got off and beat him to death with my bow. I kept on beating him awhile after he was dead, and every time I hit him I said "Hownh!" I was mad, because I was thinking of the women and little children running down there, all scared and out of breath. These Wasichus wanted it, and they came to get it, and we gave it to them. I did not see much more. I saw Brings Plenty kill a soldier with a war club. I saw Red Horn Buffalo fall. There was a Lakota riding along the edge of the gulch, and he was yelling to look out, that there was a soldier hiding in there. I saw him charge in and kill the soldier and begin slashing him with a knife.

Then we began to go towards the river, and the dust was lifting so that we could see the women and children coming over to us from across the river. The soldiers were all rubbed out there and scattered around.

The women swarmed up the hill and began stripping the soldiers. They were yelling and laughing and singing now. I saw something funny. Two fat old women were stripping a soldier, who was wounded and playing dead. When they had him naked, they began to cut something off that he had, and he jumped up and began fighting with the two fat women. He was swinging one of them around, while the other was trying to stab him with her knife. After awhile, another woman rushed up and shoved her knife into him and he died really dead. It was funny to see the naked Wasichu fighting with the fat women.

By now we saw that our warriors were all charging on some soldiers that had come from the hill up river to help the second band that we had rubbed out. They ran back and we followed, chasing them up on their hill again where they had their pack mules. We could not hurt them much there, because they had been digging to hide themselves and they were lying behind saddles and other things. I was down by the river and I saw some soldiers come down there with buckets. They had no guns, just

buckets. Some boys were down there, and they came out of the brush and
threw mud and rocks in the soldiers' faces and chased them into the river.
I guess they got enough to drink, for they are drinking yet. We killed
them in the water.

Afterwhile it was nearly sundown, and I went home with many others
to eat, while some others stayed to watch the soldiers on the hill. I hadn't
eaten all day, because the trouble started just when I was beginning to eat
my first meal.

Black Elk Continues:

After I showed my mother my first scalp, I stayed with the women
awhile and they were all singing and making the tremolo. We could not
see much of the battle for the big dust, but we knew there would be no
soldiers left. There were many other boys about my age and younger up
there with their mothers and sisters, and they asked me to go over to the
battle with them. So we got on our ponies and started. While we were
riding down hill toward the river we saw gray horses with empty saddles
stampeding toward the water. We rode over across the Greasy Grass to the
mouth of a gulch that led up through the bluff to where the fighting was.

Before we got there, the Wasichus were all down, and most of them
were dead, but some of them were still alive and kicking. Many other
little boys had come up by this time, and we rode around shooting arrows
into the Wasichus. There was one who was squirming around with arrows
sticking in him, and I started to take his coat, but a man pushed me away
and took the coat for himself. Then I saw something bright hanging on this
soldier's belt, and I pulled it out. It was round and bright and yellow and
very beautiful and I put it on me for a necklace. At first it ticked inside,
and then it did not any more. I wore it around my neck a long time before
I found out what it was and how to make it tick again.

Then the women all came over and we went to the top of the hill. Gray
horses were lying dead there, and some of them were on top of dead
Wasichus and dead Wasichus were on top of them. There were not many
of our own dead there, because they had been picked up already; but
many of our men were killed and wounded. They shot each other in the
dust. I did not see Pahuska, and I think nobody knew which one he was.
There was a soldier who was raising his arms and groaning. I shot an arrow
into his forehead, and his arms and legs quivered. I saw some Lakotas
holding another Lakota up. I went over there, and it was Chase-in-the-
Morning's brother, who was called Black Wasichu. He had been shot
through the right shoulder downward, and the bullet stopped in his left
hip, because he was hanging on the side of his horse when he was hit.
They were trying to give him some medicine. He was my cousin, and his

father and my father were so angry over this, that they went and butchered a Wasichu and cut him open. The Wasichu was fat, and his meat looked good to eat, but we did not eat any.

There was a little boy, younger than I was, who asked me to scalp a soldier for him. I did, and he ran to show the scalp to his mother. While we were there, most of the warriors chased the other soldiers back to the hill where they had their pack mules. After awhile I got tired looking around. I could smell nothing but blood, and I got sick of it. So I went back home with some others. I was not sorry at all. I was a happy boy. Those Wasichus had come to kill our mothers and fathers and us, and it was our country. When I was in the brush up there by the Hunkpapas, and the first soldiers were shooting. I knew this would happen. I thought that my people were relatives to the thunder beings of my vision, and that the soldiers were very foolish to do this.

Everybody was up all night in the village. Next morning another war party went up to the hill where the other soldiers were, and the men who had been watching there all night came home. My mother and I went along. She rode a mare with a little colt tied beside her and it trotted along with its mother.

We could see the horses and pack mules up there, but the soldiers were dug in. Beneath the hill, right on the west side of the Greasy Grass, were some bullberry bushes, and there was a big boy by the name of Round Fool who was running around the bushes. We boys asked him what he was doing that for, and he said: "There is a Wasichu in that bush." And there was. He had hidden there when the other soldiers ran to the hill-top and he had been there all night. We boys began shooting at him with arrows, and it was like chasing a rabbit. He would crawl from one side to the other while we were running around the bush shooting at him with our bows. Once he yelled "Ow." After awhile we set fire to the grass around the bushes, and he came out running. Some of our warriors killed him.

Once we went up the back of the hill, where some of our men were, and looked over. We could not see the Wasichus, who were lying in their dug-ins, but we saw the horses and pack mules, and many of them were dead. When we came down and crossed the river again, some soldiers shot at us and hit the water. Mother and I galloped back to the camp, and it was about sundown. By then our scouts had reported that more soldiers were coming up stream; so we all broke camp. Before dark we were ready and we started up the Greasy Grass, heading for Wood Louse Creek in the Big Horn Mountains. We fled all night, following the Greasy Grass. My two younger brothers and I rode in a pony-drag, and my mother put some young pups in with us. They were always trying to crawl out and I was always putting them back in, so I didn't sleep much.

By morning we reached a little dry creek and made camp and had a big feast. The meat had spots of fat in it, and I wish I had some of it right now.

When it was full day, we started again and came to Wood Louse Creek at the foot of the mountains, and camped there. A badly wounded man by the name of Three Bears had fits there, and he would keep saying: "Jeneny, jeneny." I do not know what he meant. He died, and we used to call that place the camp where Jeneny died.

That evening everybody got excited and began shouting: "The soldiers are coming!" I looked, and there they were, riding abreast right toward us. But it was some of our own men dressed in the soldiers' clothes. They were doing this for fun.

The scouts reported that the soldiers had not followed us and that everything was safe now. All over the camp there were big fires and kill dances all night long.

I will sing you some of the kill-songs that our people made up and sang that night. Some of them went like this:

> "Long Hair has never returned,
> So his woman is crying, crying.
> Looking over here, she cries."

> "Long Hair, guns I had none.
> You brought me many. I thank you!
> You make me laugh!"

> "Long Hair, horses I had none.
> You brought me many. I thank you!
> You make me laugh!"

> "Long Hair, where he lies nobody knows.
> Crying, they seek him.
> He lies over here."

> "Let go your holy irons (guns).
> You are not men enough to do any harm.
> Let go your holy irons!"

After awhile I got so tired dancing that I went to sleep on the ground right where I was.

My cousin, Black Wasichu, died that night.

LAME DEER, SEEKER OF VISIONS

by John Lame Deer and Richard Erdoes

Lame Deer, a Miniconjou Sioux, was born in 1903. His memoirs, recorded by Richard Erdoes, tell the story of one of the most colorful Americans of this century. In many ways he was a living incarnation of the trickster: like Iktome, Wakdjunkaga, and Saynday, he was a footloose prankster, a man of unbounded appetites for food and sex, and a complex figure who was simultaneously a benefactor and menace—a benefactor to the hundreds of sufferers he cured and a menace to the scores of men he cuckolded. To whites he may appear to be a hypocrite—a holy man who philandered and stole cars, a man who suffered and fasted for four days on a vision quest but was often drunk for a week or more. Lame Deer believed that a holy man must know both good and evil intimately and at first hand because God and nature have an evil as well as a good side. Therefore, he made his life a "find-out," denying himself nothing that tempted him.

Lame Deer moved easily back and forth between the white world and the red, living as a rancher, rodeo rider, doughboy, reservation policeman, and Yuwipi holy man. His hell-raising and lack of formal education should not obscure the fact that he is the author of a very profound and moving book. Having lived among both whites and Indians, he is able to evaluate both cultures. When he views life in our suburbs, he makes a powerful case that today's middle-class child is culturally deprived—shut off from nature, living in a sterile environment as a passive spectator to a moribund civilization. He makes life on the prairies, or even in the rundown shacks in Indian ghettos, sound preferable to the cellophaned existence of the pampered WASP child. He contrasts the rich religious heritage of the Sioux with the tepid existential angst of the modern American and the travesty Americans have made out of Christianity, their official religion. "You've made a blondie out of Jesus," he says, "a sanitized, Cloroxed, Ajaxed Christ." In contrast to this anemic religion, he describes in detail the intense experience of the Sioux ceremonies—the vision quest, the sun dance, and the healing rituals.

That Gun in the New York Museum Belongs to Me

In the Museum of the American Indian in New York are two glass cases. A sign over them reads: "Famous Guns of Famous Indian Chiefs." They have five or six guns there, Sitting Bull's among them. A note next to one of these old breech loaders says that it belonged to the famous Chief Lame Deer, killed in a battle with General Miles, who generously donated this gun to the New York museum. I don't know what right old Bear Coat Miles had to be that free with other people's property. That gun didn't belong to him. It belongs to me. I am the only Lame Deer left.

I am a medicine man and I want to talk about visions, spirits and sacred things. But you must know something about the man Lame Deer before you can understand the medicine man Lame Deer. So I will start with the man, the boy, and we'll get to the medicine part later.

Tahca Ushte—the first Lame Deer—was my great-grandfather on my father's side. He was killed by mistake. You could say he was murdered. A year before this so-called battle with General Miles, Lame Deer had made his final peace with the white man. He had made an agreement with the U.S. Government. By this treaty they measured off four square miles west of what is now Rapid City, South Dakota. This was to be a reservation for the chief and his people, and it was to be called Lame Deer after him. This land was to be ours forever—"as long as the sun shines and the grass grows." These days smog is hiding the sun and there's little grass left in Rapid City now. Maybe the white people had a gift of foreseeing this when they took our land before the ink on that treaty was dry.

Lame Deer said that he would sign this treaty if he and his people could go out on one last hunt and live for just one more summer in the good old way—going after the buffalo. After that they would all settle down on their new reservation and "walk the white man's road." The Government people said that this was all right and gave him permission for his last hunt. They shook hands on it.

The U.S. Government is a strange monster with many heads. One head doesn't know what the others are up to. The Army had given Lame Deer its word that he could hunt in peace. At the same time it told Bear Coat Miles that any Indians found hunting off the reservations were to be attacked as "hostiles." Lame Deer had gone north in the spring of 1877 to his favorite buffalo range between the Rosebud and Bighorn rivers. He had camped in the Wolf Mountains along Fat Horse Creek.

The old people have told me that the prairie had never been more beautiful than it was that spring. The grass was high and green. The slopes were covered with flowers, and the air was full of good smells and the song of birds. If the Indians had only one more hunt left, this was how they wished it to be. Lame Deer knew that there were soldiers around, but this did not worry him. He had a right to be where he was. Besides, any fool could see that he was not about to make war on anybody. He had all the women and children with him. His fifty lodges were full of meat and hides. His people had come as to a feast. They were dressed in their finery and beaded goods. They were enjoying their last vacation from the white man.

General Miles was stupid not to grasp this, but I think that he acted in good faith. Nobody had told him about the treaty. He had six companies of walking soldiers and several troops of cavalry, more men than all the Indians together, including the women and children. The blue coats came tearing into the camp, shooting and yelling, stampeding the horses and riding down the people. At the same time one of them carried a white flag of truce.

Seeing the peaceful camp from up close, Bear Coat Miles, I believe, changed his mind and regretted what was happening. He began waving his arms, trying to stop the killing, shouting over and over again, "*Kola, kola*—friend, friend." His Indian scouts took up the cry. They too started shouting, "We are friends!" It sure was a strange way for friends to drop in, but my great-grandfather pretended to believe them. He didn't want his people to be killed. He dropped his gun as a sign of peace.

General Miles rushed up to him, grabbed his hand and started shaking it. He kept shouting, "*Kola, kola.*" But peace was not what his soldiers wanted. They wanted Indian scalps and souvenirs. Probably they also wanted to get at the women and girls. One trooper came riding up and fired his carbine at Lame Deer. Miles hung onto my great-grandfather's arm with both hands, but the chief tore himself loose and picked up his gun, shooting the man who had fired on him. Then all the soldiers opened up with everything they had, killing Lame Deer, his second chief, Iron Star, and about a dozen more of the warriors. Then they plundered the tipis, taking what they wanted and destroying the rest. Even General Miles was not too proud to take a few things for himself, and that is why my ancestor's gun is in a New York museum instead of hanging on my wall.

About those four square miles along the Rapid River: When the treaty was signed Lame Deer said, "If I ever die, or the school closes, this land shall go to my first son and, if he dies, to his son, and so on down the line." I tried to sue the Government for this land, and they said, "No personal Indian claims allowed." Maybe it was a good thing that they would not let us Indians keep that land. Think of what would have been missed: the motels with their neon signs, the pawn shops, the Rock Hunter's Paradise, the Horned Trophies Taxidermist Studio, the giftie shoppies, the Genuine Indian Crafts Center with its beadwork from Taiwan and Hong Kong, the Sitting Bull Cave—electrically lighted for your convenience—the Shrine of Democracy Souvenir Shop, the Fun House—the talk of your trip for years to come—the Bucket of Blood Saloon, the life-size dinosaur made of green concrete, the go-go gals and cat houses, the Reptile Gardens, where they don't feed the snakes because that would be too much trouble. When they die you get yourself some new rattlers for free. Just think: If that land belonged to us there would be nothing here, only trees, grass and some animals running free. All that *real estate* would be going to waste!

My great-grandfather Lame Deer was a chief of the Mni Owoju—the Planters by the Water—one of the seven western tribes of the Sioux nation. He had three wives. His first wife had three sons: Did Not Butcher, Flying By and my own grandfather, Cante Witko, which means Crazy Heart. The second wife had one daughter. The third wife had no children. My other grandfather was named Good Fox.

Both Crazy Heart and Good Fox were famous warriors and had been in the Custer fight. Good Fox was also a survivor of the Wounded Knee massacre. Crazy Heart was a shirt-wearer, which was a great honor. He wore a yellow-and-blue shirt fringed with locks of human hair. He was listened to in our councils and the people sought his advice on all matters of importance. Good Fox, too, was respected for his wisdom. Right up to the time of his death in 1928 he was always given the job of supervising our ceremonies and smoothening up the sacred dancing ground.

I never knew Crazy Heart, but my grandpa Good Fox played a big part in my life, and I looked up to him. He had a great reputation as a warrior, but he was not a killing man. Most of his war honors came from "counting coup," riding up to the enemy, zig-zagging among them, touching them with his crooked coup stick wrapped in otter fur. He was a coup-man. That was his way of showing his bravery. Compared to my grandfathers, we reservation people of today are just plain chicken. They say, "Custer died for your sins." I say Custer is alive. We still have too many Custers and Mileses among the white people, but where is our Crazy Horse? One medicine man around here told me he had a vision that Crazy Horse would come back as a black man. That would be something.

I often asked my grandpa Good Fox to tell me about the Custer battle. "I'm not a good witness," he said, "because I was too busy fighting to pay much attention to what was going on. I raced my horse right into the middle of a big cloud of dust where the hottest action was, shouting, "It's a good day to die and a good day to fight,' but this was a day for the blue coats to die, though one of them hit me in the arm with a bullet from his carbine. It didn't even go all the way through my arm. I was told that after the battle two Cheyenne women came across Custer's body. They knew him, because he had attacked their peaceful village on the Washita. These women said, 'You smoked the peace pipe with us. Our chiefs told you that you would be killed if you ever made war on us again. But you would not listen. This will make you hear better.' The women each took an awl from their beaded cases and stuck them deep into Custer's ears. Somebody who saw this told me about it. Grandson, I tell you, hundreds of books have been written about this battle by people who weren't there. I was there, but all I remember is one big cloud of dust."

About the Wounded Knee massacre grandfather Good Fox told me, "There may be some good men among the whites, but to trust them is a quick way to get oneself killed. Every time I hear a lady or child screaming I think of that terrible day of killing. The preachers and missionaries tell you to turn the other cheek and to love your neighbor like yourself. Grandson, I don't know how the white people treat each other, but I don't think they love us more than they love themselves. Some don't love themselves. Some don't love us at all." My grandpa died in 1928. He was almost blind at the end.

My father came from Standing Rock. His name was Wawi-Yohi-Ya, which means Let-Them-Have-Enough. Silas was his first name, which the missionaries gave him. He was a very generous man. He always invited people to a feast or to a give-away ceremony. At such a time he always used to worry about everybody having enough to eat and enough presents. That's why he was known as Let-Them-Have-Enough among the Indian people.

Among the whites he was known as Silas Fire. They had a census and everybody had to go to Rosebud to be put in a big book. The superintendent told my father, "Sign here." My dad couldn't write his name. He told that white man what his name was in Indian. The superintendent said it was too long and complicated. Dad told him, "O.K., give me a short name." A lot of people had come for their rations and put up tents. Just at that moment one of them caught fire. It caused a big uproar. People were running about calling, "Fire, fire!" The superintendent heard it and said, "That's it. You are Silas Fire, short and sweet."

If that tent hadn't caught fire my name would have been Let-Them-Have-Enough. Now it's John Fire on some white man's documents, but my Indian name is Lame Deer, after my great-grandfather, and that's as it should be. My father was loved by everybody. He was a kind, smiling man. He had great patience and it was very hard to get him angry. He was the silent type, kept his mouth shut and did very little talking. Some men have their mouths open all the time, but they own only one horse or no horse at all. My dad had over two hundred. He used to tease me, pat me on the head, showing that he loved me in a hundred ways, but for weeks he did not say one goddam word to me.

My dad never went to school, couldn't read or write, but one could learn a lot from him just by watching. Dad taught me how to rope a horse or how to gentle it down for riding. First I'd watch him do it, then he made a motion with his hand. That meant: "Now you try it!" I caught on easy and I was faster than he was. Once I was thrown from a horse. I came down real hard. My father told me, "Don't kill yourself, son." It was one of the few things he ever said to me. That's why I remember it.

My mother's name was Sally Red Blanket. She was good to look at, a beautiful woman with long, curly hair. She was very skilled with her hands, doing fine beadwork. She used the tiniest beads, the ones you can't get anymore. Much later, when I was half grown, I noticed that whenever a trader looked at her work with a magnifying glass or fingered it too long, the price went up. My mother died when I was seventeen years old.

I was born a full-blood Indian in a twelve-by-twelve log cabin between Pine Ridge and Rosebud. *Maka tanhan wicasa wan*—I am a man of the earth, as we say. Our people don't call themselves Sioux or Dakota. That's white man talk. We call ourselves Ikce Wicasa—the nature humans, the free, wild, common people. I am pleased to be called that.

As with most Indian children, much of my upbringing was done by my grandparents—Good Fox and his wife, Pte-Sa-Ota-Win, Plenty White Buffalo. Among our people the relationship to one's grandparents is as strong as to one's own father and mother. We lived in that little hut way out on the prairie, in the back country, and for the first few years of my life I had no contact with the outside world. Of course we had a few white man's things—coffee, iron pots, a shotgun, an old buckboard. But I never thought much of where these things came from or who had made them.

When I was about five years old my grandma took me to visit some neighbors. As always, my little black pup came along. We were walking on the dirt road when I saw a rider come up. He looked so strange to me that I hid myself behind Grandma and my pup hid behind me. I already knew enough about riding to see that he didn't know how to handle a horse. His feet were hanging down to the ground. He had some tiny, windmill-like things coming out of his heels, making a tinkling sound. As he came closer I started to size him up. I had never seen so much hair on a man. It covered all of his face and grew way down to his chest, maybe lower, but he didn't have hair where it counted, on top of his head. The hair was of a light-brown color and it made him look like a a mattress come to life. He had eyes like a dead owl, of a washed-out blue-green hue. He was chewing on something that looked like a smoking Baby Ruth candy bar. Later I found out that this was a cigar. This man sure went in for double enjoyment, because he was also chomping on a wad of chewing tobacco, and now and then he took the smoking candy bar from his mouth to spit out a long stream of brown juice. I wondered why he kept eating something which tasted so bad that he couldn't keep it down.

This strange human being also wore a funny headgear—a cross between a skillet and a stovepipe. He had a big chunk of leather piled on top of his poor horse, hanging down also on both sides. In front of his crotch the leather was shaped like a horn. I thought maybe he kept his man-thing inside to protect it. This was the first saddle I had seen. His pitiful horse also had strings of leather on his head and a piece of iron in its mouth. Every time the horse stuck out its tongue I could hear some kind of roller or gear grinding inside it. This funny human being wore leather pants and had two strange-looking hammers tied to his hips. I later found out these were .45 Colts.

The man started to make weird sounds. He was talking, but we couldn't understand him because it was English. He pointed at my grandmother's pretty beaded moccasins and he took some square green frog hides from his pocket and wanted to trade. I guess those were dollar bills. But Grandma refused to swap, because she had four big gold coins in her moccasins. That man must have smelled them. This was the first white man I met.

When I got home I had a new surprise waiting for me. My grandpa was butchering something that I had never seen before, an animal with hoofs like a horse and the body of a dog. Maybe somebody had mated a dog with a horse and this funny creature was the result. Looking at its pink, hairless body, I was reminded of scary old tales about humans coupling with animals and begetting terrifying monsters. Grandpa was chopping away, taking the white meat and throwing the insides out. My little puppy was sure enjoying this, his first pig. So was I, but the pig smelled terrible. My grandpa said to save the fat for axle grease.

Most of my childhood days weren't very exciting, and that was all right with me. We had a good, simple life. One day passed like another. Only in one way was I different from other Indian kids. I was never hungry, because my dad had so many horses and cattle. Grandma always got up early in the morning before everybody else, taking down the big tin container with the Government-issue coffee. First I would hear her roasting the beans in a frying pan, then I would hear her grind them. She always made a huge pot holding two gallons of water, put in two big handfuls of coffee and boiled it. She would add some sweetener—molasses or maple syrup; we didn't like sugar. We used no milk or cream in our *pejuta sapa*—our black medicine.

Before anything else Grandma poured out a big soup spoon of coffee as an offering to the spirits, and then she kept the pot going all day. If she saw people anywhere near the house she called out to them, regardless of who they were, "Come in, have some coffee!" When the black medicine gave out, she added water and a lot more coffee and boiled the whole again. That stuff got stronger and stronger, thicker and thicker. In the end you could almost stick the spoon in there and it would keep standing upright. "Now the coffee is real good," Grandma would say.

To go with the coffee Grandma got her baking powder each morning and made soda bread and squaw bread. That squaw bread filled the stomach. It seemed to grow bigger and bigger inside. Every spring, as the weather got warmer, the men would fix up Grandma's "squaw-cooler." This was a brush shelter made of four upright tree trunks with horizontal lodge poles tied to the top. The whole was then covered with branches from pine trees. They rigged up an old wood burner for Grandma to cook on, a rough table and some logs to sit on. In the summer, much of our life was spent in the squaw-cooler, where you could always feel a breeze. These squaw-coolers are still very popular on the reservation.

Grandma liked to smoke a little pipe. She loved her *kinnick-innick*— the red willow-bark tobacco. One time she accidentally dropped some glowing embers into an old visitor's lap. This guy still wore a breech cloth. Suddenly we smelled something burning. That breech cloth had caught fire and we had to yank it off and beat the flames out. He almost got his child-maker burned up. He was so old it wouldn't have made a lot of difference, but he still could jump.

One of my uncles used to keep a moon-counting stick, our own kind of calendar and a good one. He had a special staff and every night he cut a notch in it until the moon "died"—that is, disappeared. On the other side of this staff he made a notch for every month. He started a new stick every year in the spring. That way we always knew when it was the right day for one of our ceremonies.

Every so often my grandparents would take me to a little celebration down the creek. Grandpa always rode his old red horse, which was well known in all the tribes. We always brought plenty of food for everybody, squaw bread, beef, the kind of dried meat we called *papa*, and *wasna*, or pemmican, which was meat pounded together with berries and kidney fat. We also brought a kettle of coffee, wild mint tea, soup or stuff like that. Grandfather was always the leader of the *owanka osnato*—the rehearsal ground. He prepared the place carefully. Only the real warriors were allowed to dance there—men like Red Fish or Thin Elk, who had fought in the Custer battle. With the years the dancers grew older and older and fewer and fewer. Grandfather danced too. Everybody could see the scars all over his arm where he had been wounded by the white soldiers.

Some women had scars, too. Grandpa's brother, White Crane Walking, had three wives. They were not jealous of one another. They were like sisters. They loved one another and they loved their husband. This old man was really taking it easy; the women did all the work. He just lay around the whole day long, doing nothing. Once in a while some men called him lazy, but he just laughed and told them, "Why don't you get a second wife?" He knew their wives were jealous and didn't want them to get a second one. When this old man finally passed away, the two wives who survived him buried him in the side of a hill. They took their skinning knives and made many deep gashes in their arms and legs to show their grief. They might have cut off their little fingers too, but somebody told them that this was no longer allowed, that the Government would punish them for this. So they cut off their hair instead. They keened and cried for four days and nights; they loved their husband that much.

I was the *takoja*—the pampered grandson—and like all Indian children I was spoiled. I was never scolded, never heard a harsh word. "*Ajustan*—leave it alone"—that was the worst. I was never beaten; we don't treat children that way. Indian kids are so used to being handled gentle, to get away with things, that they often don't pay much attention to what the grownups tell them. I'm a grandfather now myself and sometimes I feel like yelling at one of those brash kids, "Hey, you little son of a bitch, listen to me!" That would make him listen all right, but I can't do it.

When I didn't want to go to sleep my grandma would try to scare me with the *ciciye*—a kind of bogeyman. "*Takoja, istima ye*—Go to sleep, sonny," she would say, "or the *ciciye* will come after you." Nobody knew what the *ciciye* was like, but he must have been something terrible. When the *ciciye* wouldn't work anymore, I was threatened with the *siyoko*—another kind of monster. Nobody knew what the *siyoko* was like, either, but he was ten times more terrible than the *ciciye*. Grandma did not have much luck. Neither the *ciciye* nor the *siyoko* scared me for long. But when I was real bad, Grandma would say, "*Wasicun anigni kte*"—the white man will come and take you to his home," and that scared me all right. *Wasicun* were for real.

It was said that I didn't take after my grandpa Good Fox, whom I loved, but after my other grandfather, Crazy Heart, whom I never knew. They said I picked up where he left off, because I was so daring and full of the devil. I was told that Crazy Heart had been like that. He did not care what happened to other people, or to himself, once he was on his way. He

was hot-tempered, always feuding and on the warpath. At the same time
he saved lots of people, gave wise counsel, urged the people to do right.
He was a good speech-maker. Everybody who listened to him said that he
was a very encouraging man. He always advised patience, except when it
came to himself. Then his temper got in the way.

I was like that. Things I was told not to do—I did them. I liked to play
rough. We played shinny ball, a kind of hockey game. We made the ball
and sticks ourselves. We played the hoop game, shot with a bow and arrow. We had foot races, horse races and water races. We liked to play
mato kiciyapi, the bear game, throwing sharp, stiff grass stems at each
other. These could really hurt you and draw blood if they hit the bare
skin. And we were always at the *isto kicicastakapi*, the pit-slinging game.
You chewed the fruit from the rosebush or wild cherries, spit a fistful of
pits into your hand and flung them into the other fellow's face. And of
course I liked the Grab-Them-by-the-Hair-and-Kick-Them game, which
we played with two teams.

I liked to ride horseback behind my older sister, holding onto her. As I
got a little bigger she would hold onto me. By the time I was nine years
old I had my own horse to ride. It was a beautiful gray pony my father had
given me together with a fine saddle and a very colorful Mexican saddle
blanket. That gray was my favorite companion and I was proud to ride
him. But he was not mine for long. I lost him through my own fault.

Nonge Pahloka—the Piercing of Her Ears—is a big event in a little
girl's life. By this ceremony her parents, and especially her grandmother,
want to show how much they love and honor her. They ask a man who is
respected for his bravery or wisdom to pierce the ears of their daughter.
The grandmother puts on a big feed. The little girl is placed on a blanket
surrounded by the many gifts her family will give away in her name. The
man who does the piercing is much admired and gets the most valuable
gift. Afterward they get down to the really important part—the eating.

Well, one day I watched somebody pierce a girl's ears. I saw the fuss
they made over it, the presents he got and all that. I thought I should do
this to my little sister. She was about four years old at the time and I was
nine. I don't know anymore what made me want to do this. Maybe I
wanted to feel big and important like the man whom I had watched per-
form the ceremony. Maybe I wanted to get a big present. Maybe I wanted
to make my sister cry. I don't remember what was in my little boy's mind
then. I found some wire and made a pair of "ear rings" out of it. Then I
asked my sister, "Would you like me to put these on you?" She smiled.
"*Ohan—.*" I didn't have the sharp bone one uses for the ear-piercing, and
I didn't know the prayer that goes with it. I just had an old awl but

thought this would do fine. Oh, how my sister yelled. I had to hold her down, but I got that awl through her earlobes and managed to put the "ear rings" in. I was proud of the neat job I had done.

When my mother came home and saw those wire loops in my sister's ears she gasped. But she recovered soon enough to go and tell my father. That was one of the few occasions he talked to me. He said, "I should punish you and whip you, but I won't. That's not my way. You'll get your punishment later." Well, some time passed and I forgot all about it. One morning my father announced that we were going to a powwow. He had hitched up the wagon and it was heaped high with boxes and bundles. At that powwow my father let it be known that he was doing a big *otuhan*—a give-away. He put my sister on a rug, a pretty Navajo blanket, and laid out things to give away—quilts, food, blankets, a fine shotgun, his own new pair of cowboy boots, a sheepskin coat, enough to fit out a whole family. Dad was telling the people, "I want to honor my daughter for her ear-piercing. This should have been done openly, but my son did it at home. I guess he's too small. He didn't know any better." This was a long speech for Dad. He motioned me to come closer. I was sitting on my pretty gray horse. I thought we were both cutting a very fine figure. Well, before I knew it, Dad had given my horse away, together with its beautiful saddle and blanket. I had to ride home in the wagon and I cried all the way. The old man said, "You have your punishment now, but you will feel better later on. All her life your sister will tell about how you pierced her ears. She'll brag about you. I bet you are the only small boy who ever did this big ceremony."

That was no consolation to me. My beautiful gray was gone. I was heart-broken for three days. On the fourth morning I looked out the door and there stood a little white stallion with a new saddle and a silver-plated bit. "It's yours," my father told me. "Get on it." I was happy again.

After I was six years old it was very hard to make me behave. The only way one could get me to sit still was to tell me a story. I loved to listen to my grandparents' old tales, and they were good at relating the ancient legends of my people. They told me of the great gods Wi and Hanwi, the sun and the moon, who were married to each other. They told me about the old man god Waziya, whom the priests have made into Santa Claus. Waziya had a wife who was a big witch. These two had a daughter called Ite—the face—the most beautiful woman in the universe. Ite was married to Tate, the wind.

The trouble with this pairing was that Ite got it into her mind that the sun, Wi, was more handsome than her own husband, the wind. Wi, on his part, thought that Ite was much more beautiful than his own wife, the moon. Wi was having a love affair with Ite, and whenever the moon saw them misbehaving she hid her face in shame. "That's why on some nights we don't see the moon," Grandma told me.

The Great Spirit did not like these goings-on, and he punished Ite. She still remained the most beautiful creature in the world, but only if one looked at her from one side. The other half of her face had become so hideous and ugly that there were no words to describe it. From that time on she was known as Anunk-Ite, or Double-Face. When it comes to love the women always have the worst of it.

Many of these legends were about animals. Grandma told me about the bat who hid himself on top of the eagle's back, screaming, "I can fly higher than any other bird." That was true enough; even the eagle couldn't fly higher than somebody who was sitting on top of him. As a punishment the other birds grounded the bat and put him in a mouse hole. There he fell in love with a lady mouse. That's why bats now are half mouse and half bird.

Grandpa Good Fox told me about the young hunters who killed a buffalo with a big rattle for a tail. After eating of its meat these young men were changed into giant rattlesnakes with human heads and human voices. They lived in a cave beneath the earth and ruled the underworld.

The stories I liked best had to do with Iktome, the evil spiderman, a smart-ass who played tricks on everybody. One day this spider was walking by a lake where he saw many ducks swimming around. This sight gave him a sudden appetite for roast duck. He stuffed his rawhide bag full of grass and then he showed himself. When the ducks saw him they started to holler, "Where are you going, Iktome?"

"I am going to a big powwow."

"What have you got in your bag, Iktome?"

"It's full of songs which I am taking to the powwow, good songs to dance to."

"How about singing some songs for us?" begged the ducks.

The tricky spider made a big show of not wanting to do it. He told the ducks he had no time for them, but in the end he pretended to give in, because they were such nice birds. "I'll sing for you," he told the ducks, "but you must help me."

"We'll do what you want. Tell us the rules."

"Well, you must form three rows. In the front row, all you fat ones, get in there. In the second row go all those who are neither fat nor thin—the in-betweens. The poor scrawny ones go in the third row, way down there. And you have to act out the song, do what the words tell you. Now the words to my first song are 'Close your eyes and dance!'"

The ducks all lined up with their eyes shut, flapping their wings, the fat ones up front. Iktome took a big club from underneath his coat. "Sing along as loud as you can," he ordered, "and keep your eyes shut. Whoever peeks will get blind." He told them to sing so that their voices would drown out the "thump, thump" of his club when he hit them over the head. He knocked them down one by one and was already half done when one of those low-down, skinny ducks in the back row opened its eyes and saw what Iktome was up to.

"Hey, wake up!" it hollered. "That Iktome is killing us all!"

The ducks that were left opened their eyes and took off. Iktome didn't mind. He already had more fat ducks than he could eat.

Iktome is like some of those bull-shitting politicians who make us close our eyes and sing and dance for them while they knock us on the head. Democratic ducks, Republican ducks, it makes no different. The fat, stupid ones are the first in the pot. It's always the skinny, no-account, low-class duck in the back that doesn't hold still. That's a good Indian who keeps his eyes open. Iktome is an evil schemer, Grandpa told me, but luckily he's so greedy that most of the time he outsmarts himself.

It's hard to make our grandchildren listen to these stories nowadays. Some don't understand our language anymore. At the same time there is the TV going full blast—and the radio and the phonograph. These are the things our children listen to. They don't care to hear an old-fashioned Indian story.

I was happy living with my grandparents in a world of our own, but it was a happiness that could not last. "Shh, *wasicun anigni kte*—be quiet or the white man will take you away." How often had I heard these words when I had been up to some mischief, but I never thought that this threat could become true, just as I never believed that the monsters *ciciye* and *siyoko* would come and get me.

But one day the monster came—a white man from the Bureau of Indian Affairs. I guess he had my name on a list. He told my family, "This kid has to go to school. If your kids don't come by themselves the Indian police will pick them up and give them a rough ride." I hid behind Grandma. My father was like a big god to me and Grandpa had been a warrior at the Custer fight, but they could not protect me now.

In those days the Indian schools were like jails and run along military lines, with roll calls four times a day. We had to stand at attention, or march in step. The B.I.A. thought that the best way to teach us was to stop us from being Indians. We were forbidden to talk our language or to sing our songs. If we disobeyed we had to stand in the corner or flat against the wall, our noses and knees touching the plaster. Some teachers hit us on the hands with a ruler. A few of these rulers were covered with brass studs. They didn't have much luck redoing me, though. They could make me dress up like a white man, but they couldn't change what was inside the shirt and pants.

My first teacher was a man and he was facing a lot of fearful kids. I noticed that all the children had the same expression on their faces—no expression at all. They looked frozen, deadpan, wooden. I knew that I, too, looked that way. I didn't know a word of the white man's language and very little about his ways. I thought that everybody had money free. The teacher didn't speak a word of Lakota. He motioned me to my seat. I was scared stiff.

The teacher said, "Stand," "Sit down!" He said it again and again until we caught on. "Sit, stand, sit, stand. Go and stop. Yes and no." All without spelling, just by sound.

We also had a lady teacher. She used the same method. She'd hold up one stick and say, "One." Then she'd hold up two sticks and say, "Two," over and over again. For many weeks she showed us pictures of animals and said "dog" or "cat." It took me three years to learn to say, "I want this."

My first day in school was also the first time I had beans, and with them came some white stuff, I guessed it was pork fat. That night, when I came home, my grandparents had to open the windows. They said my air was no good. Up to then I had eaten nothing but dry meat, *wasna, papa,* dry corn mixed with berries. I didn't know cheese and eggs, butter or cream. Only seldom had I tasted sugar or candy. So I had little appetite at school. For days on end they fed us cheese sandwiches, which made Grandma sniff at me, saying, "Grandson, have you been near some goats?"

After a while I lost some of my fear and recovered my daring. I called the white man teacher all the bad names in my language, smiling at him at the same time. He beamed and patted me on the head, because he thought I was complimenting him. Once I found a big picture of a monkey in the classroom, a strange animal with stiff, white side whiskers. I thought this must be the Great White Father, I really did.

I went to the day school on the Rosebud Reservation, twelve miles south of Norris, South Dakota. The Government teachers were all third-grade teachers. They taught up to this grade and that was the highest. I stayed in that goddam third grade for six years. There wasn't any other. The Indian people of my generation will tell you that it was the same at the other schools all over the reservations. Year after year the same grade over again. If we ran away the police would bring us back. It didn't matter anyway. In all those years at the day school they never taught me to speak English or to write and read. I learned these things only many years later, in saloons, in the Army or in jail.

When I was fourteen years old I was told that I had to go to boarding school. It is hard for a non-Indian to understand how some of our kids feel about boarding schools. In their own homes Indian children are surrounded with relatives as with a warm blanket. Parents, grandparents, uncles, aunts, older brothers and cousins are always fussing over them, playing with them or listening to what they have to say. Indian kids call their aunt "Mother," not just as a polite figure of speech but because that aunt acts like a mother. Indian children are never alone. If the grownups go someplace, the little ones are taken along. Children have their rights just as the adults. They are rarely forced to do something they don't like, even if it is good for them. The parents will say, "He hates it so much, we don't have the heart to make him do it."

To the Indian kid the white boarding school comes as a terrific shock. He is taken from his warm womb to a strange, cold place. It is like being pushed out of a cozy kitchen into a howling blizzard. The schools are better now than they were in my time. They look good from the outside—modern and expensive. The teachers understand the kids a little better, use more psychology and less stick. But in these fine new buildings Indian children still commit suicide, because they are lonely among all that noise and activity. I know of a ten-year-old who hanged herself. These schools are just boxes filled with homesick children. The schools leave a scar. We enter them confused and bewildered and we leave them the same way. When we enter the school we at least know that we are Indians. We come out half red and half white, not knowing what we are.

When I was a kid those schools were really bad. Ask the oldtimers. I envied my father, who never had to go through this. I felt so lonesome I cried, but I wouldn't cooperate in the remaking of myself. I played the dumb Indian. They couldn't make me into an apple—red outside and white inside. From their point of view I was a complete failure. I took the rap for all the troubles in the school. If anything happened the first question always was "Did you see John do it?" They used the strap on us, but more on me than on anybody else.

My teacher was a mean old lady. I once threw a live chicken at her like a snowball. In return she hit my palms with a ruler. I fixed an inkpot in such a way that it went up in her face. The black ink was all over her. I was the first to smile and she knew who had done it right away. They used a harness thong on my back that time and locked me up in the basement. We full-bloods spent much time down there. I picked up some good fox songs in that basement.

I was a good athlete. I busted a kitchen window once playing stickball. After that I never hit so good again. They tried to make me play a slide trombone. I tore it apart and twisted it into a pretzel. That mean old teacher had a mouth like a pike and eyes to match. We counted many coups upon each other and I still don't know who won. Once, when they were after me again for something I didn't do, I ran off. I got home and on my horse. I knew the Indian police would come after me. I made it to Nebraska, where I sold my horse and saddle and bought a ticket to Rapid City. I still had twelve dollars in my pocket. I could live two days on one dollar, but the police caught me and brought me back. I think in the end I got the better of that school. I was more of an Indian when I left than when I went in. My back had been tougher than the many straps they had worn out on it.

Some doctors say that Indians must be healthier than white people because they have less heart disease. Others say that this comes from our being hungrier, having less to eat, which makes our bodies lean and healthy. But this is wrong. The reason Indians suffer less from heart disease is that we don't live long enough to have heart trouble. That's an old folks' sickness. The way we have to live now, we are lucky if we make it to age forty. The full-bloods are dying fast. One day I talk to one, the next day he is dead. In a way the Government is still "vanishing" the Indian, doing Custer's work. The strange-looking pills and capsules they give us to live on at the Public Health Service hospitals don't do us much good. At my school the dentist came once a year in his horse and buggy with a big pair of pliers to yank our teeth, while the strongest, biggest man they could find kept our arms pinned to our sides. That was the anesthesia.

There were twelve of us, but they are all dead now, except one sister. Most of them didn't even grow up. My big brother, Tom, and his wife were killed by the flu in 1917. I lost my own little boy thirty-five years ago. I was a hundred miles away, caught in a blizzard. A doctor couldn't be found for him soon enough. I was told it was the measles. Last year I lost another baby boy, a foster child. This time they told me it was due to some intestinal trouble. So in a lifetime we haven't made much progress. We medicine men try to doctor our sick, but we suffer from many new white man's diseases, which come from the white man's food and white man's living, and we have no herbs for that.

My big sister was the oldest of us all. When she died in 1914 my folks took it so hard that our life was changed. In honor of her memory they gave away most of their possessions, even beds and mattresses, even the things without which the family would find it hard to go on. My mother died of tuberculosis in 1920, when I was seventeen years old, and that was our family's "last stand." On her last day I felt that her body was already gone; only her soul was still there. I was holding her hand and she was looking at me. Her eyes were big and sad, as if she knew that I was in for a hard time. She said, "*Onsika, onsika*—pitiful, pitiful." These were her last words. She wasn't sorry for herself; she was sorry for me. I went up on a hill by myself and cried.

When grandfather Crazy Heart died they killed his two ponies, heads toward the east and tails to the west. They had told each horse, "Grandson, your owner loved you. He has need of you where he's going now." Grandfather knew for sure where he was going, and so did the people who buried him according to our old custom, up on a scaffold where the wind and air, the sun, the rain and the snow could take good care of him. I think that eventually they took the box with his body down from the scaffold and buried it in a cemetery, but that happened years later and by then he and his ponies had long gone to wherever they wanted to be.

But in 1920 they wouldn't even allow us to be dead in our own way. We had to be buried in the Christian fashion. It was as if they wanted to take my mother to a white boarding school way up there. For four days I felt my mother's *nagi*, her presence, her soul, near me. I felt that some of her goodness was staying with me. The priest talked about eternity. I told him we Indians did not believe in a forever and forever. We say that only the rocks and the mountains last, but even they will disappear. There's a new day coming, but no forever, I told him. "When my time comes, I want to go where my ancestors have gone." The priest said, "That may be hell." I told him that I'd rather be frying with a Sioux grandmother or uncle than sit on a cloud playing harp with a pale-faced stranger. I told him, "That Christian name, John, don't call me that when I'm gone. Call me Tahca Ushte—Lame Deer."

With the death of my mother one world crumbled for me. It coincided with a new rule the Government made about grazing pay and allotments. Barbed-wire fences closed in on us. My dad said, "We might just as well give up." He went back to Standing Rock, where he was from. He left my sister about sixty horses, forty scrub cows and one bull. I had about sixty head of broken saddle horses and fifty cows. My dad turned me loose. "Hey, I give you these horses; do as you please. If you want to live like a white man, go and buy a car till you are broke and walk on foot." I guess Dad knew what was in my mind.

I started trading my stock for a Model-T Ford and bought things that were in style for the rodeo—fancy boots, silver spurs, gaudy horse-trappings, a big hat. I followed the rodeo circuit, but I wasn't too interested in competing as a rider. It was just an excuse to travel to different reservations. My life was changed and I myself was changing. I hardly recognized myself anymore. I was a wanderer, a hippie Indian. I knew nothing then. Right or wrong were just words. My life was a find-out. If somebody said, "That's bad," I still wanted to experience it. Maybe it would turn out to be good. I wasn't drinking then but soon would be. My horses and cows were gone. Instead I was the owner of a half-dozen wrecked jalopies. Yet I felt the spirits. Always at night they came down to me. I could hear them, something like the whistling from the hearing aid that I am wearing now. I could feel their touch like a feather on a sore spot. I always burned a little sweet grass for them. Though I lived like a hobo, I was visiting many old medicine men, trying to learn their ways.

I didn't need a house then or a pasture. Somewhere there would be a cave, a crack in the rocks, where I could hole up during a rain. I wanted the plants and the stones to tell me their secrets. I talked to them. I roamed. I was like a part of the earth. Everything had been taken from me except myself. Now and then, in some place or other, I looked at my face in a mirror to remind myself who I was. Poverty. hardship, laughter, shame, adventure—I wanted to experience them all. At times I felt like one of those modern declawed cats, like a lone coyote with traps, poisoned meat, and a ranger's gun waiting for him, but this did not worry me. I was neither sad nor happy. I just was.

I knew an old Indian at this time who was being forced to leave his tent and to go live in a new house. They told him that he would be more comfortable there and that they had to burn up his old tent because it was verminous and unsanitary. He looked thin and feeble, but he put up a terrific fight. They had a hard time dragging him. He was cursing them all the time: "I don't want no son-of-a-bitch house. I don't want to live in a box. Throw out the goddam refrigerator, drink him up! Throw out the chair, saw off the damn legs, sit on the ground. Throw out that thing to piss in. I won't use it. Dump the son-of-a-bitch goldfish in there. Kill the damn cow, eat him up. Tomorrow is another day. There's no tomorrow in this goddam box!"

I felt proud of this old man. He expressed what I felt. He gave me courage. I was cut loose, drifting like a leaf the wind tore from a tree. I listened to many white preachers of all denominations simply because I was curious to hear what they had to say. But I had no need of their churches. I carried my own church within me. I went to peyote meetings and had visions. I wanted to feel, smell, hear and see, but not see with my eyes and my mind only. I wanted to see with *cante ista*—the eye of the heart. This eye had its own way of looking at things. I was going through a change. I didn't resist it. I gave myself up to it wholly. Always I tried to find out. I met a medicine man, one of my uncles. "Tell me about the Great Spirit," I asked him. "He is not like a human being, like the white god. He is a power. That power could be in a cup of coffee. The Great Spirit is no old man with a beard." This answer made me happy, but I would ask the same question again from somebody else.

I had a thirst for women. I wanted to know them. I loved many girls, more than a hundred. Their soft moaning had something to teach me. It could also get me killed. At a dance on one reservation—I won't mention the name of the place, because they could come and want to shoot me again—I met a girl and took her out, brought her to my hideout nearby. Then I noticed that I had left my coat at the powwow and went to get it. When I got there I ran into her husband, pawing the ground, looking mean. Of all things he turned out to be one hell of a big policeman and he had seen me sneaking off with his wife. He had his gun out in a flash and started banging away at me, calling me some very bad names at the time. I didn't stop to listen but jumped on the nearest horse and away I went. He fired all six shots after me. He didn't hit me, but one of the bullets hit the horse in the rump. Poor horse, he hadn't done a thing.

In 1930 I got what I deserved. I was married by force. The girl's father was a big cheese, a Christian with plenty of pull. They put the pressure on me. I didn't have any choice. I was like the coyote caught with his leg in a trap. At some time I would bite the leg off.

These people were Catholics and I went to their church with them. It didn't work well. People paid more attention to me than to the preacher. Some white people didn't want to sit next to me. It was the boarding school all over again. After three years my wife divorced me. She said I was good during the day but bad in the nighttime.

I was out of the trap. I hadn't been ready to settle down anyway. There were still many things I had to be—an outlaw and a lawman, a prisoner and roamer, a sheepherder and a bootlegger, a rodeo rider and a medicine man. I still wanted to lead many lives, finding out who I was. The fever was still strong in me. Like my great-grandfather Lame Deer, I wanted to go on one more big hunt, though I didn't know then what I was hunting for or how long the hunt would last, and whether it would kill me, as it had killed my ancestor. Maybe I was looking for his gun. I still say it is mine.

Talking to the Owls and Butterflies

Let's sit down here, all of us, on the open prairie, where we can't see a highway or a fence. Let's have no blankets to sit on, but feel the ground with our bodies, the earth, the yielding shrubs. Let's have the grass for a mattress, experiencing its sharpness and its softness. Let us become like stones, plants, and trees. Let us be animals, think and feel like animals.

Reprinted by permission of Simon & Schuster, Inc. from *Lame Deer, Seeker of Visions*, by John Lame Deer and Richard Erdoes (New York, 1972). Copyright © 1972 John Fire/Lame Deer and Richard Erdoes.

Listen to the air. You can hear it, feel it, smell it, taste it. *Woniya wakan*—the holy air—which renews all by its breath. *Woniya, woniya wakan*—spirit, life, breath, renewal—it means all that. *Woniya*—we sit together, don't touch, but something is there; we feel it between us, as a presence. A good way to start thinking about nature, talk about it. Rather talk to it, talk to the rivers, to the lakes, to the winds as to our relatives.

You have made it hard for us to experience nature in the good way by being part of it. Even here we are conscious that somewhere out in those hills there are missile silos and radar stations. White men always pick the few unspoiled, beautiful, awesome spots for the sites of these abominations. You have raped and violated these lands, always saying, "Gimme, gimme, gimme," and never giving anything back. You have taken 200,000 acres of our Pine Ridge reservation and made them into a bombing range. This land is so beautiful and strange that now some of you want to make it into a national park. The only use you have made of this land since you took it from us was to blow it up. You have not only despoiled the earth, the rocks, the minerals, all of which you call "dead" but which are very much alive; you have even changed the animals, which are part of us, part of the Great Spirit, changed them in a horrible way, so no one can recognize them. There is power in a buffalo—spiritual, magic power—but there is no power in an Angus, in a Hereford.

There is power in an antelope, but not in a goat or in a sheep, which holds still while you butcher it, which will eat your newspaper if you let it. There was great power in a wolf, even in a coyote. You have made him into a freak—a toy poodle, a Pekingese, lap dog. You can't do much with a cat, which is like an Indian, unchangeable. So you fix it, alter it, declaw it, even cut its vocal cords so you can experiment on it in a laboratory without being disturbed by its cries.

A partridge, a grouse, a quail, a pheasant, you have made them into chickens, creatures that can't fly, that wear a kind of sunglasses so that they won't peck each other's eyes out, "birds" with a "pecking order." There are some farms where they breed chickens for breast meat. Those birds are kept in low cages, forced to be hunched over all the time, which makes the breast muscles very big. Soothing sounds, Muzak, are piped into these chicken hutches. One loud noise and the chickens go haywire, killing themselves by flying against the mesh of their cages. Having to spend all their lives stooped over makes an unnatural, crazy, no-good bird. It also makes unnatural, no-good human beings.

That's where you fooled yourselves. You have not only altered, declawed and malformed your winged and four-legged cousins; you have done it to yourselves. You have changed men into chairmen of boards, into office workers, into time-clock punchers. You have changed women into housewives, truly fearful creatures. I was once invited into the home of such a one.

"Watch the ashes, don't smoke, you stain the curtains. Watch the gold-fish bowl, don't breathe on the parakeet, don't lean your head against the wallpaper; your hair may be greasy. Don't spill liquor on that table; it has a delicate finish. You should have wiped your boots; the floor was just varnished. Don't, don't, don't . . ." That is crazy. We weren't made to endure this. You live in prisons which you have built for yourselves, calling them "homes," offices, factories. We have a new joke on the reservation: "What is cultural deprivation?" Answer: "Being an upper-middle-class white kid living in a split-level suburban home with a color TV."

Sometimes I think that even our pitiful tar-paper shacks are better than your luxury homes. Walking a hundred feet to the outhouse on a clear wintry night, through mud or snow, that's one small link with nature. Or in the summer, in the back country, leaving the door of the privy open, taking your time, listening to the humming of the insects, the sun warming your bones through the thin planks of wood; you don't even have that pleasure anymore.

Americans want to have everything sanitized. No smells! Not even the good, natural man and woman smell. Take away the smell from under the armpits, from your skin. Rub it out, and then spray or dab some non-human odor on yourself, stuff you can spend a lot of money on, ten dollars an ounce, so you know this has to smell good. "B.O.," bad breath, "Intimate Female Odor Spray"—I see it all on TV. Soon you'll breed people without body openings.

I think white people are so afraid of the world they created that they don't want to see, feel, smell or hear it. The feeling of rain and snow on your face, being numbed by an icy wind and thawing out before a smoking fire, coming out of a hot sweat bath and plunging into a cold stream, these things make you feel alive, but you don't want them anymore. Living in boxes which shut out the heat of the summer and the chill of winter, living inside a body that no longer has a scent, hearing the noise from the hi-fi instead of listening to the sounds of nature, watching some actor on TV having a make-believe experience when you no longer experience anything for yourself, eating food without taste—that's your way. It's no good.

The food you eat, you treat it like your bodies, take out all the nature part, the taste, the smell, the roughness, then put the artificial color, the artificial flavor in. Raw liver, raw kidney—that's what we old-fashioned full-bloods like to get our teeth into. In the old days we used to eat the guts of the buffalo, making a contest of it, two fellows getting hold of a long piece of intestines from opposite ends, starting chewing toward the middle, seeing who can get there first; that's eating. Those buffalo guts, full of half-fermented, half-digested grass and herbs, you didn't need any pills and vitamins when you swallowed those. Use the bitterness of gall for flavoring, not refined salt or sugar. *Wasna*—meat, kidney fat and berries all pounded together—a lump of that sweet *wasna* kept a man going for a whole day. That was food, that had the power. Not the stuff you give us today: powdered milk, dehydrated eggs, pasteurized butter, chickens that are all drumsticks or all breast; there's no bird left there.

You don't want the bird. You don't have the courage to kill honestly— cut off the chicken's head, pluck it and gut it—no, you don't want this anymore. So it all comes in a neat plastic bag, all cut up, ready to eat, with no taste and no guilt. Your mink and seal coats, you don't want to know about the blood and pain which went into making them. Your idea of war—sit in an airplane, way above the clouds, press a button, drop the bombs, and never look below the clouds—that's the odorless, guiltless, sanitized way.

When we killed a buffalo, we knew what we were doing. We apologized to his spirit, tried to make him understand why we did it, honoring with a prayer the bones of those who gave their flesh to keep us alive, praying for their return, praying for the life of our brothers, the buffalo nation, as well as for our own people. You wouldn't understand this and that's why we had the Washita Massacre, the Sand Creek Massacre, the dead women and babies at Wounded Knee. That's why we have Song My and My Lai now.

To us life, all life, is sacred. The state of South Dakota has pest-control officers. They go up in a plane and shoot coyotes from the air. They keep track of their kills, put them all down in their little books. The stockmen and sheepowners pay them. Coyotes eat mostly rodents, field mice and such. Only once in a while will they go after a stray lamb. They are our natural garbage men cleaning up the rotten and stinking things. They make good pets if you give them a chance. But their living could lose some man a few cents, and so the coyotes are killed from the air. They were here before the sheep, but they are in the way; you can't make a profit out of them. More and more animals are dying out. The animals which the Great Spirit put here, they must go. The man-made animals are allowed to stay—at least until they are shipped out to be butchered. That terrible arrogance of the white man, making himself something more than God, more than nature, saying, "I will let this animal live, because it makes money"; saying, "This animal must go, it brings no income, the space it occupies can be used in a better way. The only good coyote is a dead coyote." They are treating coyotes almost as badly as they used to treat Indians.

You are spreading death, buying and selling death. With all your deodorants, you smell of it, but you are afraid of its reality; you don't want to face up to it. You have sanitized death, put it under the rug, robbed it of its honor. But we Indians think a lot about death. I do. Today would be a perfect day to die—not too hot, not too cool. A day to leave something of yourself behind, to let it linger. A day for a lucky man to come to the end of his trail. A happy man with many friends. Other days are not so good. They are for selfish, lonesome men, having a hard time leaving this earth. But for whites every day would be considered a bad one, I guess.

Eighty years ago our people danced the Ghost Dance, singing and dancing until they dropped from exhaustion, swooning, fainting, seeing visions. They danced in this way to bring back their dead, to bring back the buffalo. A prophet had told them that through the power of the Ghost Dance the earth would roll up like a carpet, with all the white man's works—the fences and the mining towns with their whorehouses, the factories and the farms with their stinking, unnatural animals, the railroads and the telegraph poles, the whole works. And underneath this rolled-up white man's world we would find again the flowering prairie, unspoiled, with its herds of buffalo and antelope, its clouds of birds, belonging to everyone, enjoyed by all.

I guess it was not time then for this to happen, but it is coming back, I feel it warming my bones. Not the old Ghost Dance, not the rolling-up—but a new-old spirit, not only among Indians but among whites and blacks, too, especially among young people. It is like raindrops making a tiny brook, many brooks making a stream, many streams making one big river bursting all dams. Us making this book, talking like this—these are some of the raindrops.

Listen, I saw this in my mind not long ago: In my vision the electric light will stop sometime. It is used too much for TV and going to the moon. The day is coming when nature will stop the electricity. Police without flashlights, beer getting hot in the refrigerators, planes dropping from the sky, even the President can't call up somebody on the phone. A young man will come, or men, who'll know how to shut off all electricity. It will be painful, like giving birth. Rapings in the dark, winos breaking into the liquor stores, a lot of destruction. People are being too smart, too clever; the machine stops and they are helpless, because they have forgotten how to make do without the machine. There is a Light Man coming, bringing a new light. It will happen before this century is over. The man who has this power will do good things, too—stop all atomic power, stop wars, just by shutting the white electro-power off. I hope to see this, but then I'm also afraid. What will be will be.

I think we are moving in a circle, or maybe a spiral, going a little higher every time, but still returning to the same point. We are moving closer to nature again. I feel it, you feel it, your two boys here feel it. It won't be bad, doing without many things you are now used to, things taken out of the earth and wasted foolishly. You can't replace them and they won't last forever. Then you'll have to live more according to the Indian way. People won't like that, but their children will. The machine will stop, I hope, before they make electric corncobs for poor Indians' privies.

We'll come out of our boxes and rediscover the weather. In the old days you took your weather as it came, following the cranes, moving south with the herds. Here, in South Dakota, they say, "If you don't like the weather, wait five minutes." It can be 100 degrees in the shade one afternoon and suddenly there comes a storm with hailstones as big as golf balls, the prairie is all white and your teeth chatter. That's good—a reminder that you are just a small particle of nature, not so powerful as you think.

You people try to escape the weather, fly to Miami where it's summer all the time, miss the rains, miss the snow. That's pitiful. Up to 1925 we had some old men who had a sort of a club where they could get together. Somehow they could tell what the weather would be. They needed no forecaster with all those gimmicks, satellites and what have you. They just had their wisdom, something which told them what nature was up to.

Some medicine men have the power to influence the weather. One does not use it lightly, only when it is absolutely necessary. When we hold our sun dance, we always try to have perfect weather. When we had a wedding ceremony in Winner, last spring, you saw me draw a design in the earth, the figure of a turtle. I picked this up from the old people. When I was a little boy I had a party where we played games. It was drizzling and I was mad. We wanted to play and the weather wouldn't let us. My grandma said, "Why don't you make the picture of turtle?" Before we were through making it, the rain stopped. I could dry the country up, or make a special upside-down turtle and flood everything. You have to know the right prayer with it, the right words. I won't tell what they are. That's too dangerous. You don't fool around with it. I see that white man's look on your face. You don't believe. Ask my friend Pete Catches here, a brother medicine man.

PETE CATCHES: "John is right. That sun dance he was referring to, when we chopped down the sun-dance pole, we had to catch the tree. It is not supposed to touch the ground. We stood in line and I was close to the trunk of the tree, and when it fell it hit me right above the knee. I went through the sun dance with that suffering in me. And I really like it. My sun dance was as near close to authentic as I could make it. I pierced my flesh in the morning and broke loose around three o'clock in the afternoon, the longest piercing since we revived this sacred dance. And after I broke loose, there was a big thundercloud forming in the west. A lot of people wanted to get away, to go home before the storm broke. And it was nearing, coming on fast. So, during the course of the dance, they handed me my pipe, the pipe that I always use. I call it my chief pipe. So I took that and asked the Great Spirit to part that thunder, part it in half, so we can finish our ceremony. Before all the people that great storm parted, right before their eyes. The one part went to the north, wrought havoc in the White River country, clear on in, tore off the roofs, destroyed gardens and acted like that. The part of the storm which went south, toward Pine Ridge, covered everything with hail, but on the dance ground the sun kept shining. So, to me, that sun dance in 1964 was the best one I ever did.

"And the power of the turtle design, what John told you about it, we know this to be true. The heart of Keha, the turtle, is about the strongest thing there is. It keeps on beating and beating for two days after you kill the turtle. There is so much strength and endurance in it. To eat such a heart makes you tough. It imparts its power to whoever has eaten of it. My sister ate that turtle heart. They had to cut it in half for her to make it possible to swallow it. This made her into a strong woman, stouthearted like a warrior. She had a growth on her breast. The doctors said it was cancer. She lit five cigarettes. She told the children to puff on them, to keep those cigarettes glowing. Then she took the lighted cigarettes, one after the other, and burned this evil thing out of her. On and on she went, deep into her breast, and her face remained calm all the while; not one muscle twitched. She is cured now. A turtle heart will do this for you.

"But all animals have power, because the Great Spirit dwells in all of them, even a tiny ant, a butterfly, a tree, a flower, a rock. The modern, white man's way keeps that power from us, dilutes it. To come to nature, feel its power, let it help you, one needs time and patience for that. Time to think, to figure it all out. You have so little time for contemplation; it's always rush, rush, rush with you. It lessens a person's life, all that grind, that hurrying and scurrying about. Our old people say that the Indians of long ago didn't have heart trouble. They didn't have that cancer. The illnesses they had they knew how to cure. But between 1890 and 1920 most of the medicines, the animal bundles, the pipes, the ancient, secret things which we had treasured for centuries, were lost and destroyed by the B.I.A., by the Government police. They went about tearing down sweat lodges, went into our homes, broke the pipes, tore up the medicine bags, threw them into the fire, burned them up, completely wiped out the wisdom of generations. But the Indian, you take away everything from him, he still has his mouth to pray, to sing the ancient songs. He can still do his *yuwipi* ceremony in a darkened room, beat his small drum, make the power come back, make the wisdom return. He did, but not all

of it. The elk medicines are gone. The bear medicine, too. We had a medicine man here, up the creek, who died about fifteen years ago. He was
the last bear medicine man that I knew about. And he was good, too. He
was really good."

But it is coming again, the bear power. We make bear sounds, talk bear
language when we are in a fighting mood. "Harrnh"—and you are as good
as gone. A bear claw, properly treated, you pierce a man for the sun dance
with it, he won't feel the pain. Let me tell you about the power of the
bear, natural animal power when it comes up against one of those artificial, non-animals.

Medicine Good and Bad

I am a medicine man—a *wićaśa wakan*. "Medicine man"—that's a white
man's word like squaw, papoose, Sioux, tomahawk—words that don't exist
in the Indian language. I wish there were better words to make clear what
"medicine man" stands for, but I can't find any, and you can't either, so I
guess medicine man will have to do. But it doesn't convey the many different meanings that come to an Indian's mind when you say "medicine man."

We have different names for different men doing different things for
which you have only that one puny name. First, we distinguish the
healer—*pejuta wićaśa*—the man of herbs. He does not cure with the
herbs alone; he must also have the *wakan* power to heal. Then we have
the *yuwipi*, the tied-one, the man who uses the power of the rawhide and
the stones to find and to cure. We also speak of the *waayatan*—the man of
vision who can foretell events which will happen in the future, who has
been given the power to see ahead. Things that have come true according
to such a man's prediction are called *wakinyanpi*. This word also means
the winged-ones, those who fly through the air, because the power to
foretell the future comes from them.

Then there is the *wapiya*—the conjurer—what you might call a witch
doctor. If he is a good man he does the *waanazin*—the shooting at the
disease, the drawing up and sucking out of your body evil things which
have been put into a person by a bad spirit, such as a particular kind of
gopher that will shoot sharp blades of grass and tiny bits of porcupine
quills from his hole in the ground into your body, causing it to break out in
boils.

If such a conjurer is bad, he himself will put a sickness into you which only he can cure—for a price. There are some fakers among this group. They give a little medicine to a soldier boy which is supposed to protect him from harm, make him bulletproof and ensure his coming home safely. If he comes back in one piece, they collect. If he doesn't—well, that's just too bad.

Another kind of medicine man is the *heyoka*—the sacred clown—who uses his thunder power to cure some people. If you want to stretch the word out like a big blanket to cover everybody, even a peyote roadman could squeeze underneath it and qualify as a medicine man. But the more I think about it, the more I believe that the only real medicine man is the *wićaśa wakan*—the holy man. Such a one can cure, prophesy, talk to the herbs, command the stones, conduct the sun dance or even change the weather, but all this is of no great importance to him. These are merely stages he has passed through. The *wićaśa wakan* has gone beyond all this. He has the *wakanya wowanyanke*—the great vision. Sitting Bull was such a man. When he had his sun-dance vision at Medicine Deer Rock he saw many blue-coated soldiers fall backward into the Indian camp and he heard a voice telling him, "I give you these, because they have no ears." Sitting Bull knew then that the Indians would win the next battle. He did not fight himself, he commanded no men, he did not do anything except let his wisdom and power work for his people.

The *wićaśa wakan* wants to be by himself. He wants to be away from the crowd, from everyday matters. He likes to meditate, leaning against a tree or rock, feeling the earth move beneath him, feeling the weight of that big flaming sky upon him. That way he can figure things out. Closing his eyes, he sees many things clearly. What you see with your eyes shut is what counts.

The *wićaśa wakan* loves the silence, wrapping it around himself like a blanket—a loud silence with a voice like thunder which tells him of many things. Such a man likes to be in a place where there is no sound but the humming of insects. He sits facing the west, asking for help. He talks to the plants and they answer him. He listens to the voices of the *wama kaśkan*—all those who move upon the earth, the animals. He is as one with them. From all living beings something flows into him all the time, and something flows from him. I don't know where or what, but it's there. I know.

This kind of medicine man is neither good nor bad. He lives—and that's it, that's enough. White people pay a preacher to be "good," to behave himself in public, to wear a collar, to keep away from a certain kind of women. But nobody pays an Indian medicine man to be good, to behave himself and act respectable. The *wićaśa wakan* just acts like himself.

He has been given the freedom—the freedom of a tree or a bird. That freedom can be beautiful or ugly; it doesn't matter much.

Medicine men—the herb healers as well as our holy men—all have their own personal ways of acting according to their visions. The Great Spirit wants people to be different. He makes a person love a particular animal, tree or herb. He makes people feel drawn to certain favorite spots on this earth where they experience a special sense of well-being, saying to themselves, "That's a spot which makes me happy, where I belong." The Great Spirit is one, yet he is many. He is part of the sun and the sun is a part of him. He can be in a thunderbird or in an animal or plant.

A human being, too, is many things. Whatever makes up the air, the earth, the herbs, the stones is also part of our bodies. We must learn to be different, to feel and taste the manifold things that are us. The animals and plants are taught by Wakan Tanka what to do. They are not alike. Birds are different from each other. Some build nests and some don't. Some animals live in holes, others in caves, others in bushes. Some get along without any kind of home.

Even animals of the same kind—two deer, two owls—will behave differently from each other. Even your daughter's little pet hamsters, they all have their own ways. I have studied many plants. The leaves of one plant, on the same stem—none is exactly alike. On all the earth there is not one leaf that is exactly like another. The Great Spirit likes it that way. He only sketches out the path of life roughly for all the creatures on earth, shows them where to go, where to arrive at, but leaves them to find their own way to get there. He wants them to act independently according to their nature, to the urges in each of them.

If Wakan Tanka likes the plants, the animals, even little mice and bugs, to do this, how much more will he abhor people being alike, doing the same thing, getting up at the same time, putting on the same kind of store-bought clothes, riding the same subway, working in the same office at the same job with their eyes on the same clock and, worst of all, thinking alike all the time. All creatures exist for a purpose. Even an ant knows what that purpose is—not with its brain, but somehow it knows. Only human beings have come to a point where they no longer know why they exist. They don't use their brains and they have forgotten the secret knowledge of their bodies, their senses, or their dreams. They don't use the knowledge the spirit has put into every one of them; they are not even aware of this, and so they stumble along blindly on the road to nowhere—a paved highway which they themselves bulldoze and make smooth so that they can get faster to the big, empty hole which they'll find at the end, waiting to swallow them up. It's a quick, comfortable superhighway, but I know where it leads to. I have seen it. I've been there in my vision and it makes me shudder to think about it.

I believe that being a medicine man, more than anything else, is a state of mind, a way of looking at and understanding this earth, a sense of what it is all about. Am I a *wićaśa wakan?* I guess so. What else can or would I be? Seeing me in my patched-up, faded shirt, with my down-at-the-heels cowboy boots, the hearing aid whistling in my ear, looking at the flimsy shack with its bad-smelling outhouse which I call my home—it all doesn't add up to a white man's idea of a holy man. You've seen me drunk and broke. You've heard me curse or tell a sexy joke. You know I'm not better and wiser than other men. But I've been up on the hilltop, got my vision and my power; the rest is just trimmings. That vision never leaves me— not in jail, not while I'm painting funny signs advertising some hash-house, not when I am in a saloon, not while I am with a woman, especially not then.

I am a medicine man because a dream told me to be one, because I am commanded to be one, because the old holy men—Chest, Thunderhawk, Chips, Good Lance—helped me to be one. There is nothing I can, or want, to do about it. I could cure you of a sickness just with a drink of pure cold water and the workings of my vision. Not always, but often enough. I want to be a *wićaśa wakan*, a man who feels the grief of others. A death anywhere makes me feel poorer. A young woman and her child were killed the other night on the highway. I feel so deeply about them. At sundown I will talk to the Great Spirit for them. I will fill my pipe and offer it on their behalf. I do this always. Would you believe it, that when Robert Kennedy was assassinated shortly after he had come out here to talk to us Indians, I went into my sweat lodge and made an offering for him. Could you imagine a white man praying for Crazy Horse? I have passed through all the phases, the healing with herbs, the *uywipi*, the peyote. I just took my pipe and went from this to a higher spot.

I want to speak some more about the ways of our medicine men, those still alive and those who have passed away. I'll close my eyes, thinking while I talk, let the spirit talk through me. This is a remembering. We have a word for this special kind of remembering, *waki-ksuya.* It means to recall, to travel back into the past, to hold communion with the spirits, to receive a message from them, to bring to one's mind the dead friends, to hear their voices once again, even to the point of having a vision. Don't let me spook you. I don't want to do all this now. I just want to lean back, close my eyes, let somebody else do the driving. I'll just keep talking and let the words find their own way.

You become a *pejuta wićaśa,* a medicine man and healer, because a dream tells you to do this. No one man dreams of all the medicines. You doctor where you know you have the power. You don't inherit it; you work for it, fast for it, try to dream it up, but it doesn't always come. It is true that some families produce a string of good medicine men, and it helps to have a holy man among your relatives who teaches you and tries to pass his power on to you. It works sometimes, but not always. Medicine men aren't horses. You don't breed them. You can give a boy a car for a present and teach him how to drive, but if there's no gas in the tank, the learning and the car won't do him any good. Sometimes the power skips a generation and reappears in a grandchild.

A medicine man, when he's old, tries to pass his vision and his knowledge to his son. There's a power line there, but sometimes no juice is coming through. If in spite of all the learning and trying and begging for a vision a man doesn't obtain this power, he'll know it. Most of the time he'll be honest about it and just stop trying. But sometimes a man will fake it, pretend to be something he isn't. In the end it will only bring misfortune on his own home. Trying to trick others, he'll only trick himself. So most men won't try this.

One of our greatest Sioux holy men was old Chips. Without him, maybe our religion would have died out. During the darkest years he kept his vision alive, worked it for the good of the people. He was a real *wičaśa wakan*. If he hadn't taught us, there would be no medicine men left among us now. He did it almost all by himself. Well, he passed his power on to his son, Ellis Chips, and he is a good man. But the real great power of the old holy man has passed on to his grandson Godfrey, who is still only a boy of sixteen. First the power was given to an elder brother. But this young man did not know how to handle it. He was too fond of the hard stuff, liking to have a glass or two now and then. "Take this burden away from me," he said. "It is no good to me."

But the power turned up in the younger boy Godfrey. Nobody had tried to pass it on to him. The spirits, the *yuwipi*, picked him and talked to him for about three months. He didn't understand them and they scared him at first. He told his father about this. His father said, "Why don't you ask them for something to put in your ear so you will understand them. Well, he did, and the *yuwipi* gave him something and told him to look for a certain herb. His dad told him to rub it in his ear and right then and there he understood what the spirits were saying. They told him he was going to be their interpreter and he was supposed to relate everything exactly as the *yuwipi* told him. So from that night on he's been their spokesman. He was only thirteen years old when this happened. He is our youngest *yuwipi* man.

Otherwise he is a cheerful, normal boy. He plays the usual boys' games and he likes to take machinery and gadgets apart to see how they work.

The only way he is different from other kids is that he will not get into any fights anymore. If another boy hits him, he won't strike back. Also he won't go near a girl who has her monthly sickness, because this could be very bad for both of them. So in everyday life he is just another good-looking kid, but at night he is a very powerful *yuwipi*. The Chips family was related to Chief Crazy Horse, and people say that the spirit of this great warrior is sometimes present during young Chips's ceremonies. One of the spirits there is powerful, all right. It sometimes breaks things, smashes dishes, nearly wrecks the place.

Well, Crazy Horse was a warrior, not a medicine man. He was a man-killer, but he had strange powers, like the pebble behind his ear which made him bulletproof. He also wore an herb—*santu bu*, red grass—as his *wotawe*, his special medicine. Crazy Horse's power is still around, like two flintstones clashing, powerful. I have a son whom you have never met. I sometimes think he got some of that warrior power. For years he used to be an Indian stunt man in Hollywood, doing crazy, dare-devil things. But he was never hurt or even scratched. Like Crazy Horse, he was injury-proof. It gave him a confidence.

When it became clear that young Chips was going to be a medicine man, his parents kept him out of school. We usually do this in a case like Chips's. Going to a white school and walking a medicine man's road, you can't do both. I know one father of a youngster who was showing signs of being *wakan*. The father drove the truant officers off with his shot-gun. That boy can't read or write, but he grew up to become a fine medi-cine man.

In the case of Godfrey Chips, the Indian police came after him and their car swerved and turned over, one officer coming out of it with a dis-located shoulder. After this they never bothered him again. He now has a certificate which says that he is living according to the traditional Indian way and that he doesn't have to go to school.

We all knew right away that his powers were great. One family traveled 200 miles to seek his help. They had lost their little boy, who had disap-peared without a trace. They asked young Chips to find him for them. They had this ceremony and Godfrey asked the spirits. He told the par-ents, "I see your son, and you'll see him too, in seven days, but I don't know whether you'll be happy to see him." And he told them where to find him. Later he took me aside and said, "Uncle, I have seen this boy. I didn't want to tell this to his father, but the child is dead. I saw him. He was still alive, but then, in my vision, I watched him drown in the Mis-souri River. I could describe him as he is now, but I don't want to. I know I must tell the truth, but maybe not all of it at once." Chips was still so young himself, telling those parents was a great burden to him. It was almost too much. They found that poor boy seven days later, just as God-frey Chips had foreseen.

So you can become a medicine man in different ways, like Chips, by the *yuwipis* talking to you, or like me, through a *hanblechia*—a vision quest. You could be lucky and have a holy man give you his power. It will soon be time for me to look for a young man to give my power to. When he appears I'll know him. I'll sense: This is the one! This power is some-thing like AC and DC. The white preacher goes on AC. He takes what-ever he has and it just goes straight on and vanishes. It never comes back. I'm on DC. The line can be cut, it still comes back, it moves like a circle without end. I'm watching my line to the other medicine men, on the lookout for power breaks. Also I'm watching for my successor.

As I said, most of the time a person becomes a medicine man through his own vision. His dream is his very own; nobody else has it exactly the same. There'll be a certain something in it which will be just for him—his own special secret. On the other hand, part of his dream he'll share with the other medicine men—a common vision which holds them all to-gether, which comes out of our common blood, out of the prairie itself. Being a medicine man ties a man to his people as with a *yuwipi's* rawhide.

I respect other religions, but I don't like to see them denatured and made into something else. You've made a blondie out of Jesus. I don't care for those blond, blue-eyed pictures of a sanitized, Chloroxed, Ajaxed Christ. How would you like it if I put braids on Jesus and stuck a feather in his hair? You'd call me a very crazy Indian, wouldn't you? Jesus was a Jew. He wasn't a yellow-haired Anglo. I'm sure he had black hair and a dark skin like an Indian. The white ranchers around here wouldn't have let him step out with their daughters and wouldn't have liked him having a drink in one of their saloons. His religion came out of the desert in which he lived, out of his kind of mountains, his kind of animals, his kind of plants. You've tried to make him into an Anglo-Saxon Fuller Brush sales-man, a long-haired Billy Graham in a fancy night shirt, and that's why he doesn't work for you anymore. He was a good medicine man, I guess. As you read it in the Bible, he sure had the power, the healing touch. He was a hippie, too. *Hipi*—in our language that means "He is here, we are here, it is here"—something like that. So I don't mind a young white man with long hair and a beaded headband coming to me, asking to learn about our Indian religion, even praying with us. But I would mind it if he tried to change our beliefs, adapt them to his kind of culture, progress, civilization and all that kind of stuff. I would mind that very much. You can't take our beliefs out of our Badlands and prairies and put them into one of your factories or office buildings.

A big Catholic church is being built for Indians on one of our Sioux reservations. It is shaped like a giant tipi. Over its altar hangs a huge peace pipe together with the cross. It tries to make you believe that Jesus was a *yuwipi*. It says: Come all you peyote men, medicine men, *heyokas* and elk dreamers, come all you Indians and worship here. This is like a *hanblechia*, or a peyote meeting; it's all the same, there is no difference. I don't like it and many others besides me don't like it. It is dishonest. Because there is a difference, and there will always be a difference, as long as one Indian is left alive. Our beliefs are rooted deep in our earth, no matter what you have done to it and how much of it you have paved over. And if you leave all that concrete unwatched for a year or two, our plants, the native Indian plants, will pierce that concrete and push up through it.

In order to be a medicine man one should find the visions there, in nature. To the west a man has the power from the buffalo. From the north he gets the power from the thunder-beings. From the east his strength comes from the spirit horse and the elk. From the south he has the ghost power. From above, from the sky, he will receive the wisdom of the great eagle. From beneath, from the earth, he will receive the mother's food. This is the way to become a *wićaśa wakan*, to learn the secret language, to speak about sacred things, to work with the stones and herbs, to use the pipe.

Much power comes from the animals, and most medicine men have their special animal which they saw in their first vision. One never kills or harms this animal. Medicine men can be buffalo, eagle, elk or bear dreamers. Of all the four-legged and winged creatures a medicine man could receive a vision from, the bear is foremost. The bear is the wisest of animals as far as medicines are concerned. If a man dreams of this animal he could become a great healer. The bear is the only animal that one can see in a dream acting like a medicine man, giving herbs to people. It digs up certain healing roots with its claws. Often it will show a man in a vision which medicines to use.

The old medicine men used to have bear claws in their sacred bundles. These claws, pressed into the flesh of a sick person, would make the healing bear medicine penetrate into his body. Many songs of the bear dreamers end with the words *Mato hemakiye*—a bear told me this. Then everybody knows who gave this medicine man his powers. One great gift of the bear dreamers was fixing up broken bones. They had a special bear medicine—*huhuwehanhan pejuta*—which they mixed with fat and smeared on a broken arm or leg. They had a way of setting the bone, pulling it into place, then wrapping the whole up tightly with a moistened rawhide, and in a month that man would walk again on that broken leg, draw a bow with his doctored arm. This the old people told me. It was cheaper than a hospital, too, I tell you.

Those bear medicine men knew how to cure. We used to have people ninety and a hundred years of age and they still had all their teeth left. Now you look around and you see all those commodities-fed young Indians with most of their teeth gone. The modern food, the shiny new hospitals and bad teeth seem to go together. But we used to be a healthy people. Those old men, the warriors who had fought Custer, still used to meet in the 1930s and 1940s. Some were over a hundred years old, still able to sit on a horse, still liking to chew on tough meat. They had their spiritual meetings in the dark. I helped them sing. I learned most of the *yuwipi* songs from a pair of twin brothers. We had to sneak off for these parties because the Government was trying to discourage us so they could take away the power the Indian doctors had.

THE WAY TO RAINY MOUNTAIN

by N. Scott Momaday

N. Scott Momaday is Kiowa on his father's side and Cherokee on his mother's. He considers himself Kiowa. He was born in 1934 in southwest Oklahoma, which is Kiowa country, but moved with his family to New Mexico when he was one. His parents were with the Indian Service, and he spent most of his childhood among Navajos and Tanoans where they were working. In 1946 his father became principal of the day school at Jemez, New Mexico, the town Momaday depicts in his novel House Made of Dawn. *Momaday graduated from the University of New Mexico and went on to get an M.A. and Ph.D. in English literature at Stanford University. He now teaches at the University of Arizona.*

House Made of Dawn *won the Pulitzer Prize for fiction in 1969 and established Momaday as the most prominent Indian writer today. But to say that he is our most prominent Indian writer is like calling Sandy Koufax a great Jewish pitcher: both statements are true, of course, but far too restrictive. Momaday is one of the best novelists of any sort in America today. He is also a poet of considerable talents—in fact, he was a poet before he was a novelist—and the great strength of both* The Way to Rainy Mountain *and* House Made of Dawn *is the power of his language and his poetic way of looking at things.*

The Way to Rainy Mountain *is Momaday's account of his quest to learn what it means to be Kiowa. Since most of his youth had been spent with Indians of other tribes, he had, until his pilgrimage to Rainy Mountain, a less-than-fully-developed sense of his own Indianness. The trip was an odyssey that was destined to inculcate in him Kiowa culture and history at the last historical moment when he could learn it from people who actually participated in it. In particular, he learned from the memory of his grandmother, Aho, whose grave he sought at Rainy Mountain, and from Ko-Sahn, a Kiowa woman who was one hundred years old. The route he traveled, from the mountains at Yellowstone to the plains of southwest Oklahoma, is the same route the Kiowas traveled as they evolved from a "bent and blind woodland people" to the proud rulers of the southern plains.* The Way to Rainy Mountain *thus is both an account of Momaday's personal journey and an account of the history of the Kiowas—not only*

The "Introduction" is reprinted with the permission of the University of New Mexico Press from N. Scott Momaday, *The Way to Rainy Mountain* (© copyright 1969 by University of New Mexico Press). It was first published in *The Reporter*, January 26, 1967.

*their physical travels, which extended past Oklahoma as far as Central
America, but also their spiritual journey, in which they acquired the sun-
dance religion of the Plains tribes.*

Introduction

A single knoll rises out of the plain in Oklahoma, north and west of the
Wichita Range. For my people, the Kiowas, it is an old landmark, and
they gave it the name Rainy Mountain. The hardest weather in the world
is there. Winter brings blizzards, hot tornadic winds arise in the spring,
and in summer the prairie is an anvil's edge. The grass turns brittle and
brown, and it cracks beneath your feet. There are green belts along the
rivers and creeks, linear groves of hickory and pecan, willow and witch
hazel. At a distance in July or August the steaming foliage seems almost to
writhe in fire. Great green and yellow grasshoppers are everywhere in
the tall grass, popping up like corn to sting the flesh, and tortoises crawl
about on the red earth, going nowhere in the plenty of time. Loneliness is
an aspect of the land. All things in the plain are isolate; there is no confu-
sion of objects in the eye, but *one* hill or *one* tree or *one* man. To look
upon that landscape in the early morning, with the sun at your back, is to
lose the sense of proportion. Your imagination comes to life, and this, you
think, is where Creation was begun.

I returned to Rainy Mountain in July. My grandmother had died in the
spring, and I wanted to be at her grave. She had lived to be very old and
at last infirm. Her only living daughter was with her when she died, and I
was told that in death her face was that of a child.

I like to think of her as a child. When she was born, the Kiowas were
living that last great moment of their history. For more than a hundred
years they had controlled the open range from the Smoky Hill River to
the Red, from the headwaters of the Canadian to the fork of the Arkansas
and Cimarron. In alliance with the Comanches, they had ruled the whole
of the southern Plains. War was their sacred business, and they were
among the finest horsemen the world has ever known. But warfare for the
Kiowas was preeminently a matter of disposition rather than of survival,
and they never understood the grim, unrelenting advance of the U.S.
Cavalry. When at last, divided and ill-provisioned, they were driven onto
the Staked Plains in the cold rains of autumn, they fell into panic. In Palo
Duro Canyon they abandoned their crucial stores to pillage and had nothing then but their lives. In order to save themselves, they surrendered to
the soldiers at Fort Sill and were imprisoned in the old stone corral that

now stands as a military museum. My grandmother was spared the humiliation of those high gray walls by eight or ten years, but she must have known from birth the affliction of defeat, the dark brooding of old warriors.

Her name was Aho, and she belonged to the last culture to evolve in North America. Her forebears came down from the high country in western Montana nearly three centuries ago. They were a mountain people, a mysterious tribe of hunters whose language has never been positively classified in any major group. In the late seventeenth century they began a long migration to the south and east. It was a journey toward the dawn, and it led to a golden age. Along the way the Kiowas were befriended by the Crows, who gave them the culture and religion of the Plains. They acquired horses, and their ancient nomadic spirit was suddenly free of the ground. They acquired Tai-me, the sacred Sun Dance doll, from that moment the object and symbol of their worship, and so shared in the divinity of the sun. Not least, they acquired the sense of destiny, therefore courage and pride. When they entered upon the southern Plains they had been transformed. No longer were they slaves to the simple necessity of survival; they were a lordly and dangerous society of fighters and thieves, hunters and priests of the sun. According to their origin myth, they entered the world through a hollow log. From one point of view, their migration was the fruit of an old prophecy, for indeed they emerged from a sunless world.

Although my grandmother lived out her long life in the shadow of Rainy Mountain, the immense landscape of the continental interior lay like memory in her blood. She could tell of the Crows, whom she had never seen, and of the Black Hills, where she had never been. I wanted to see in reality what she had seen more perfectly in the mind's eye, and travelled fifteen hundred miles to begin my pilgrimage.

Yellowstone, it seemed to me, was the top of the world, a region of deep lakes and dark timber, canyons and waterfalls. But, beautiful as it is, one might have the sense of confinement there. The skyline in all directions is close at hand, the high wall of the woods and deep cleavages of shade. There is a perfect freedom in the mountains, but it belongs to the eagle and the elk, the badger and the bear. The Kiowas reckoned their stature by the distance they could see, and they were bent and blind in the wilderness.

Descending eastward, the highland meadows are a stairway to the plain. In July the inland slope of the Rockies is luxuriant with flax and buckwheat, stonecrop and larkspur. The earth unfolds and the limit of the land recedes. Clusters of trees, and animals grazing far in the distance, cause the vision to reach away and wonder to build upon the mind. The sun follows a longer course in the day, and the sky is immense beyond all comparison. The great billowing clouds that sail upon it are shadows that move upon the grain like water, dividing light. Farther down, in the land of the Crows and Blackfeet, the plain is yellow. Sweet clover takes hold of the hills and bends upon itself to cover and seal the soil. There the Kiowas paused on their way; they had come to the place where they must change their lives. The sun is at home on the plains. Precisely there does it have the certain character of a god. When the Kiowas came to the land of the Crows, they could see the dark lees of the hills at dawn across the Bighorn River, the profusion of light on the grain shelves, the oldest deity ranging after the solstices. Not yet would they veer southward to the caldron of the land that lay below; they must wean their blood from the northern winter and hold the mountains a while longer in their view. They bore Tai-me in procession to the east.

A dark mist lay over the Black Hills, and the land was like iron. At the top of a ridge I caught sight of Devil's Tower upthrust against the gray sky as if in the birth of time the core of the earth had broken through its crust and the motion of the world was begun. There are things in nature that engender an awful quiet in the heart of man; Devil's Tower is one of them. Two centuries ago, because they could not do otherwise, the Kiowas made a legend at the base of the rock. My grandmother said:

Eight children were there at play, seven sisters and their brother. Suddenly the boy was struck dumb; he trembled and began to run upon his hands and feet. His fingers became claws, and his body was covered with fur. Directly there was a bear where the boy had been. The sisters were terrified; they ran, and the bear after them. They came to the stump of a great tree, and the tree spoke to them. It bade them climb upon it, and as they did so it began to rise into the air. The bear came to kill them, but they were just beyond its reach. It reared against the tree and scored the bark all around with its claws. The seven sisters were borne into the sky, and they became the stars of the Big Dipper.

From that moment, and so long as the legend lives, the Kiowas have kinsmen in the night sky. Whatever they were in the mountains, they could be no more. However tenuous their well-being, however much they had suffered and would suffer again, they had found a way out of the wilderness.

My grandmother had a reverence for the sun, a holy regard that now is all but gone out of mankind. There was a wariness in her, and an ancient awe. She was a Christian in her later years, but she had come a long way about, and she never forgot her birthright. As a child she had been to the Sun Dances; she had taken part in those annual rites, and by them she had learned the restoration of her people in the presence of Tai-me. She was about seven when the last Kiowa Sun Dance was held in 1887 on the Washita River above Rainy Mountain Creek. The buffalo were gone. In order to consummate the ancient sacrifice—to impale the head of a buffalo bull upon the medicine tree—a delegation of old men journeyed into Texas, there to beg and barter for an animal from the Goodnight herd. She was ten when the Kiowas came together for the last time as a living Sun Dance culture. They could find no buffalo; they had to hang an old hide from the sacred tree. Before the dance could begin, a company of soldiers rode out from Fort Sill under orders to disperse the tribe. Forbidden without cause the essential act of their faith, having seen the wild herds slaughtered and left to rot upon the ground, the Kiowas backed away forever from the medicine tree. That was July 20, 1890, at the great bend of the Washita. My grandmother was there. Without bitterness, and for as long as she lived, she bore a vision of deicide.

Now that I can have her only in memory, I see my grandmother in the several postures that were peculiar to her: standing at the wood stove on a winter morning and turning meat in a great iron skillet; sitting at the south window, bent above her beadwork, and afterwards, when her vision failed, looking down for a long time into the fold of her hands; going out upon a cane, very slowly as she did when the weight of age came upon her; praying. I remember her most often at prayer. She made long, rambling prayers out of suffering and hope, having seen many things. I was never sure that I had the right to hear, so exclusive were they of all mere custom and company. The last time I saw her she prayed standing by the side of her bed at night, naked to the waist, the light of a kerosene lamp moving upon her dark skin. Her long, black hair, always drawn and braided in the day, lay upon her shoulders and against her breasts like a shawl. I do not speak Kiowa, and I never understood her prayers, but there was something inherently sad in the sound, some merest hesitation upon the syllables of sorrow. She began in a high and descending pitch, exhausting her breath to silence; then again and again—and always the same intensity of effort, of something that is, and is not, like urgency in the human voice. Transported so in the dancing light among the shadows of her room, she seemed beyond the reach of time. But that was illusion; I think I knew then that I should not see her again.

Houses are like sentinels in the plain, old keepers of the weather watch. There, in a very little while, wood takes on the appearance of great age. All colors wear soon away in the wind and rain, and then the wood is burned gray and the grain appears and the nails turn red with rust. The windowpanes are black and opaque; you imagine there is nothing within, and indeed there are many ghosts, bones given up to the land. They stand here and there against the sky, and you approach them for a longer time than you expect. They belong in the distance; it is their domain.

Once there was a lot of sound in my grandmother's house, a lot of coming and going, feasting and talk. The summers there were full of excitement and reunion. The Kiowas are a summer people; they abide the cold and keep to themselves, but when the season turns and the land becomes warm and vital they cannot hold still; an old love of going returns upon them. The aged visitors who came to my grandmother's house when I was a child were made of lean and leather, and they bore themselves upright. They wore great black hats and bright ample shirts that shook in the wind. They rubbed fat upon their hair and wound their braids with strips of colored cloth. Some of them painted their faces and carried the scars of old and cherished enmities. They were an old council of warlords, come to remind and be reminded of who they were. Their wives and daughters served them well. The women might indulge themselves; gossip was at once the mark and compensation of their servitude. They made loud and elaborate talk among themselves, full of jest and gesture, fright and false alarm. They went abroad in fringed and flowered shawls, bright beadwork and German silver. They were at home in the kitchen, and they prepared meals that were banquets.

There were frequent prayer meetings, and great nocturnal feasts. When I was a child I played with my cousins outside, where the lamplight fell upon the ground and the singing of the old people rose up around us and carried away into the darkness. There were a lot of good things to eat, a lot of laughter and surprise. And afterwards, when the quiet returned, I lay down with my grandmother and could hear the frogs away by the river and feel the motion of the air.

Now there is a funeral silence in the rooms, the endless wake of some final word. The walls have closed in upon my grandmother's house. When I returned to it in mourning, I saw for the first time in my life how small it was. It was late at night, and there was a white moon, nearly full. I sat for a long time on the stone steps by the kitchen door. From there I could see out across the land; I could see the long row of trees by the creek, the low light upon the rolling plains, and the stars of the Big Dipper. Once I looked at the moon and caught sight of a strange thing. A cricket had perched upon the handrail, only a few inches away from me. My line of vision was such that the creature filled the moon like a fossil. It had gone there, I thought, to live and die, for there, of all places, was its small definition made whole and eternal. A warm wind rose up and purled like the longing within me.

The next morning I awoke at dawn and went out on the dirt road to Rainy Mountain. It was already hot, and the grasshoppers began to fill the air. Still, it was early in the morning, and the birds sang out of the shadows. The long yellow grass on the mountain shone in the bright light, and a scissortail hied above the land. There, where it ought to be, at the end of a long and legendary way, was my grandmother's grave. Here and there on the dark stones were ancestral names. Looking back once, I saw the mountain and came away.

POETRY

FOR SOME REASON there are more good Indian poets than fiction writers today. Whether the reason is cultural, artistic, or connected somehow to the dynamics of getting published, the fact is that there are far more poets reading and writing in Indian country than there are novelists and short-story writers.

The first Indian to publish a book of poems in this country was George Copway, whose *The Ojibway Conquest* appeared in 1850. Alexander Posey, a Creek, and E. Pauline Johnson, a Mohawk, were probably the best-known Indian poets writing in mainstream genres during the early part of the present century. The first poetry collections of the 1960s Indian literary Renaissance were published by John Milton as special issues of the *South Dakota Review* in the summers of 1969 and 1970. Other sources of Indian poetry in mainstream publications in the early 1970s were the poetry page of *Akwesasne Notes*, a journal published by the Mohawks of New York State, and the publications of the Blue Cloud Abbey, a Benedictine monastery in Marvin, South Dakota.

Although Indian fiction has achieved a good deal of attention—Scott Momaday won the Pulitzer Prize, and he along with James Welch, Gerald Vizenor, Louise Erdrich, and Michael Dorris have had novels reviewed in the *New York Times Book Review*—Indian poetry, even that of Momaday, Welch, Erdrich, and Vizenor, has been largely ignored. Many major anthologies of contemporary American verse—for example, *The Harvard Book of Contemporary American Poetry*, *New American Poets of the 80s*, and *The Norton Anthology of American Literature*—have no Indian poetry whatever.

By and large, Indian poets employ the same styles as other American poets. Lance Henson is an exception at times: some of his poems incorporate Cheyenne symbols and sound patterns. And, Momaday and Louise Erdrich have a few prose poems that resemble Indian narratives. For the

211

most part, however, Indian poetry is no different stylistically from that produced by members of other ethnic groups. Much contemporary poetry is difficult and obscure, and Indian poetry is no exception. In contemporary poetry, allusions are often personal rather than cultural, and structure is associational rather than logical, and this holds true for a good deal of Indian poetry as well. Also, poets like James Welch, Gus Palmer, and even occasionally Momaday, employ surrealism in their work, and this can be a problem for readers.

Thematically, Indians tend most of the time to write about Indian subjects—in particular, about being Indian, or more often, mixed-blood, in America today. Common subjects are their relationship to their tribes and to the land.

In the selections that follow I have tried to strike a balance between the works of writers who are established, like Momaday, Welch, and Simon Ortiz, and those who are in the process of developing their reputations, like Gus Palmer, nila northSun, and Charlotte DeClue.

MAURICE KENNY

Maurice Kenny was born in the Akwesasne country of northern New York in 1929. He is Mohawk. In addition to being an excellent poet, he has achieved much success as an editor (*Contact/II*), publisher (Strawberry Press), and professor (North Country Community College and the University of Oklahoma).

Kenny's books include *The Mama Poems*, for which he won the American Book Award in 1984; *Is Summer This Bear* (1985); *Rain and other Fictions* (1985); *Greyhounding This America* (1986); and *Between Two Rivers: Selected Poems* (1987).

Kenny's poetry reflects the oral traditions of the Mohawks: it employs the strong rhythms of declamation and a tone that resembles incantation.

Corn Planter

I plant corn four years:
ravens steal it;
rain drowns it;
August burns it;
locusts ravage leaves.

I stand in a circle and throw seed.
Old men laugh because they know the wind
will carry the seed to my neighbor.

I stand in a circle on planted seed.
Moles burrow through the earth
and harvest my crop.

I throw seed to the wind
and wind drops it on the desert.

The eighth year I spend planting corn;
I tend my fields all season.
After September's harvest I take it to the market.
The people of my village are too poor to buy it.

The ninth spring I make chicken feather headdresses,
plastic tom-toms and beaded belts.
I grow rich,
buy an old Ford,
drive to Chicago,
and get drunk
on welfare checks.

Aiionwatha
(b. circa 1400)

I have listened
and I will aid the stutterer[1]
to unite the people
of this river country.
I will start with the Mohawk,
carry the word to Atotarho of the Onondaga,
advise him to take the bones
from the pot and water the pine.

I will travel and tell this
to both the younger brothers
and the elder brothers.
I will show them
the white roots of peace
as he has instructed.
We will mold a Nation.

Sometimes . . . Injustice

The day I was born my father bought me a .22.
A year later my mother traded it for a violin.
Ten years later my big sister traded that
for a guitar, and gave it to her boyfriend . . .
who sold it.

---

[1] Aiionwatha (Hiawatha) was inspired by Deganawidah, the Peacemaker, to found the Iroquois Confederacy and establish the rule of law, which for the Woodland Iroquois was symbolized by the white pine's "roots of peace." According to Iroquois tradition, the Peacemaker stuttered, and it was partly for that reason that he needed Aiionwatha to transmit his message. Atotarho, an evil wizard and a chief of the Onondaga nation, was another important convert of the Peacemaker. The bones that were to be taken from the pot were human: part of the Peacemaker's message was that the Iroquois nations were to give up warring amongst themselves and cannibalism. See Paul A. Wallace, *The White Roots of Peace* (1946; reprint, Saranac Lake, N.Y.: Chauncy Press, 1986).

Now you know why I never learned to hunt,
or learned how to play a musical instrument,
or became a Wall St. broker.

Mama Failed to Kill the Rat . . .

Mama failed to kill the rat
when it ran across my bed
that November my father tore the wall away
building the new addition to the house.
Snow seeped in, and not only snow:
raccoon thought it a good winter place;
squirrel cached hickory nuts.
Mama stood in the doorway
with a lamp in her grip
and told me not to move.

Since then rodents, mice have
always meant change to me, dead
or alive; a different course.

When corn leans, chestnuts fall;
when neighbors take in the screens
and fishermen put away
hooks and poles, late autumn,
I don't sleep so very well,
but still see Mama in the doorway
in the light of that kerosene flame
her face contorted in the mask
of chilled horror.

Mice have always meant change to me.
I hear rats gnawing the floor.

The Last Word
(In memory of my Father)

He was an ornery cuss,
bull-headed as a Hereford,
sensitive as a sitting hen.

No doubt he gave you a rough time,
probably whacked you once or twice.
(I remember taking the broom to him,
and that finished our affair for life.)
He was known to take a glass of beer,

and I've heard it said he'd pinch
a waitress' buttocks, never refused a bed.
He taught you how to drive his car
and promptly took the Ford away.
He'd buy you a new dress and grumbled
if you wore it. He even upbraided you
for buying a pound of butter
at fifteen cents a pound.
One year he furiously threw
the Christmas tree down the cellar stairs
when he couldn't nudge the lights to blink.
After he bought the radio
he never went to Mass,
but never missed a funeral.
He dressed in tailor-made suits
and wore white shirts you pressed.
Monday through Thursday he was a gentle man,
coy as a kitten, soft as a rabbit.
He showed his colors Friday nights
when we kids went through his pockets
for dimes and nickles which rolled
from his pants along the kitchen floor.

But he paid Agnes' way to Missouri
and gave Mary a husband to keep
'till death did them part, and he got me
out of trouble as fast as I got in.
Even after the divorce he made payments
on your insurance policy.

                                    He died.
The very last word he said was, "Doris."

Misbegotten Sonnet

There's not much sense to love,
nor much understanding . . . mainly
for kids who can't imagine why you'd
give up one man for another.

We change loves as wolves shed
winter fur for spring weather.
We change one face for another
without having learned the first.

Divorce is final, walls
between understanding.
It solves nothing;
a clean apron over a dirty dress.

LAND

1976

Torn, tattered, yet rugged
in the quick incline of bouldered hills
crab appled, cragged, lightning-struck birch, cedar;
wilderness muzzled; forests . . . kitchen tables and bedposts
of foreign centuries; meadows cowed
beyond redemption, endurance, violated
by emigres' feet, and vineyards alien
to indigenous squash and berry,
fragile lupine and iris of the pond;
while wounded willows bend in the snow
blown north by the west wind.

1820

spring lifts under drifts, saplings
hold to the breeze, larks sing, strawberries
crawl from under snow, woodchucks run
stone walls of new cemeteries and orchards;
apples blossom, thistle bloom

(Madame de Feriet's ghost prowls the miraged bridge
spanning Black River and her mansion lanterns
glow in the clear darkness of the French dream,
hazeled in the richness of her opulence

the lands she would hold out to tenants for rent
have neither clearings nor plows;
the disillusionment loried her trucks to France,
her mansion to ashes, her bridge to dust in 1871,
her savings to pittance, her dream to agony

Madame de Feriet gave her French aristocratic manner
to a signpost at the edge of the county road,
tangled now by yellow roses and purple vetch)

1976

April lifts from under the drifts of grey
snow piled by plows ruthless in their industrial
might to free roads and make passage
for trucks and automobiles to hurry to the grave
with dead horses in the far pasture
that no longer sustains the hunger of bleating lambs

virgin spring lifts, its muddy face scarred
and mapped with trails of progress, its smoke
rising in pine, maple, flowering aspen,
chicory weed and clods, manure of waste, whey,
abandoned farm houses and barns shaking in the wind . . .
blind old men caught without canes in the storm;
spring bloody in its virginity, its flow corrupted,
raped in zoned courts of law that struck quarried hills . . .
a great god's lance thrust in the quickness of electric sun

rage of spring rivers, swollen with anger . . .
cold voice growling through the night . . . swirling,
swallowing the soft shoulders of shoreline;
the rage of the aged shackled to history
and the crumbling bones of its frame, fisted against
the night, shaking the cane against the dark, the bats
fluttering in the balmy summer eve, fireflies creeping
through the young green grass of the long fresh meadows

1812

the north, the north aches in the bones, the land,
in the elms' limbs gently singing in that August
breeze, bereft of holiday and festival, ghost and voice . . .
tunneled by gophers; ticks and fleas stuck to an old dog's back

(General Brown marched his men to Sacketts Harbor,
struck the British in the red belly
and went home to lift a pint to his deeds
and captured vices, to ville a town, erect a fence)

1976

the gooseberry is diseased, and the elm,
stone walls broken, sky cracked, pheasants
and young muskrats sterilized, and fields

Saranac Lake, N.Y.
August—1985

I stood outside this fancy hotel
feeling pretty good to be out of Brooklyn
awhile in mountain cool, mountain breeze,
staring at the mystery of those Adirondacks,
those crystal lakes . . . though dead in acid rain.

The breeze not only lifted my long, clean
pony-tail but also cooled my tennis-shod feet;
a freshly laundered t-shirt was on my back
with lettering stencilled in gold against purple dye;
my face had been washed that morning and teeth brushed,
nails were even clipped. Well, there I stood outside
that fancy hotel proud in my Mohawk blood
and writing gifts with sun shining on my bronzed
cheeks thinking of teaching this autumn
in the local comm. college when out the door
frumped an older couple. The lady's lioness hair
breezed in the same wind as mine and the gentleman
wore tennis sneaks exactly as mine, yet there was
disdain . . . not on my lips . . . a coldness not
frozen in my heart by those mountain winds.

She to him . . . looking me dead in the eye . . . "This
hotel has gone to ruin." She added an acute barb:
"And so has that college." They strode down the street
leaving me not only speechless and feeling
dirty but about to resign my new teaching job
at that denigrated college . . . a job I'd been
fighting against taking all my life.

Heard Poem
Studio Museum Book Fair

"I used
to have
a Cherokee
boyfriend.
I knew
he was
Indian
because

he could see
a road sign
three miles
away."

After the Reading
Bernard/Laguna

We shook hands when Pat smiled our names.
His eyes bleary in mistrust, spoke
of a can or two of beer . . . "You Indian,
white man. Don't look Indian to me.
We saw you in the street we'd blow you off."

Through the reading he mumbled pretty loud.
Geary gave him a kick as I read rather quietly,
down-beat but didn't offer Bernard
an enrollment number, my grandmother's headstone
nor admit to the Irish grandpa.
                               A number
of poems read and tucked away, he asked questions,
began to make statements: "I see
your country." Last poem finished, he jumped
up, clapped an arm about my shoulder and grinned:
"I know who you are . . . a Mohawk."
He bought a book, my *MAMA POEMS*, and paid for it
with a checque on Pat's account. I offered
my hand in "so long." "Brother, we don't
need to shake. I know you now. We're cousins."
He left in night stars to find a friend to tell he knew
a white Mohawk with a center and blue eyes.
Magic was on his cheek, verbena on his arm.

I write this early the next morning
while riding Greyhound to Las Cruces after
two containers of black coffee and one Coke
which will stiffen the frame for the next
encounter, round, with students who want
wild iris in their hands, coyotes in their eyes.

CARTER REVARD

Carter Revard, whose Osage name is Nom-Pa-Wa-The, or "Fear-inspiring," was born in 1931 in Pawhuska, Oklahoma, where he grew up with four half-brothers and sisters who are half Osage, and with Ponca cousins and relatives. The most famous of those Poncas is Carter Camp, the AIM leader who was sentenced to three years in prison for his part in the occupation of Wounded Knee. Of his own ethnicity Revard says: "I think I have Indianness in me, but I am only a small part Osage. . . . When I jumped into my genes they were mostly white, but the red ones spelled OSAGE. Still it is delicate being mixed—neither red or white nor pink, could never serve as a barber pole I guess."[1]

Revard went to the University of Tulsa on a Quiz Kids scholarship, then on to Yale, where he got his doctorate, and further graduate study at Oxford, where he rowed on the Merton crew. He is currently a professor of English literature at Washington University in St. Louis, where he teaches Chaucer and historical linguistics.

After experimenting extensively, Revard seems to have found his poetic voice, using the speech patterns of his native Oklahoma. Revard says of his poetry: "I think of my poems as being implicit rather than explicit about themes and ideas—mostly I prefer not to state, trying to turn sounds into music without going through a particular instrument, only the mind."[2] He cites the influence of Hopkins, Frost, Wordsworth, and Stevens on his work, though obviously he transmutes thoroughly everything that he borrows from them.

Wazhazhe Grandmother

They chose their allotted land
   out west of the Agency
               at the prairie's edge,
     where the Osage Hills begin they built
       their homestead, honeymooned there
   near Timber Hill,
       where Bird Creek meanders in
from the rolling grassy plains with their prairie chicken dancing in spring,

[1] Carter Revard in a letter to Alan R. Velie, September 7, 1975.
[2] Ibid.

built in a timbered hollow where deer came down
            at dusk with the stars
        to drink from the deep pools
            near Timber Hill
                            and below the
            waterfall that seemed
        so high to me the summer
    when I was six and walked up near its clearness gliding
        some five or six feet down from the flat
            sandstone ledge to its pools
                    she called it in Osage, *ni-xe ga-thpe,*
    where the dark water turning into
                    a spilling of light
                                    was a curtain clear and flowing, under
            the blue flash of a kingfisher's diving
                into the pool above the falls
                    and his flying up
            again to the dead white branch of his willow—
    the whole place was so quiet
                in the way Grandma was quiet,
        it seemed a place to be still,
                    seemed waiting for us,
            though no one lived there by then
                        since widowed during the war she'd moved
                    to the place south of Pawhuska,
    and why we had driven down there from Timber Hill, now,
            I can't quite remember—
                                was it a picnic, or some kind
        of retreat or vacation time
            out of the August heat of Pawhuska?
                                    The pictures focus sharp-edged:
            a curtain of dark green ivy ruffled
        a bit by breeze and water beside
                    the waters falling there
    and a dirt road winding red and rocky
            across tree-roots, along which, carefully,
        my mother eased our rumbling Buick Eight
            in that Depression year when Osage oil
                still poured to float us into
                        a happy future—
    but whether I dreamed, or saw real things in time,
        their road, their house, the waterfall back in the woods are all
                        at the bottom of Lake Bluestem now,
        because Bird Creek,
                blessed with a dam,

is all psyched out
of its snaggly, snaky self into a
windsparkling lake
whose deep blue water, the politicians promise, will soon
come piped into Pawhuska pure and drinkable,
filling with blue brilliance municipal pools
and sprinkling the lawns to green or pouring freshets
down asphalt gutters to cool the shimmering
cicada-droning fevers of August streets
even as
in Bird Creek's old channel under Lake Bluestem big
catfish grope slowly in darkness
up over the sandstone ledge of the drowned
waterfall, or
scavenge through the ooze of
the homestead and along the road where
the bride and groom came riding one special day
and climbed down from the buggy in all their
best finery
to live in their first home.

Support Your Local Police Dog

The night before my Uncle Carter got shot
Trying to hijack a load of bootleg whiskey,
He dressed fit to kill, put on his lilac hairoil,
And leaned down to the mirror in our living room
To comb the hair back over his bald spot, humming
'Corinne, Corinne, where have you been so long?'
I don't know if 'Corrine' tipped the other bunch off,
But I hope he put it to her before they killed him.
I bet if there was any he was getting his.
—Jesus, I never saw him standing still
Or lying down, till they led me past his coffin.
He should have been a lord in Boswell's time,
Though he'd most likely been laid up with gout
Before he was forty, had that kind of drive.
More drive than brains though. Hell, man out on parole
For robbing a bank, and his hip not very long healed
Where the cop in ambush shot him trying to surrender,
Had no more sense than go after those bottled-in-bonders
From Kansas City. You KNOW they'd be in cahoots
With all the local crooks and laws. We couldn't
See why he'd let himself get talked into trying.

My Uncle Dwain said it was a put-up job,
Carter knew too much, the gang had him bumped off.

Well, the last time I was home for a visit,
Leaving behind these earnest city people
Who keep DISCOVERING crime and poverty
Like tin cans tied to their suburbs' purebred tails
Till they run frothing, yapping for law and order,
I thought of the big police dog Carter brought home
His last time there and kenneled by the chickenhouse:

Nobody was going to steal OUR stock, by God.
(Later the damn dog got to killing turkeys
On a neighbor's place; we had to let it be shot.)
—The gilt mirror he'd gazed at his bald spot in
Had been demoted, now hung dim in the bathroom.
I patted my Old Spice lather on and shaved
As suavely as he had combed, and smelled as good.
He never lived to grow white whiskers like mine;
I knew the smartest crooks don't ever need guns,
And I would never walk out into the night
To get myself shot down, the way he did.
I've got more brains. But while he lived, I admit,
He was my favorite uncle; guts, charm, and drive.
He would have made a perfect suburban mayor—
Or maybe, manager for some liquor chain.

Driving in Oklahoma

On humming rubber along this white concrete
     lighthearted between the gravities
of source and destination like a man
          halfway to the moon
     in this bubble of tuneless whistling
at seventy miles an hour from the windvents,
          over prairie swells rising
     and falling, over the quick offramp
that drops to its underpass and the truck
          thundering beneath as I cross
with the country music twanging out my windows,
     I'm grooving down this highway feeling
technology is freedom's other name when
          —a meadowlark
     comes sailing across my windshield
          with breast shining yellow
     and five notes pierce

the windroar like a flash
of nectar on mind
gone as the country music swells up and
drops me wheeling down
my notch of cement-bottomed sky
between home and away
                              and wanting
to move again through country that a bird
has defined wholly with song
                    and maybe next time see how
he flies so easy, when he sings.

N. SCOTT MOMADAY

Momaday began writing poetry in college at the University of New Mexico. Later, at Stanford University, his mentor Yvor Winters exerted the major influence on his verse. Winters was one of the few American poets influenced by Indian poetry. He had studied the translations of Frances Densmore and was particularly influenced by her collection of Chippewa songs. Momaday credits Winters with teaching him poetic technique.

Winters placed Momaday in a group he called the "post-Symbolists," which was made up of American poets possessing certain similarities with the French Symbolists, particularly Mallarmé, Rimbaud, and Verlaine. Included in the group were Frederick Goddard Tuckerman, Emily Dickinson, Wallace Stevens, Edgar Bowers, and Louise Bogan.[1] The post-Symbolists use what Winters described as "closely controlled association" for the structure of their poems. According to the doctrine of association—originally promulgated by Hobbes and Locke—all ideas arise from the complex association of sense perceptions. Our train of thought is not logical in nature; instead, ideas are linked because they derive from the same experience. That is, if a man is hit by a car while standing in the rain, he may think of automobile accidents whenever it rains. What this means for poetry is that the tight logical organization that marked English Renaissance verse gives way, in eighteenth- and nineteenth-century poetry, to an organization based on reverie. One thought leads to another in a pattern that makes sense to the thinker, but the pattern may be difficult to follow for anyone else. With the Symbolists, the process often leads to obscurity. Because the post-Symbolists carefully control association, their poetry is usually less obscure. Both Symbolists and post-Symbolists make heavy use of sensory perception and put a great deal of emphasis on natural detail.

The main difference between Symbolism and post-Symbolism is that post-Symbolist imagery is "weighted with intellect," as Winters put it, and has moral meaning. Momaday's "Angle of Geese" is a good example of the post-Symbolist method. The poem is about death and the inadequacy of language to cope with the experience of death. It begins by discussing the death of a friend's child and proceeds by an associative leap to Momaday's memory of killing a goose on a childhood hunting trip. There is a careful rendering of detail, and the detail is charged with abstract meaning. Al-

---

[1] Yvor Winters, *Forms of Discovery* (Denver: Alan Swallow, 1967), pp. 251–98.

N. Scott Momaday's poems are reprinted with his permission.

though Momaday is ostensibly describing only one dying goose, in fact he
is making a statement about death itself.
For more information on Momaday, see page 204.

Simile

What did we say to each other
that now we are as the deer
who walk in single file
with heads high
with ears forward
with eyes watchful
with hooves always placed on firm ground
in whose limbs there is latent flight

The Bear

What ruse of vision,
escarping the wall of leaves,
rending incision
into countless surfaces,

would cull and color
his comnolence, whose old age
has outworn valor,
all but the fact of courage?

Seen, he does not come,
move, but seems forever there,
dimensionless, dumb,
in the windless noon's hot glare.

More scarred than others
these years since the trap maimed him,
pain slants his withers,
drawing up the crooked limb.

Then he is gone, whole,
without urgency, from sight
as buzzards control,
imperceptibly, their flight.

Before an Old Painting of the Crucifixion

The Mission Carmel
June, 1960

I ponder how He died, despairing once.
I've heard the cry subside in vacant skies,
In clearings where no other was. Despair,
Which, in the vibrant wake of utterance,
Resides in desolate calm, preoccupies,
Though it is still. There is no solace there.

That calm inhabits wilderness, the sea,
And where no peace inheres but solitude;
Near death it most impends. It was for Him,
Absurd and public in His agony,
Inscrutably itself, nor misconstrued,
Nor metaphrased in art or pseudonym:

A vague contagion. Old, the mural fades . . .
Reminded of the fainter sea I scanned,
I recollect: How mute in constancy!
I could not leave the wall of palisades
Till cormorants returned my eyes on land.
The mural but implies eternity:

Not death, but silence after death is change.
Judean hills, the endless afternoon,
The farther groves and arbors seasonless
But fix the mind within the moment's range.
Where evening would obscure our sorrow soon,
There shines too much a sterile loveliness.

No imprecisions of commingled shade,
No shimmering deceptions of the sun,
Herein no semblances remark the cold
Unhindered swell of time, for time is stayed.
The Passion wanes into oblivion,
And time and timelessness confuse, I'm told.

These centuries removed from either fact
Have lain upon the critical expanse
And been of little consequence. The void
Is calendared in stone; the human act,
Outrageous, is in vain. The hours advance
Like flecks of foam borne landward and destroyed.

Angle of Geese

How shall we adorn
Recognition with our speech?—
    Now the dead firstborn
Will lag in the wake of words.

    Custom intervenes;
We are civil, something more:
    More than language means,
The mute presence mulls and marks.

    Almost of a mind,
We take measure of the loss;
    I am slow to find
The mere margin of repose.

    And one November
It was longer in the watch,
    As if forever,
Of the huge ancestral goose.

    So much symmetry!
Like the pale angle of time
    And eternity.
The great shape labored and fell.

    Quit of hope and hurt,
It held a motionless gaze,
    Wide of time, alert,
On the dark distant flurry.

The Fear of Bo-Talee

Bo-talee rode easily among his enemies, once, twice,
three—and four times. And all who saw him were
amazed, for his was utterly without fear; so it seemed.
But afterwards he said: Certainly I was afraid. I was
afraid of the fear in the eyes of my enemies.

The Great Fillmore Street Buffalo Drive

Insinuate the sun through fog
upon Pacific Heights, upon the man on horseback,
upon the herd ascending. *There* is color and clamor.

And there he waves them down,
those great, humpbacked animals,
until their wild grace gone
they lumber and lunge
and blood blisters at their teeth,
and their hooves score the street—

and among boulders they settle on the sea.

He looks after them, twisted round upon his sorrow,
the drape of his flag now full and formal,
ceremonial.

One bull, animal representation of the sun,
he dreams back from the brink
to the green refuge of his hunter's heart.
It grazes near a canyon wall,
along a ribbon of light, among Red Bud trees,
eventually into shadow.

Then the hold of his eyes is broken:
on the farther rim the grasses flicker and blur,
a hawk brushes rain across the dusk,
meadows recede into mountains, and here and there
are moons like salmonberries
upon the glacial face of the sky.

PAULA GUNN ALLEN

Paula Gunn Allen, a mixed-blood Laguna, Sioux, and Lebanese, was born in Cubero, New Mexico, in 1939. She currently teaches in the Native American Studies Department of the University of California, Berkeley.

Widely anthologized, Allen is the author of four chapbooks; a collection of poems, Shadow Country *(1982); a novel,* The Woman Who Owned the Shadows; *and a collection of essays,* The Sacred Hoop: Recovering the Feminine in American Indian Traditions *(1986). She edited the highly influential* Studies in American Indian Literature *for the Modern Languages Association.*

Shadows are the primary metaphor of Allen's works: she borrows the concept from Black Elk, who spoke of the shadow cast on earth from the heavens, meaning that reality is in the spirit world and not in this. This world is a dazzling and confusing place: in the introduction to Shadow Country, *Kenneth Lincoln describes Allen's vision as the "polychromatic shock of Indian modernism."*

Powwow 79, Durango

haven't been to one in almost three years
there's six drums and 200 dancers a few
booths piled with jewelry and powwow stuff
some pottery and oven bread
everyone gathers
stands for the grand entry
two flag songs
and the opening prayer by some guy
works for the BIA
who asks our father
to bless our cars
to heal our hearts
to let the music here tonight
make us better, cool
hurts and unease
in his son's name, amen.
my daughter arrives, stoned,
brown face ashy from the weed,

Paula Gunn Allen's poems are reprinted with permission from her book *Shadow Country* (Los Angeles: American Indian Studies Center, UCLA, 1982).

there's no toilet paper
in the ladies room she accuses me
there's never any toilet paper
in the *ladies* room at a powwow she glares
changes
calms
its like being home after a long time
are you gonna dance I ask
here's my shawl
not dressed right she says
the new beaded ties I bought her swing
from her long dark braids
why not you have dark blue on I say
look.
we step inside the gym
eyes sweep the rubber floor
jackets, jeans, down-filled vests,
sweatshirts all dark blue.
have to look close to pick out
occasional brown or red on older folks
the dark brown faces rising on the bleachers
the dark hair on almost every head
ever see so many Indians
you're dressed right
we look at the bleachers
quiet like shadows
the people sit watching the floor below
where dancers circle the beating drums
exploding color in the light.

Crow Ambush
(*Song for '76*)

crow
circling overhead
stands on a broken branch
to consider his reflection
in the pool

moon
riding herd on utility poles
wonders
when the converging lines
will surround him

wind
lulling grass into submission
mutters to the drying hills
        (eating pemmican)

            nothing obvious
        a natural sort of understanding
        elusive as half-meant charity as
        singing a boarding-school song
        from Indian 49:

"HII-AA HA HA HAA. HII-AA HA HA HAA.
I'd rather be a drunkard than a fool."

Los Angeles, 1980

The death culture swarms
over the land bringing
honeysuckle eucalyptus palm
ivy brick and unfinished wood
torn from forests to satisfy organic
craving. The death society walks
hypnotized by its silent knowledge
nor does it hear the drum quiet
to the core.
The trees know.
Look.
They are dying.
The small birds who walk heedless
of the people swarming around them
know: they peck at sesame seeds trucked
from factories far away and crumbs
dropped from Rainbow buns. They
do not fly at human approach. They
act as if we are not there.

The dying generation does not know.
Boys offer me papers that shriek
of impending death: *Klan and Nazis Unite!*
the headlines proclaim. I must be aware, be
ware. The rally forming on the steps
beyond the plaza swirls with belief
that protest can change something, a
transformation needed, longed for,
that does not ever seem to come.
"It's getting worse," the young beard

assures me. His hair, teeth, skin
gleam with assured elegance.
"I know," I reply.

The dying generation moves purposefully:
well-dressed in Jantzen and Wrangler,
Gucchi and Adidas, clothes, bodies,
smiles gleaming, cool in the practiced
superiority of well-cut, natural fiber
clothes and vitamin-drenched consciousness,
they live their truth. They cannot count
the cost. But their silent hearts beat
slow with knowledge their bodies share
with the birds.

On my way to this New Jerusalem
on a smog-shrouded hill, I passed
fine stores filled with hidden omen,
dedicated to health and cleanliness,
luxury and the One True Path.
I could see they were there to save
my life. One brick-front shop's
bronze-tasteful sign announced:
Weight and Smoking Control Center.
In its smoky glass I saw
my own reflection:
short, fat, a black cigarette
in my hand, my self-cut hair
greying, my worn clothes mocking
the expensive, seductive sign.
I could see how I am
neither healthy nor wealthy.
But I am wise
enough to know
that death comes in pretty packages too,
and all around me
the dying air agreed.

The death people do not know
what they create, or how they hide
from the consequences of their dreams.
Wanting the good they slide
into an unforgiving destiny.
Alfalfa sprout, sesame seed,
no meat, no cigarettes: what will change
the inexorable dying we are facing?

No rally, no headline, no designer jean
can do more than hasten it.
We are related, after all,
the beautiful
wealthy
sun children and I.
We wander together into a smoky tomorrow,
seeing the clouds of darkness gather
on the surrounding hills,
shroud the sea, cover and oppose our
brightest dreams.
The dying grows silent
around us
and we walk
still believing it need not be.

Hoop Dancer

It's hard to enter
circling clockwise and counter
clockwise moving no
regard for time, metrics
irrelevant to this dance
where pain is the prime number
and soft stepping feet
praise water from the skies:

I have seen the face of triumph
the winding line stare down all moves
to desecration: guts not cut from arms,
fingers joined to minds,
together Sky and Water
one dancing   one
circle of a thousand turning lines
beyond the march of gears—
out of time,   out of
time, out
of time.

JAMES WELCH

James Welch is Blackfoot on his father's side and Gros Ventre on his mother's. He was born in 1940. After attending school on Montana reservations, he bounced around several colleges before graduating from the University of Montana. He subsequently taught creative writing at Montana for several years before devoting himself full time to his own writing.

Welch's poetry alternates between a realistic depiction of vivid details and a peculiar Indian form of surrealism that he has adapted from the work of Cesar Vallejo and James Wright. Indian poets find surrealism attractive because the surrealist's interest in dreams corresponds in some ways to the Indians' traditional practice of basing their spiritual life on visions. "Magic Fox" is a surrealistic poem about dreaming. The rules of the world of dreams govern the poem. The dreamers—"those men that rattled in their sleep"—dream of leaves, horses, fish, stars, and a beautiful girl. Their dreams are controlled by a magic fox, a sort of trickster figure with power to transform things. The fox transforms the dreamers' horses into fish. Or does he? The dreamers are not sure because, in the uncertain world of dreams, images shift constantly.

"Getting Things Straight" describes a hawk hunting and the last of the Indian giants, who has a vision on Heart Butte. Welch asks if the hawk is his own vision. An Indian vision differs in important ways from the dreams that are the basis of traditional surrealistic poetry, but there is a similarity. In both cases, seemingly mundane things are invested with intense symbolic importance, and distinctions between the real and the unreal are blurred.

"The D-Y Bar" shows Welch's ability to distill art from the most banal and unpoetic material. The setting is a cowboy bar in the Montana boondocks; the subject, a drunken Indian named Bear Child, whom Welch transmutes into a fascinating and mysterious creature. "Arizona Highways" deals with an experience from Welch's days on the road as a poet in the schools. Eulynda was an Indian girl whose untamed vibrancy made Welch, the college-educated Blackfoot, feel soft, white, and overcivilized. "Plea to Those Who Matter" treats his feelings at not being invited to a party which his wife attended. Probably the best of Welch's poems is "Grandma's Man," a masterpiece of irony about a Don Quixote figure, who undoubtedly is the fool his wife thinks he is and yet is also the only one around able to perceive and appreciate the beauty of the world.

James Welch's poems are reprinted with his permission.

Magic Fox

They shook the green leaves down,
those men that rattled
in their sleep. Truth became
a nightmare to their fox.
He turned their horses into fish,
or was it horses strung
like fish, or fish like fish
hung naked in the wind?

Stars fell upon their catch.
A girl, not yet twenty-four
but blonde as morning birds, began
a dance that drew the men in
green around her skirts.
In dust her magic jangled memories
of dawn, till fox and grief
turned nightmare in their sleep.

And this: fish not fish but stars
that fell into their dreams.

Getting Things Straight

Is the sun the same drab gold?
The hawk—is he still rising, circling,
falling above the field? And the rolling day,
it will never stop? It means nothing?
Will it end the way history ended when
the last giant climbed Heart Butte, had his vision,
came back to town and drank himself
sick? The hawk has spotted a mouse.
Wheeling, falling, stumbling to a stop,
he watches the snake ribbon quickly
under a rock. What does it mean?
He flashes his wings to the sun, bobs
twice and lifts, screaming
off the ground. Does it mean this to him:
the mouse, a snake, the dozen angry days
still rolling since his last good feed?
Who offers him a friendly meal?
Am I strangling in his grip?
Is he my vision?

Harlem, Montana: Just Off the Reservation

We need no runners here. Booze is law
and all the Indians drink in the best tavern.
Money is free if you're poor enough.
Disgusted, busted whites are running
for office in this town. The constable,
a local farmer, plants the jail with wild
raven-haired stiffs who beg just one more drink.
One drunk, a former Methodist, becomes a saint
in the Indian church, bugs the plaster man
on the cross with snakes. If his knuckles broke,
he'd see those women wail the graves goodbye.

Goodbye, goodbye, Harlem on the rocks,
so bigoted, you forget the latest joke,
so lonely, you'd welcome a battalion of Turks
to rule your women. What you don't know,
what you will never know or want to learn—
Turks aren't white, Turks are olive, unwelcome
alive in any town. Turks would use
your one dingy park to declare a need for loot.
Turks say bring it, step quickly, lay down and dead.

Here we are when men were nice. This photo, hung
in the New England Hotel lobby, shows them nicer
than pie, agreeable to the warring bands of redskins
who demanded protection money for the price of food.
Now, only Hutterites out north are nice. We hate
them. They are tough and their crops are always good.
We accuse them of idiocy and believe their belief all wrong.

Harlem, your hotel is overnamed, your children
are raggedy-assed but you go on, survive
the bad food from the two cafes and peddle
your hate for the wild who bring you money.
When you die, if you die, will you remember
the three young bucks who shot the grocery up,
locked themselves in and cried for days, we're rich,
help us, oh God, we're rich.

D-Y Bar

The tune is cowboy; the words, sentimental crap.
Farther out, wind is mending sagebrush,
stapling it to earth in rows only a badger

would recommend. Reservoirs are dry,
the sky commands a cloud high
to skip the Breaks bristling with heat
and stunted pine.

In stunted light, Bear Child tells a story
to the mirror. He acts his name out,
creeks muscling gorges fill his glass
with gumbo. The bear crawls on all fours
and barks like a dog. Slithering snake-wise
he balances a nickel on his nose. The effect,
a snake in heat.

We all know our names here. Summer is a poor
season to skip this place or complain
about marauding snakes. Often when wind
is cool off mountains and the flats
are green, cars stop for gas, motors clicking
warm to songs of a junction bar, head down,
the dormant bear.

Arizona Highways

I see her seventeen,
a lady dark, turquoise
on her wrists. The land
astounded by a sweeping rain
becomes her skin. Clouds
begin to mend my broken eyes.
I see her singing by a broken shack,
eyes so black it must be dawn.
I hum along, act sober,
tell her I could love her
if she dressed better, if her father
got a job and beat her more.
Eulynda. There's a name
I could live with. I could
thrash away the nuns, tell them
I adopt this girl, dark,
seventeen, silver on her fingers,
in the name of the father, son,
and me, the holy ghost.
Why not? Mormons do less
with less. Didn't her ancestors
live in cliffs, no plumbing,
just a lot of love and corn?

Me, that's corn, pollen
in her hair. East, south, west, north—
now I see my role—religious.
The Indian politician made her laugh.
Her silver jingled in her throat,
those songs, her fingers busy
on his sleeve. Fathers, forgive me.
She knows me in her Tchindii dream,
always a little pale, too much
bourbon in my nose, my shoes
too clean, belly soft as hers.

I'll move on. My schedule
says Many Farms tomorrow, then
on to Window Rock, and finally home,
that weathered nude, distant
as the cloud I came in on.

The Man from Washington

The end came easy for most of us.
Packed away in our crude beginnings
in some far corner of a flat world,
we didn't expect much more
than firewood and buffalo robes
to keep us warm. The man came down,
a slouching dwarf with rainwater eyes,
and spoke to us. He promised
that life would go on as usual,
that treaties would be signed, and everyone—
man, woman and child—would be inoculated
against a world in which we had no part,
a world of money, promise and disease.

In the American Express Line

Chrysanthemums in her crimson hair,
scattered, baiting, waiting
for the fool's dark hands
to rearrange her life. She claimed
to be the kind of innocent
I could get to know in stages.

She had been to Istanbul,
had known the seedy breath
of genuflecting Turks, the producer

in Crete who imagined her a boy.
How could I refuse: American Express
checks flocked to her willow body,
paper pressed against a fence
on a frumpy day.

Her boyfriend, a nasal drip, touched
my arm, marched her off.
Something he offered made her laugh.
Later I found my wife, browsing
in fields of one drachma postcards.
I touched her hip. The day fired.

Plea to Those Who Matter

You don't know I pretend my dumb.
My songs often wise, my bells could chase
the snow across these whistle-black plains.
Celebrate. The days are grim. Call your winds
to blast these bundled streets and patronize
my past of poverty and 4-day feasts.

Don't ignore me. I'll build my face a different way,
a way to make you know that I am no longer
proud, my name not strong enough to stand alone.
If I lie and say you took me for a friend,
patched together in my thin bones,
will you help me be cunning and noisy as the wind?

I have plans to burn my drum, move out
and civilize this hair. See my nose? I smash it
straight for you. These teeth? I scrub my teeth
away with stones. I know you help me now I matter.
And I—I come to you, head down, bleeding from my smile,
happy for the snow clean hands of you, my friends.

Grandma's Man

That day she threw the goose over the roof
of the cowshed, put her hand to her lips
and sucked, cursing, the world ended. In blood
her world ended though these past twenty years
have healed the bite and that silly goose
is preening in her favorite pillow.

Her husband was a fool. He laughed too long
at lies told by girls whose easy virtue disappeared

when he passed stumble-bum down the Sunday street.
Baled hay in his every forty, cows on his allotted range,
his quick sorrel quarter-horse, all neglected for
the palms of friends. Then, he began to paint LIFE.

His first attempt was all about a goose that bit
the hand that fed it. The obstacles were great.
Insurmountable. His fingers were too quick to grip
the brush right. The sky was always green
the hay spoiled in the fields. In wind,
the rain, the superlative night, images came, geese
skimming to the reservoir. This old man listened.
He got a bigger brush and once painted the cry
of a goose so long, it floated off the canvas
into thin air. Things got better. Sky turned white.
Winter came and he became quite expert at snowflakes.
But he was growing wise, Lord, his hair white as snow.

Funny, he used to say, how mountains are blue
in winter and green in spring. He never ever
got things quite right. He thought a lot about the day
the goose bit Grandma's hand. LIFE seldom came
the shade he wanted. Well, and yes, he died well,
but you should have seen how well his friends took it.

SIMON ORTIZ

Simon Ortiz, born in 1941, is from Acoma, New Mexico. Although his poems are disarmingly informal and colloquial in diction, they are also profoundly moving and filled with mordant irony. His book Going for the Rain *(part of Harper and Row's Native American publishing program) is a collection of short poems describing his odyssey across the country looking for Indians and looking at America. The trip, like Momaday's in* The Way to Rainy Mountain, *has a spiritual dimension. As Ortiz puts it: "A man leaves; he encounters all manners of things. He has adventures, meets people, acquires knowledge, goes different places; he is always looking. Sometimes the travelling is hazardous; sometimes he finds meaning and sometimes he is destitute. But he continues; he must. His travelling is a prayer as well, and he must keep on."* [1]

A Barroom Fragment

He was talking,
"I invited her to Las Vegas,
and when we got to the hotel
she asked for a separate room.
I told her, 'Shit, if you want
a room to yourself, why baby
that's alright, have it.'
I had brought her up there
on a four-million-dollar airplane,
and I told her, 'You can
go across the street
and take a thirty-thousand-dollar bus
back to Burbank.'"
That was Coyote talking.

Washyuma Motor Hotel

Beneath the cement foundations
of the motel, the ancient spirits
of the people conspire sacred tricks.
They tell stories and jokes and laugh
and laugh.

[1] Simon Ortiz, *Going for the Rain* (New York: Harper and Row, 1976), p. xiii.
Simon Ortiz's poems are reprinted with his permission.

The American passerbys
get out of their hot, stuffy cars
at evening, pay their money wordlessly,
and fall asleep without benefit of dreams.
The next morning, they get up,
dress automatically, brush their teeth,
get in their cars and drive away.
They haven't noticed that the cement
foundations of the motor hotel
are crumbling, bit by bit.

The ancient spirits tell stories
and jokes and laugh and laugh.

The Significance of a Veteran's Day

I happen to be a veteran
but you can't tell in how many ways
unless I tell you.

A cold morning waking up on concrete;
I never knew that feeling before,
calling for significance,
and no one answered.

Let me explain it this way
so that you may not go away
without knowing a part of me:

that I am a veteran of at least 30,000 years
when I travelled with the monumental yearning
of glaciers, relieving myself by them,
growing, my children seeking shelter
by the roots of pines and mountains.

When it was that time to build,
my grandfather said, "We cut stone and mixed mud
and ate beans and squash and sang
while we moved ourselves. That's what we did."
And I believe him.

And then later on in the ancient and deep story
of all our nights, we contemplated,
contemplated not the completion of our age,
but the continuance of the universe,
the travelling, not the progress,
but the humility of our being there.

Caught now, in the midst of wars
against foreign disease, missionaries,
canned food, Dick & Jane textbooks, IBM cards,
Western philosophies, General Electric,
I am talking about how we have been able
to survive insignificance.

To & Fro

On the train to California,
a Black porter told me,
"We don't serve Indians hard liquor, chief."
I said, "That's okay, man."
When I got home my wife asked,
"What are you doing back here?"
I said, "I came home."

Actually, I was a fugitive.
I had decided that at 8:00 A.M.
in the East Commons
over scalding coffee, sitting
at an imitation-wood table
as I watched crowds of students
mangle each other before breakfast.

I had several strange moments
thinking of Charles Olson
and language, thinking about a point
in particular the night before
when the night and the connections
were one and the same,
and I had touched a sustaining motion,
realizing the energy that language is
and becomes.

I had to leave California
I told my wife later
but kept secret that dove I heard
one precarious morning
when I was sick and moaned for home,
pushing back the memory of a boy
in Summer morning fields.

GEARY HOBSON

Geary Hobson, a Cherokee-Quapaw-Chickasaw, was born in 1941 in Chicot County, Arkansas. A college professor and administrator, he served as director of the Native American Studies Program at the University of New Mexico before joining the English Department of the University of Oklahoma, where he teaches and coordinates courses in Indian literature.

Hobson writes both fiction and poetry, and is active as a scholar. His current project is compiling a literary and critical history of North and Central American Indian literature. Geary believes that Indian writing should be treated as a separate Anglophone literature. He states, "I feel that Native American literature will one day be recognized as a full-fledged body of literature, not merely as a quaint appendage to mainstream American literature."[1]

Deer Hunting

1.

"God dammit, Al. Are you gonna help me
cut up this deer, or
are you gonna stand there all day
drinking beer and yakking?"
 Knives flash in savage motion
flesh from hide quickly severs
as the two men rip the pelt tail downwards
from the head. The hide but not
the head is kept. Guts spew forth
in a riot of heat and berries and shit,
as is quickly kicked into the trash hole.
 Hooves are whacked off,
and thrown also to the waste hole—
a rotted hallow stump.
But the antler rack is saved,
sawed from the crown with a hand-saw,
trophy of-the hunt,
like gold teeth carried home
from the wars
in small cigar boxes.

---

[1] Hal May, ed., *Contemporary Authors* (Detroit: Gale Research Co., 1987), 122:231. Geary Hobson's poems are printed with his permission.

Men stand around in little groups,
bragging how the deer fell to their rifles
and throw their empties into the stump-hole.
    Al walks to the stump, unzips his pants.
"Hell, Bob, you're so fucking slow,
I could skin ten deer while you're doing one
and I'll show you up just as soon
as I take a piss."
    The hounds,
tired from the slaughter,
watch the men. They whine
for flesh denied them
and turn to pans filled with Purina.

2.

"Now, watch me, ungilisi, grandson,
as I prepare this deer
which the Great Spirit has given to us
for meat."
    The old man hangs the carcass
feet-first from the pecan tree
with gentleness
like the handling of spider-webbing
for curing purposes.
    Slow cuts around the hooves,
quick slices of the knives as
the grandfather and father
part the hide from the meat.
The young boy—now a man—
stands shy and proud,
his initiating kill before him,
like a prayer unexpected,
his face still smeared
with the deer's blood of blessing.
    The hide is taken softly,
the head and antlers brought easily with it,
in a downward pull by the two men.
    Guts in a tumbling rush
fall into the bucket
to be cooked with the hooves
into a strength stew
for the hunting dogs
brothers who did their part in the chase.
    The three men share the raw liver,
eating it to become
part of the deer.

The older man cuts
a small square of muscle
from the deer's dead flank,
and tosses it solemnly into the bushes
behind him, giving back part of the deer's
swiftness
to the place from which it came.
     Softly, thankfully, the old man
breathes to the woods,
and turns and smiles at his grandson,
now become a man.

Lonnie Kramer

The morning is hot and windy.
What more to expect of March
in its last days
than wind and dust?

But this morning I meet
an old ghost from the '60's:
Lonnie Kramer
(bony elbows   skimpy moustache
pimpled face) now as then
Though then executive chairman
of the campus Young Socialist Alliance
who once condemned me
as a capitalist lackey
stating to the assembled true-believers
in an evening meeting
how I craved beer   bourbon shots
and pool games in a railroaders' bar
a scuzzy place patronized by
Pimas   Papagos   bikers
hippies and needle-freaks
He impaled me with the charge
I didn't think constantly
of Marx   Lenin   Che
and the workers of the world
or what national HQ
thought we should do
(when to march   when to strike
when to shit   and what color)
and I guess he was right.

And now   Lonnie
chief regional salesman
of Dutton (or Bratton?) Industries
makers of microwave ovens
and other assorted time-saving gadgets
for the American homemaker
with a territory
"big as all outdoors"
with "the sky as limit."

We talk over old times
though not about national HQ
or Marx and Che
The March wind carries our words
like feathers
toward the city's outskirts
half-heard   and half-listened to
lost in dust and heat.
The frayed elbows of my jacket
are under his close scrutiny
and I see he doesn't approve
my long hair either.

I still know very little
about microwave ovens
even less about Dutton (or Bratton?)
Industries.
But I still like beer   bourbon shots
pool games
I still hang out in scuzzy bars
full of Indians   street-people
and other workers of the world.

A Discussion about Indian Affairs

She was a white woman
from some little town
in one of the Dakotas.
    "I've heard about Cherokees
—everybody's heard about Cherokees—
but I always thought Chickasaws
were some made-up tribe—
one that never existed—
invented by someone like Al Capp,
a word like 'Kickapoo," you know?"

"There's a Kickapoo tribe, too."
I said.   "Oh," she said,
and having nothing more to say
on the subject, said nothing.
   I wondered if we'd ever have
anything to say to one another.

For My Brother and Sister Southwestern Indian Poets

I come from a wet land
        (bayous hills old stomp-dance
        grounds flood-plain delta)
and I never learned to sing for rain.

Buffalo Poem #1
(OR)
ON HEARING THAT A SMALL HERD OF BUFFALO HAS "BROKEN LOOSE" AND IS "RUNNING WILD" AT THE ALBUQUERQUE AIRPORT—SEPTEMBER 26, 1975

—roam on, brothers . . .

Central Highlands, Viet Nam, 1968

1.

An eagle glides above the plain
where mice scurry in a vortex
of smoke and blood.
Wings dip, soar downward
in a clash
of fire
and upheaval
of earth and bone.

2.

You will die, Dull Knife,
and your people,
and your vanquisher's descendants
will weep over their father's deeds.

3.

In the mountains of Viet Nam
the Meo people, too,
will pass
from this world in napalm flashes

and burnt-out hillsides
and all that will be left
to give
will be
the helpless tears
of history future.

4.

The eagle flies blindly
into the smoke of his past.

RAYNA GREEN

Rayna Green (born 1942) is a Cherokee from Oklahoma. She earned a Ph.D. in folklore from Indiana University and currently heads the American Indian Program Office of the Department of History of Science at the Smithsonian. She considers her primary work to be in the field of Native American scientific and technical development. Her poetry, which is notable for its biting wit, has been widely anthologized. She is currently working on a detective novel.

Another Dying Chieftain

he was a braids-and-shades dog soldier
AIM all the way

reduced to telling white women
about coup counting
in a hotel room
late

where they wanted his style
and he wanted the reporters
back again

so he seduced them with lectures
on the degrees of Sioux adoption
trying to make the talk
pass for battle

when the others came in
Indian women and not his tribe
they knew what kind of war was being fought

and one asked
when he was finished
what degree were you adopted in
when he shook his fist at her
it didn't make headlines
there's no good day to die
in these wars

Rayna Green's poems are reprinted with the permission of Indiana University Press from *That's What She Said: Contemporary Poetry and Fiction by Native American Women,* edited by Rayna Green (Bloomington, 1984), pp. 114–17.

Road Hazard

the car-tape machine
plays the music I want
and it is pow-wow trash, a forty-nine
nothing sacred
still, the drums have a way

I forget the other cars
and I am on another highway
north of Talihina
going to the Choctaw all-night sing

Grandma relished
that Choc singing
brush arbor Christian music

and so I stay up all night
and drive for no reason
but the singing
to get somewhere
with the singing
to be out there
in the singing

it's not the booze or pick-ups
that will kill me
on this road

Old Indian Trick

I thought she was white
but she missed her calling
really Indian and fooled me
with all that talk
Not one silence the whole
evening filled
no place to rest my head
All the tequila didn't shut her up
or the crazy ride home either

I thought maybe the danger
would stop her voice
and make her show respect
for the possibilities
there on the road

But she won
making me think she was white
I forgot to shield myself
and she got inside my silence

a good disguise, little sister

hide your thoughts with words
like white girls
so blood, crushed bone, burned flesh
terrify only as ghosts
of brown women's lives

Indian silence
leaves no room to hide
except in dreams
visions of light and spirit
to wipe terror away

Coosaponakeesa (Mary Mathews Musgrove Bosomsworth), Leader of the Creeks, 1700–1783

for Joy Harjo

what kind of lovers could they have been
these colonists

good enough to marry them everyone
or was it something else that made her take them on

all woman
part swamp rat
half horse
she rode through Georgia
It was hers and the Creeks'
and Oglethorpe wanted it all

But she rolled with him too
and kept them at bay
for too long
'til they said
she'd sold out for the goods

the money and velvet was what she loved
sure enough
but Ossabaw and Sapelo and Savannah more

so she fought them with sex and war
and anything that worked
until they rolled over her

The Creeks say Mary came back as Sherman
just to see what they'd taken away
burned to the ground
and returned to her once more

The Creek girls in Oklahoma
laugh like Mary now
wild and good
they'll fight you for it
and make you want everything all over again

no deals this time though
it's all
or nothing

GUS PALMER, JR.

Augustine Palmer, Jr., a Kiowa, was born in Anadarko, Oklahoma, in 1943. He attended the University of Oklahoma as an undergraduate and has done graduate work in English and creative writing at Oklahoma and at Stanford University. Like fellow Kiowa poet Scott Momaday, Palmer has been strongly influenced by Yvor Winters. He is fond of the one-line poem, a form Winters adapted from Chippewa songs. In addition to poetry, Palmer has written, directed, and produced a film entitled Mina. *He also translates Kiowa narratives and writes short fiction.*

Frieze

"A ghost can't whistle"
An owl doesn't talk
But a raven that can sing
That is a different thing

Message to Spring,
or, The Choctaw Virgin Moon

Full being a whole month
being with you.

I count on you
I beautify you
I laud you
I give you my shirt
Dis-assemble the moon

When nights wide awake I cry I describe your radiance, the stars break.
They quake. They groan. They grumble.
Moths breathe fire. They lose their breaths.

If I were you these days, wanton days, I'd resemble Carthage.
I'd grow pyres strong enough to hold Moses.
Mightier than the hills, I should think to rise above the Pyrenees
ranging like an eagle.
Radiant, I would raze the entire Himalayas, if I could. And I do,
knowing me.

Gus Palmer, Jr.'s poems are printed with his permission.

Ask any fool the sky bulges and burns, and I would pretend as frogs
leaping frozen, frantic against the rain. I guess I might live a
thousand years.
With your quiver and dull arrow you hunt me, braving my element.
Yet somewhere, and you may never know
there is a city rich with me.
Don't tell. Don't tell.
Where the city is doom to itself.
And the mouse that coughs tuberculin
is scant in his cold, secret cave.
There, it is there that you must look.
Don't faint. Don't feint.

I am the sky
I am the red
I am the raw melon-moon
your curdling young, rebel blood

•

Noon
where is your shadow?

•

Winter
did I catch you napping there?

For Paolo and Francesca, Lovers, In Cold

The winds I've heard their farthest gale
The fringe of coming cold
Except where limbs that farther blow
A constant fleeter's rail

In dance, in poise, in love reposed
The gangly manor's row
Where thought sufficed a fainter gale
The reeds transfix, then fold

For Theodore Roethke: 1908–1962

I. Quiet while first we court these dreams
Be still so no one hears
Be gracious lest the forceful fraught
The throes of nothing got
Bequeath the ever-joisting scene
T'when time's a meaner team

In earnest sum of sumptuousness
The flagrant wrother, fests

II. Believe with me these minor years
Believe with me of lose
Believe with me and I'll strike down
The dregs of rancor time
Believe with me as I with you
Believe, Believe, Believe
At some point in this strange transport
We'll deign this havoc closed

The Poignant Beast

"In painting the canvas is not a picture."
It is an eye.
In seeing the eye is no mere stone.
It is an ear to fight you with.

In living the artist is no beast.
He is a centaur defeated by love.
Do not be fooled by him,
for he will lead a legion to destroy you.

His is the vast domain.
And he is the creature at its center.
He thrashes in gold and vermillion and brown.

In gold he washes the underside of Earth.
In vermillion he paints heaven's bowels.
His brushes are brazen and clean.
They hold close to his fingers like the marrow of bone.

The underside of the earth is visible and black.
He voyages through it alone.
Terrible is his sheath.
He carries its path scorched white above his head.

Stone Carvers

The dense popularity of stone
wages war against unkempt school children.
So, the carver, disgusted at love, weasels
about how he broke both his legs
when he fell facedown in the sight of Love,
how he hen-pecked her to death.

I don't complain. I use both sides of my eyes
to understand him.
And we compliment one another,
all the way home.

Language and Other Redemptive Things

1. *The Pasture Below Our House*
   It is freshly mowed and
   undulates fearsomely
   in the jumping light of the sun
   so that, strangely, I am filled
   with a strange power I want
   to protect, for it might
   never come again.
   And yes, I have dreamed of you.
   Holding you, I watched those trees
   across the road from our house
   shut their eyes
   and turn every which way.
   I looked through the tree green
   of trees we loved and there was
   more of something there than I
   dreamed.

   2. Sometimes I wrap myself
      in an old overcoat and go wild
      in an open field and let the wind do
      what it wants to me. In possession of
      my powerful Indian medicine, I have nothing
      to fear. See, I often sing
      close to the trees
      and leave them in exactly
      the same way I did when I first came here.
      If they want help, they'll have to ask as men.
      That is all there is to it.

Creek

It is the sky we hear first.
Its cocoon color washed out several times until it comes
cool white like the trunk of a stripped cottonwood,
the kind we saw split into firewood all those years.

The sky is somewhere above.
The commonest velvet of these leaves rubs off dusty,
like off moth wings.
Down in a creek it is the most ordinary of days.
Volatile, lithe as a deer, you move inside brambles
raking your arms.
Barely visible now, we are in a furrow of moisture and
green, barely moving, shut in next to the creek
and smelling it, smelling ourselves in it.

Waiting

Having taken
off its armored head
we spread the salmon
on the kitchen table
so that at once
it was bright
and smoothed down.

With animal fat oozing
it lay flat and heavier than anything
off the gaff end.
Its broken, contaminated eye
swam in full round view
where we sat and
back of us.

The room hummed quietly.
At length, it seemed
a grown man lay before us,
ruined and naked.
We regarded it closely,
sure what happened next
might change our lives
forever.

Dawn, rosey and bright, poured
in the back screen door that was
frozen in place.
We could find no words. A stench heavy
as crude oil filled the room,
live and deadly.

An Eclipse

See, my son yells,
the body of the moon
has eaten through
the sun.

I think to myself:
What do the people in this town care.
Oscillating slowly, it will finally be
enough of something and sink
like the head of a man on the horizon.
Like a red fruit we will talk about
in the stillness of night
in the unmoving unmoveable nature
of ourselves, as we do when confronting
the stillborn.

Right now above, I say.
I say, right now in the dying presence
of the sun, we must dance once more.
We must dance before it turns into
the great solitary stone
we fear.
But more humane, lovelier
than you or me.

Legend People

Possessed of a kind of magic,
we command a river out of these rocks.
All day the errant hawk sails over sacred grounds.
He too is in possession of power, with ready beak
and searching yellow eyes.
Alert as deer, we move into the full circle
of field light, going deliberately, sometimes
not. Other times we point northward
as if to warn our children,
as if to warn.

The iron hard land holds bones in concealed layers,
now exposed to wind, other times to the sun's
bleaching power. They are the bones of our mothers,
our brothers, our sisters.
While we move into the deep remembered woods, we can hear

the tall men coming, coming as promised.
I can tell you they will come with their
powder and lead. I can tell you.

It is like looking through a fog.
To see the other side of these woods requires something
our common knowledge lacks.
Men are in the shadows waiting, waiting.
We know they have come closer this time because
we smell the burning. Like a knife it sinks in our guts.

Listen. We know they are here.
We crawl from them unafraid, our hearts
beating like the pond whose icy edge is broken
and breathes.
We scatter because the deer taught us how.

Haunted now, you break with tradition,
pretend as bear whose blood-red eyes watch and become power,
create a story the men are themselves hunted.
Mutants. All of us.
Now brown tufts of fur hang, dragging burned-out ends
that flame up when they vibrate or touch the bushes
we hide in.
You lumber through trees, shafts of light.
Know me. Who I am. Alone.
Wounded.

Soon wind will crash through the trees.
At dawn, winter will bring its low music.
We prefer the deep recesses of the woods this time.
Where pools of light gather and stand all afternoon.
We clench together in the bracken and bramble,
now that we know it is useless to wait.
We have come here nameless.
Night will bring us closer to the caves.
Lifting our heads, shadows will point the way, and
when the moon falls in pieces, you will be there
among us.
You will see everything, how it happened and know.
The moon will see to it. You will see we have
come this far,
this far.

LANCE HENSON

Lance Henson, a Cheyenne, was born in Washington, D.C., in 1944 and raised in Oklahoma and Texas. He did his undergraduate work at Oklahoma College of Liberal Arts, Chickasha, and received an M.A. in creative writing from Tulsa University. As an ex-Marine, he was inducted into the Dog Soldiers, a Cheyenne military society.

Henson's aesthetic theory is drawn from traditional Cheyenne philosophy, which he blends with ideas drawn from Jung, Hawthorne, Melville, and Twain. He feels that since European Americans have "wilfully deserted any truth-based philosophy," the hope for America lies in the mysterious power it can draw from its darker peoples, particularly Native Americans: "For a century and a half this country . . . has been under the watchful eye of a great natural power, a power drawn from a people reborn through death. . . . Symbols and signals that remain among a once dying race have a peculiar resurrective essence."[1] Noting Jung's observation that, "In dreams of white men, the forbidden is often represented by a colored man," Henson believes that the red man has the ability to pull the white man from "the fetters of adolescence into the dark mysterious world of manhood."[2]

Henson's first book of poems, Keeper of Arrows, *was subtitled* Poems for the Cheyenne. *His poems are that, since they use traditional Cheyenne symbols and subjects, but they are also poems for all of us, teaching us to reestablish the close relationship with nature that the Cheyennes had. "Cheyenne Winter" starts with the image of the albino buffalo, traditionally a sacred animal to the Plains tribes. The Cheyenne chiefs wore white buffalo robes, and the animal was mystically tied to the tribe's most powerful medicine. The appearance of the albino buffalo was auspicious to the Cheyenne: it brought sacred messages to them, and, if it appeared in times of trouble, it portended rescue. The central image in "flock" compares blowing snow to a herd of albino buffalos.*

"extinction" deals with the cultural assimilation of the Indian into American society. After surviving—barely—the onslaughts of the cavalry, who massacred Cheyenne women and children at the battles of Sand Creek and the Washita, and the destruction of the buffalo they depended on for food, clothing, and shelter, the Cheyennes face today an even greater threat to their survival: assimilation. Fewer and fewer Cheyennes

---

[1] Lance Henson, "Modern Indian Poetry: A Preface," unpublished manuscript, p. 2.
[2] Ibid.

Lance Henson's poems are reprinted here with his permission.

*can speak the Cheyenne language (at one time children at Indian board-
ing schools were forbidden to speak their native tongues), and fewer and
fewer know the old customs. Today the Cheyennes, like other tribes, are
trying to revive as much of the old culture as they can, but it is a difficult task in the face of the distractions and blandishments of twentieth-
century American life.*

*The next group of poems deals with the peyote ritual, the central reli-
gious ceremony of traditionalist Indians today. Peyote is a small, spineless
cactus, of which the round, buttonlike top is cut off and eaten in the ritual. It contains stimulants related to strychnine and sedatives related to
morphine and acts as a hallucinogen, generally producing kaleidoscopic
color visions.[3] Although it is not habit-forming, it is classed as a dangerous drug and its use is forbidden to the American populace at large. As an
exception to the law, the members of the Native American Church are
permitted to use the drug in their ritual. The church is Christian in theol-
ogy, and the peyote ritual is a form of communion, with the peyote taking
the place of communion wine, though much stronger.[4]*

*The last group of poems were published originally in Italy, where
Lance Henson is very popular.*

cheyenne winter

albino buffalo
stands in white void

there is no applause
for the hawk
flying into the sun

winter
                winter

the mole
sleeps

extinction

along the bleak
        sun
            brow

day goes out alone

[3]Peter Farb, *Man's Rise to Civilization* (New York: Avon Books, 1969), p. 340.
[4]Lately, Vine Deloria and others have advocated a return of the Native American Church
to the old religion of the Plains Indians.

we lift our eyes to
the same
nothingness

in my hands i hold

the last
          aching
                 sparrow

who
remembers
me

flock

across the road
ice huddles against the trees

there is only a whisper of
leaves among the cottonwoods

and over the joyless valley

snow moves
like an ancient herd

bay poem

where from the watch towers
the rust of
shipwrecks
shine

bar
where the sailor
remembered
peace and
laughed

epitaph soaked
        sponges
across bars

endless
        damp
streets

lovely moonshine
at
          2
a m

on the edge
of
rain

impressions of the peyote ritual

oh heavenly father
bless us your children
as we sit around the
bone white moon

hear us now as we
turn to your face
look behind our words
as we pray

give us what is pure
bring us from the
half sound

heal us from our wounds

father

i call you from within the gourd sound
i call you from my smoke
i call my whole self which lives in you

you answer from everywhere

holy spirit of no place
forever soul

pity me
give me
light

prairie wind
let your midnight
song find me among
blessed ones

bone flute
sound of endless
humanity
show me how i may
better know my
mother earth

sound of my father
            i
                pray
bring peace to all
                    cheyenne

great spirit
now we are one
long have we suffered
without your wisdom

our water
corn
we share with you

rope of leather

river

                brother sun

dusted eagle wing
sweet prairie medicine
comfort me your lonely son

i listen to the river of
ghosts and weep for my
brothers who call through
the wind

maheo

it is good to see you
sitting among them

our smoke has gone four ways
it calls for us

my brothers smile with tears
we may never meet again

eagle of fire whose
wings are scented cedar

moon of forever who
guards the sacred seed

keep us strong
to meet the
coming days

oklahoma twilights, I

near wewoka in the first storm i have witnessed since
returning from the east coast

i watch to the north dark thunderclouds steeped in
furrows of wind

a long hungered autumn loosens its clouds upon the earth

plagued by a winterfull of whispers
i feel my life watching me

from a swaying treeline . . .

counting losses in october

a wind grows out of itself from the north
follows the flight of geese
the first i have witnessed this season
over my grandfathers land

mid october
i keep the sweat fire coals glowing into dusk
thinking of brother songs

evening in a dark shawl watches from a grove
of elm trees

there is the joy of a small wind rising
and the unforgiving darkness of night

dream of home

the house grown cold
drifts of last nights darkness gather
inside this clove of silence

the hour goes by in its voice of bright shell

trying to sleep i see the fragile leaf of a face
of a woman looking across a field

it is spring

a small hand fits gently into her own
there is a tiny whispering on their shoulders
and they walk home together

for soft dresser[1]

when we sing
we are not playing
we are praying for life

    owl song
    ojibway

the horned owl thats night of hunting ends
in the bare and dying elm behind my house
stares toward dawn and stops singing

the suns great heart with all its knowings
passes the hour alone

in the northeast pasture
a shadow of song pauses in morning air

the white stone marker of soft dresser leans
from its shadow

as i lean from mine.

[1] ma ha it

CHARLOTTE DECLUE

Charlotte DeClue, an Osage, was born in Enid, Oklahoma, in 1946. Her poems have appeared in numerous literary journals in this country and Europe. She has had two chapbooks published: Without Warning *(Bowling Green Station, N.Y.: Strawberry Press, 1985) and* Ten Good Horses *(Kansas City, Mo.: Howling Dog Press, 1990). Her husband, Ben Carnes, a Choctaw, is a prison activist, the winner of the 1987 Oklahoma Human Rights Award.*

DeClue's poetry is marked by its skillful use of the conversational idiom and its trenchant wit.

Mmmmm. . . . Whiteman's Powwow

(Kansas City, 1989)

> Star quilt
> hanging above empty chutes
> mirrors sky.
> Kansas farms to the south,
> big city blur to the north.
> Misty river roads,
> tailgates & 6. beer,
> mark midsummer in a place
> where we scratch for work
> & a little bit of ground.
> All we know
> is motel room is guaranteed,
> groceries
> if we put up a tent.
> "Mountain men," an Osage girl
> says, even smell like weasels,
> pose beside backward teepee.
> While small town Missouri woman,
> camera, beads & feathers
> around her neck
> whines
> about Oklahoma people
> walking away
> with all the competition money.

Charlotte DeClue's poems are printed with her permission.

She is consoled
by the red, white & blue
blanket
she wins in a raffle.
Surburban boys
with water-filled condoms
& plastic M-16's
aim for my new white straw Bradford
surprised
to find a "mama" under the brim.
          Tug at my ear
signals me to listen.
Bright yellow half-face,
smile like a rattler
snag corner of my mouth.
They'll be a '9
when the dance turns RED.

Young Wife

          It's Friday night, the Panhandle
and poker at the Western.
Words out the company men are gonna play,
means high stakes.
The drillers can afford to lose,
but our men, well
I told my man if he goes down there
don't bother comin' home.
He's young but he's smart,
he'll be home.
          Lying in bed
silence next to me.
Lump under my pillow is the pistol
for protection.
Outside the wind,
always the wind,
moves like a restless man.
          The woman next door is crying,
can hear her through paper thin walls
separating our lives.
Her name is Wanda.
Just got to know her last week
chasing sheets
through the dust and tumbleweeds.

I caught her staring at me
kind of sad and knowing.
        I got a baby on the way
(a baby with a baby, Wanda says)
come due the middle of winter.
But I'm not afraid anymore,
afraid of the baby,
afraid of the wind.
It's all a part of me now.

(for Lisa
and those Northern girls)

Mr. Jack slurs your speech
but
"you never listen
anyway
damn you."
No one listens anymore, do they?
"When did you ever make me happy?"
Only fools want someone
who makes them unhappy.
"Get out"
damn you
anyway.
"When did you stand up for me?"
I put you to bed
more times than I have memory.
And laid there
and ached
and ached.
(The cops are nervous
standing there
amidst scattered toys
and broken dishes.
They're trained to know
DOMESTICS ARE DEADLY.)
Fight for me
demand me back.
Demand the wind
the flint & alabaster
the shell for my ears.
"Damn all of you."
No one knows anymore
what it's like
to be worth ten good horses.

Out on the "run" [1]

Smokey came down the hill overlookin'
the lake. Ruts and ravines hammered into his
face. He pointed to a place not far from where
we stood.
    "Over there. . . . best fishin' around."
Then he lowered his bow (shot four rounds
into its head) and laid the body onto the
earth.
    "Here. . . . doeskin," he said handing me
a fur that would make those Park Avenue women
scream with envy.
The softest skin, pale like winter grass,
caressed my hips. (Later I would hang tails
to chase when I kicked my knee.)
    "Far out, Uncle," I said, and went back
to my broom, heart pounding.
Shawnees always did come down off hills
like that.

Dialectic

*"Get your mind outa the gutter,
Head-Cutter." . . . Kansas City.*

TV blares
thru rigged antenna,
EVENING NEWS:
soft porn king
draped in american flag/first amendment rights
debates woman
with organizational skills
who sighs thru accusations
"you're just mad
because you don't look that way."
    They never ask
the right ones
who have been there and back,
just off the Greyhound,
red clay stained heels,
the street lookin' mean at you,

[1] The "run" is the passage outside a prison cell.

a sister screamin "this ain't oklahoma,
girl,
this is the fuckin' DMZ."
And he did say
they wanted innocence
at 50 bucks an hour.
All it takes
is lowerin' your face.

Separation

The women at work
tolerate my ways,
never remembering the days of the week,
setting the clock
by the first robin,
the first rays of morning sun
streaming across half-empty bed.
There's nothing in the mirror
I recognize anymore.
No simmering pots of chili
in the kitchen,
no beans to soak and salt.
No cast iron skillet
waiting for floured hands
patting out dough
with a pinch of cinnamon.
My son worries
about me,
the way I push food away,
my one syllable sentences,
sorrow that comes and goes
behind my eyes.
I mark the calendar,
Raccoon Moon waning,
winter coming.
I think it will never end.
This leaving
comes hard.

Hookin' Honkies . . .

A young Cheyenne woman
signs the Lord's prayer
hands sweeping across her chest

       . . . for thine is the kingdom
while the audio man tries competing
with the popcorn machine
    she makes a fist
         . . . and the power
smell of cotton candy and oil
from the Tilt-A-Whirl
make me want a beer
    another hand comes out
    this time across the sky
         . . . and the glory
I call for a round
but no one hears me
(at $1.75 a draw
everyone's waiting
for the beer garden to open).
Last year Alice
made me sit thru Amazing Grace
for thinking upon the thighs
of a potential snag
who bills himself as an international star.
I know not to complain
    an arm comes out
    envisioning the horizon
         . . . forever
the show barely went on
the fancy dancer
having locked his feathers in the car
along with the keys
    we will go on though
         . . . and ever
parking lot
looking more like a stand-off
between Kiowa and Pawnee clans,
one of the elders having been informed
by a woman from California
he is the father of her 21 year old son
    hands go down politely
    eyes lowered
(now that I know)
         . . . A-M-E-N.

LINDA HOGAN

Linda Hogan (born 1947) is a Chickasaw from Gene Autry, Oklahoma. She is currently teaching in the English Department at the University of Colorado. Although best known for her poetry, she has also written a novel, A Crate of Wooden Birds. *She has been active politically, especially in the peace movement and in the American Indian Movement.*

She says of her writing: "Literature has been an important part of my growing-up experience. My grandparents and my father kept the history and legends of their people alive for me by re-creating it orally. Out of the stories and out of the remembered landscape of Oklahoma come the poems which make up this book." [1]

turtle

I'm dreaming the old turtle back.
He walks out of the water,
slow,
that shell with the water on it
the sun on it,
dark as the wet trunks of hackberry trees.

In water
the world is breathing,
in the silt.
There are fish
and their blood changes easy
warm to cold.

And the turtle,
small yellow bones of animals inside
are waking
to shine out from his eyes.
Wake up the locusts whose dry skins
are still sleeping on the trees.

[1] *Calling Myself Home* (Greenfield Center, N.Y., Greenfield Review Press, 1978), back cover.

Linda Hogan's poems are reprinted with her permission from her books *Calling Myself Home* (Greenfield Center, N.Y.: Greenfield Review Press, 1978), *Savings* (Minneapolis: Coffee House Press, 1988) and *Seeing Through the Sun* (Amherst: University of Massachusetts Press, 1985).

276

We should open his soft parts,
pull his shells apart
and wear them on our backs
like old women who can see the years
back through his eyes.

Something is breathing in there.
Wake up, we are women.
The shells are on our backs.
We are amber,
the small animals
are gold inside us.

Celebration: Birth of a Colt

When we reach the field
she is still eating
the heads of yellow flowers
and pollen has turned her whiskers
gold. Lady,
her stomach bulges out,
the ribs have grown wide.
We wait,
our bare feet dangling
in the horse trough,
warm water
where goldfish brush
our smooth ankles.
We wait
while the liquid breaks
down Lady's dark legs
and that slick wet colt
like a black tadpole
darts out
beginning at once
to sprout legs.
She licks it to its feet,
the membrane still there,
red,
transparent
the sun coming up shines through,
the sky turns bright with morning
and the land
with pollen blowing off the corn,
land that will always own us,
everywhere it is red.

Heritage

From my mother, the antique mirror
where I watch my face take on her lines.
She left me the smell of baking bread
to warm fine hairs in my nostrils,
she left the large white breasts that weigh down
my body.

From my father I take his brown eyes,
the plague of locusts that leveled our crops,
they flew in formation like buzzards.

From my uncle the whittled wood
that rattles like bones
and is white
and smells like all our old houses
that are no longer there. He was the man
who sang old chants to me, the words
my father was told not to remember.

From my grandfather who never spoke
I learned to fear silence.
I learned to kill a snake
when begging for rain.

And grandmother, blue-eyed woman
whose skin was brown,
she used snuff.
When her coffee can full of black saliva
spilled on me
it was like the brown cloud of grasshoppers
that leveled her fields.
It was the brown stain
that covered my white shirt.
That sweet black liquid like the food
she chewed up and spit into my father's mouth
when he was an infant.
It was the brown earth of Oklahoma
stained with oil.
She said tobacco would purge your body of poisons.
It has more medicine than stones and knives
against your enemies.

That tobacco is the dark night that covers me.

She said it is wise to eat the flesh of deer
so you will be swift and travel over many miles.

She told me how our tribe has always followed a stick
that pointed west
that pointed east.
From my family I have learned the secrets
of never having a home.

Coyote

Steel jaws are tense to clamp shut.
The man is leaving,
the small coyote comes sniffing
soft, soft
feathers from the sky go out quiet like wings.

Such fragile things we all are,
such bones,
such silk nests of hair, fine nerves
touching the smooth beads of vertebrae
that string us together.
Coyote with invisible breath
calling for snow and wind.

Now the evergreen is turning slowly
from your eyes. Something, a bird,
goes up in the air.

Coyote, you weren't much,
nothing more than a shadow with eyes,
a wisp of air waiting to leave
through the thin bones.

All of us have stolen something
in the night
the long night ending in sweat,
the blackest sweat
of morning on the ground.

Mosquitoes

To keep them from you,
paint yourself
red as the natives.
They will not drink
blood exposed to air
only pure blood
embedded deep in flesh.

If you hate them
hum D minor, the breeding song.
They will be drawn to you,
forgetting to mate
and loving only the sound
of your voice.

Or when one lands
drinking at the rivers of your arm,
make a fist, clenched
and pulsing blood into the thin needle
of mosquito until it swells
with your life and bursts
red into air.

I will not sleep with nets,
burn a yellow light
or citron candle.
When one hums silently
around my ears,
bends its knees upon my arm,
I will be still as a stone
at the edge of water,
watching my blood carried into air.

All Winter

In winter I remember
how the white snow
swallowed those who came before me.
They sing from the earth.
This is what happened to the voices.
They have gone underground.

I remember how the man named Fire
carried a gun. I saw him
burning.
His ancestors live in the woodstove
and cry at night and are broken.
This is what happens to fire.
It consumes itself.

In the coldest weather, I recall
that I am in every creature
and they are in me.
My bones feel their terrible ache
and want to fall open

in fields of vanished mice
and horseless hooves.

And I know how long it takes
to travel the sky,
for buffalo are still living
across the drifting face of the moon.

These nights the air is full of spirits.
They breathe on windows.
They are the ones that leave fingerprints
on glass when they point out
the things that happen,
the things we might forget.

The New Apartment: Minneapolis

The floorboards creak.
The moon is on the wrong side of the building,

and burns remain
on the floor.

The house wants to fall down
the universe when earth turns.

It still holds the coughs of old men
and their canes tapping on the floor.

I think of Indian people here before me
and how last spring white merchants hung an elder

on a meathook and beat him
and he was one of The People.

I remember this war
and all the wars

and relocation like putting the moon in prison
with no food and that moon already a crescent,

but be warned, the moon grows full again
and the roofs of this town are all red

and we are looking through the walls of houses
at people suspended in air.

Some are baking, with flour on their hands,
or sleeping on floor three, or getting drunk.

I see the business men who hit their wives
and the men who are tender fathers.

There are women crying or making jokes.
Children are laughing under beds.

Girls in navy blue robes talk on the phone all night
and some Pawnee is singing 49's, drumming the table.

Inside the walls
world changes are planned, bosses overthrown.

If we had no coffee,
cigarettes or liquor,

says the woman in room 12,
they'd have a revolution on their hands.

Beyond walls are lakes and plains,
canyons and the universe;

the stars are the key
turning in the lock of night.

Turn the deadbolt and I am home.
I have walked dark earth,

opened a door to nights where there are no apartments,
just drumming and singing;

The Duck Song, The Snake Song,
The Drunk Song.

No one here remembers the city
or has ever lost the will to go on.

Hello aunt, hello brothers, hello trees
and deer walking quietly on the soft red earth.

Wall Songs

The Southern jungle is a green wall.
It grows over the roads
men have hacked away
that they may keep things separate
that they may pass through life
and not be lost in it.

There are other walls
to keep the rich and poor apart
and they rise up like teeth out of the land
snapping, Do Not Enter.
Do not climb the wire fences

or cross ledges embedded with green
and broken glass.

These walls have terrible songs
that will never stop singing
long after the walls have collapsed.

On one side of the wall there is danger.
On the other side
is danger.

There is a song
chanting from out of the past,
voices of my evicted grandmothers
walking a death song
a snow song
wrapped in trade cloth
out of Mississippi.

Open the cloth
and I fall out.

And the confines of this flesh
were created by my grandfather's song:
No Whites May Enter Here.

My own walls are smooth river stones.
They sing at night
with the beat of crickets.
They stand firm at 5 a.m.
when the talking world wants to invade
my skin
which is the real life
of love and sorrow.

My skin. Sometimes a lover
and I turn our flesh to bridges
and the air between us disappears
like in the jungle
where I am from.
Tropical vines grow together, lovers,
over roadways men have slashed,
surviving
the wounds of those lost inside
and the singing of machetes.

May all walls be like those of the jungle,
filled with animals
singing into the ears of night.

Let them be
made of the mysteries further in
in the heart, joined with the lives of all,
all bridges of flesh,
all singing,
all covering the wounded land
showing again, again
that boundaries are all lies.

The Truth Is

In my left pocket a Chickasaw hand
rests on the bone of the pelvis.
In my right pocket
a white hand. Don't worry. It's mine
and not some thief's.
It belongs to a woman who sleeps in a twin bed
even though she falls in love too easily,
and walks along with hands
in her own empty pockets
even though she has put them in others
for love not money.

About the hands, I'd like to say
I am a tree, grafted branches
bearing two kinds of fruit,
apricots maybe and pit cherries.
It's not that way. The truth is
we are crowded together
and knock against each other at night.
We want amnesty.

Linda, girl, I keep telling you
this is nonsense
about who loved who
and who killed who.

Here I am, taped together
like some old civilian conservation corps
passed by from the great depression
and my pockets are empty.
It's just as well since they are masks
for the soul, and since coins and keys
both have the sharp teeth of property.

Girl, I say,
it is dangerous to be a woman of two countries.

You've got your hands in the dark
of two empty pockets. Even though
you walk and whistle like you aren't afraid
you know which pocket the enemy lives in
and you remember how to fight
so you better keep right on walking.
And you remember who killed who.
For this you want amnesty
and there's that knocking on the door
in the middle of the night.

Relax, there are other things to think about.
Shoes for instance.
Now those are the true masks of the soul.
The left shoe
and the right one with its white foot.

JOY HARJO

Joy Harjo, a Creek, was born in Tulsa, Oklahoma, in 1951. She currently teaches in the English Department at the University of Arizona. She has published four books of poetry: The Last Song, What Moon Drove Me To This, She Had Some Horses, *and* In Mad Love and War. *She is also an artist and filmmaker. Her poetry is noteworthy for its lyricism and daring use of metaphor.*

Anchorage

for Audre Lorde

This city is made of stone, of blood, and fish.
There are Chugatch Mountains to the east
and whale and seal to the west.
It hasn't always been this way, because glaciers
who are ice ghosts create oceans, carve earth
and shape this city here, by the sound.
They swim backwards in time.

Once a storm of boiling earth cracked open
the streets, threw open the town.
It's quiet now, but underneath the concrete
is the cooking earth,
                    and above that, air
which is another ocean, where spirits we can't see
are dancing   joking   getting full
on roasted caribou, and the praying
goes on, extends out.

Nora and I go walking down 4th Avenue
and know it is all happening.
On a park bench we see someone's Athabascan
grandmother, folded up, smelling like 200 years
of blood and piss, her eyes closed against some
unimagined darkness, where she is buried in an ache
in which nothing makes
                              sense.

We keep on breathing, walking, but softer now,
the clouds whirling in the air above us.
What can we say that would make us understand
better than we do already?
Except to speak of her home and claim her
as our own history, and know that our dreams
don't end here, two blocks away from the ocean
where our hearts still batter away at the muddy shore.

And I think of the 6th Avenue jail, of mostly Native
and Black men, where Henry told about being shot at
eight times outside a liquor store in L.A., but when
the car sped away he was surprised he was alive,
no bullet holes, man, and eight cartridges strewn
on the sidewalk
            all around him.

Everyone laughed at the impossibility of it,
but also the truth. Because who would believe
the fantastic and terrible story of all of our survival
those who were never meant
                        to survive?

Night Out

I have seen you in the palms of my hands
late nights in the bar
                just before the lights
are about to be turned on. You are powerful horses
by then, not the wrinkled sacks of thin, mewing
spirit,
        that lay about the bar early in the day
                    waiting for minds and bellies.
You are the ones who slapped Anna on the back,
    told her to drink up
        that it didn't matter anyway.
You poured Jessie another Coors, and another one
                            and another.
            Your fingers were tight around hers
        because she gave herself to you.
    Your voice screamed out from somewhere in the
darkness
        another shot, anything to celebrate this deadly
        thing called living. And Joe John called out to bring

another round, to have another smoke, to dance dance it good
because tomorrow night is another year—

in your voice.

I have heard you in my ownself.
And have seen you in my own past vision.

Your hearts float out in cigarette

smoke, and your teeth are broken and scattered in my hands.
It doesn't end
For you are multiplied by drinkers, by tables, by jukeboxes
by bars.
You fight to get out of the sharpest valleys cut down into
the history of living bone.

And you fight to get in.

You are the circle of lost ones

our relatives.

You have paid the cover charge thousands of times over
with your lives

and now you are afraid

you can never get out.

What I Should Have Said

There's nothing that says you can't
call. I spend the weekdays teaching
and moving my children from breakfast
to bedtime. What else, I feel like a traitor
telling someone else things I can't tell
to you. What is it that keeps us together?
Fingertip to fingertip, from Santa Fe
to Albuquerque?
I feel bloated with what I should say
and what I don't. We drift and drift, with
few storms of heat inbetween the motions.
I love you. The words confuse me.
Maybe they have become a cushion
keeping us in azure sky and in flight
not there, not here.
We are horses knocked out with tranquilizers
sucked into a deep deep sleeping for the comfort
and anesthesia death. We are caught between
clouds and wet earth
and there is no motion

either way

no life
to speak of.

Alive

The hum of the car
is deadening.
It could sing me
to sleep.

I like to be sung to:
deep-throated music
of the south, horse songs,
of the bare feet sound
of my son walking in his sleep.

Or wheels turning,
spinning
spinning.

Sometimes I am afraid
of the sound
of soundlessness.
Like driving away from you
as you watched me wordlessly
from your sunglasses.
Your face opened up then,
a dark fevered bird.
And dived into me.
No sound of water
but the deep, vibrating
echo
        of motion.

I try to touch myself.
There is a field
of talking blood
that I have not been able
to reach,
not even with knives,
not yet.

"I tried every escape",
she told me. "Beer and wine
never worked. Then I
decided to look around, see
what was there. And I saw myself
naked. And alive. Would you
believe that?
Alive."

Alive. This music rocks
me. I drive the interstate,
watch faces come and go on either
side. I am free to be sung to;
I am free to sing. This woman
can cross any line.

nila northSun

nila northSun was born in Nevada in 1951. She is Shoshone on her mother's side, Chippewa on her father's. As is common among Indians, she associates herself more closely with her mother's people.

northSun has published three volumes of poetry: Diet Pepsi & Nacho Cheese; Small Bones, Little Eyes *(with Jim Sagel); and* Coffee, Dust Devils, and Old Rodeo Bulls. *She favors the e.e. cummings style of punctuation and capitalization, and like cummings she employs a conversational tone and displays a keen sense of humor, sharp eye for detail, and original way of looking at things.*

up & out

we total it up for
income tax
hoping to get a little
something back
but it seems we've moved ourselves
out of the poverty level
we made more money than
we've ever made before
but felt poorer
we made better money cause we
moved to the city
left the reservation where
there were no jobs
the city had jobs but it also
had high rent high food high medical
high entertainment high gas
we made better money but it
got sucked up
by the city by cable tv by
sparklettes water by laundromats
by lunches in cute places
by drinking in quaint bars instead
of at home like we did on the reservation
there we lived in gramma's old house
no rent

nila northSun's poems are reprinted with her permission from *Small Bones, Little Eyes,* by nila northSun and Jim Sagel (Fallon, Nev.: Duck Down Press, 1982).

the wood stove saved electricity &
heating bills
we only got one tv channel but we
visited with relatives more
there was no place to eat on the res
except a pool hall with chips & coke
there was only one movie house in town
& nothing good ever showed
we got government commodities that tasted
like dog food but it was free
we got government doctors those that
graduated last in their class
but it was free
if a car broke down there was always
the old pick up truck or a cousin with
a little mechanical know-how
god how I hated living on the reservation
but now
it doesn't look so bad.

nevada

dust & cracked earth
pickups jacked up standing 8 ft tall
guns in the rack on the rear window
CB antennas wagging
those caps with john deere or cat emblems
bumper stickers that say
eat more beef or
cowboys do it better
saltgrass growing up thru asphalt roads
tumbleweeds stuck in barbed wire
the smell of cow manure
country music on the only station
mosquitos buzzing & biting
jackrabbits squashed in the road
broken bottles glittering in
the sand and dirt
bugs all over the windshield & grill
hills like the humps of old rodeo bulls
& the bluest skies this side of heaven.

barrel-racer cowboy chaser

small farm town girl
never left nevada
reads *glamour* magazine
so she won't be bypassed
when it comes to the
latest styles
trouble is she only sees
the old ones left in the
laundermat
she thinks the heavy black
eyeliner & bleached hair
make her look her best
it probably does
thick pancake make-up tries
to hide her acne & scars
looks like a guy in drag
no offense to guys in drag
cruises the strip in
her mother's pickup truck
bumper sticker says
cowgirls are kiss-a-bull
whistles & shouts to the
same old gang
had a baby at 14 years
3 miscarriages since
reads *true confessions* &
can identify with every other story
19 years old
she'll never wiggle her hot pants
for anybody but the local cowboys.

the paper

the old woman told me:

i 'member my dad used to
tell us kids this story
he said long time ago
a indian was walking on
a trail
there was a paper

laying on the ground
but he didn't pick it up
instead a whiteman
walking on the trail picked
it up
that's why whitemen learned
how to read & write
indians were dumb
if he picked up the paper
we would be smart
that's what my dad
always told us
that's why we have to
work for those people
if only we picked up that
paper
we'd have the factories
we'd be the bosses &
everything.

be careful

in ponema
there still are witches
people with power
people with strong medicine
they can make
you sick or
lame or kill you
you can't take pictures of
their medicine lodge
your camera will break
you cannot cross
in front of them
you will lose your step
hang a little mirror
on your clothing then
if they should try to
cast bad medicine on you
it will reflect back.

i was thinking about death again

there's so many ways to do it
accidentally or on purpose

cancer & cars get most i guess
people have definite opinions
of ways they'd like to die
if they had to die that is
jumping from high places
letting your body momentarily fly
down
or sleeping pills for that
final good long rest with no worries
i don't understand shooting oneself
you could miss & hurt yourself
or hanging
i don't even like tight collars
or rough hickies
& what about those weirdos that
pour gasoline & set themselves on fire
that would be most gruesome of all to
feel your own flesh sizzle like bacon &
blood shooting thru your veins like drano
nope not for me
to grow old & die in your sleep
that always sounded good
as long as you were happy being old
in the first place
that being old didn't mean loneliness
or broken hips or arthritis or deafness
or blindness or malfunctioning innards
too bad it couldn't be easy for everyone
a good life
& then a good death
& then who knows what happens after that

i'm glad i don't believe in hell

another one bites the dust

he's a pretty good looking indian
about 24 years old
his waist length hair is adorned
with a couple nice feathers
he wears a cowboy shirt & jeans
next to his beaded buckle
hangs a knife in a buckskin sheath
walking in his scuffed boots he
moves like nobody would stand in
his way

like he's a mean mother
but he's small bones and not very tall
still there is a feeling
he has a lot of energy & is not
a fair fighter
so far in his short life
he has fathered 3 children
the oldest is seven
he doesn't know any of them
for some reason girls want to
have his children
he has totaled 4 cars
with the most damage to himself
being a broken ankle
his passengers have not been
as lucky but lived to tell of
riding the reservation roads
with this crazy indian
the fights in his life are too
numerous & too much the same
he loses & he wins & usually can't
even remember the next day
what has happened the bloody
ripped shirts & dirty scabs
being the only reminder
of course he drinks too much
& scores smoke whenever he can
he got his regular bunch of
rowdy friends a white bunch
& a indian bunch though he doesn't
mix the two
he's really like so many
i've known
they more or less
fit the same description
they usually die young
like a pool cue to the back
of the head
or a jealous girlfriend with
a gun
or taking a curve too drunkenly fast
an action packed indian with no
goals or hopes or aspirations
like so many i've known

RICHARD AITSON

Richard Aitson was born in Anadarko, Oklahoma, in 1953. He is the youngest of the Kiowa writers, an impressive group. Momaday is the dean, born in 1934; others are Russell Bates, Gus Palmer, Jr., and playwright Haney Geiogamah, who were all born in the forties.

Aitson's poetry is characterized by an Indian kind of surrealism which combines the dream vision with animism to produce strikingly powerful imagery. His technique has been much influenced by the surrealist verse of the Chilean poet Pablo Neruda. His material he draws from Kiowa folklore and tradition. He is a painter as well as a poet, which accounts for the vivid use of color in his poems.

The Sun Is Blue

The sun is blue and I have forgotten all the
words to make it red. I do not sing today, I do
not sing tomorrow. My voice is dust and my eyes
are blind, the sun is blue, a word caught between
my teeth. Eagles and hawks make me listen to
chants, but I do not believe in that way.
"It is evil!" I say. They reply that it is
dead. I try to remember my grandfather. He said
"The sun is blue." Old wrinkled meat women
carry guns in their hair. Children without
homes follow me, but I am hiding. Roads lead to
the mountains. Horses without riders eat the
clay. Blood is in the water bag, my mouth is dry.
Tobacco smoke reeks with the odor of cedar and
sage. The sun is blue. A stolen woman cannot be
my wife, but a stolen child may be my son. My
father had Mexican eyes. Paintings on my tepee
tell of a battle. The sun is blue.

The sun is blue and words fail to say what I
feel. Shells decorate my shirt. I paint my face
for battle. There is no reason to fear dogs.
Rain makes the air heavy with gall. Turtles eat
women when they are of no use.
Wind dances around me in whirlpools. Dust
sticks to me, I am brown. The sun is blue

Richard Aitson's poems are printed with his permission.

Winter

hiding myself
from the grandmother
breath of winter,
the footstep breath of horses,
the pure breed of snow.

hiding myself
in the windbreak of an eyelash
and the entrails of smoke.

winter's dogs sleep within the marrow,
even the blood fears to travel.

●

We count in prayers,
            peyote mornings
            and plumes of crows.

Day moves our hands
      like ropes in winter,
      slow,
      enduring,
      constant,
      the voice of wolves in famine,
      the voice of shells in dance.

●

   end of winter comes like
tomorrows of old men
dogs crawl within themselves to escape it

it hangs in the trees
autumn's prayers drip homeward
the cloud's children mingle

we look to the east
and forget to suffer

Old Man Poem

As a child I knew how to look around
   how to savor a color,
   a movement or a shadow.
I want for two things:
   to know the print of my hand
   and the smell of marrow.

Yet my eyes desire another darkness,
Whispers pass me by.
At times I hide behind a mask of feathers and of songs,
  pitiful, the smoke's shawl.

In death my hair will grow.

Walk
(for Downing)

What love will occur
  for the shoes my feet have forsaken
And will the feet listen
  for the whispers
    straying

I believe I am walking
  quietly
    to you

And yet the stone's dusty children
  arise,
  angry
(My feet awaken their fate)

Tomorrow
  they will be still—
  allow the wind's dreams to carry them
  under a shawl of pollen
    and cedar breath

Swallows sing promises,
I will be with you

DIANE BURNS

Diane Burns, born in 1957, is Chemehuevi on her father's side, Ani-shinabe (Chippewa) on her mother's. Although the Chemehuevi, whose tribal lands include part of Palm Springs, California, are the richest tribe in America on a per capita basis, Diane associates more with her mother's people, who come from Lac Court Oreilles in Wisconsin.

Diane is a protégé of Maurice Kenny's. Her poetry is notable for its trenchant humor and unrelenting honesty.

Gadoshkibos

Gadoshkibos
the warrior
He would sign no treaties
"Foolish" he called them
The whites are crazy
The whites are crazy
they sang around the fires at night
when the Anishinabe knew the trappers were gone.

Gadoshkibos
great grandfather
died in ecstacy
Nakota arrow in his throat, cries
The whites are crazy
Why fight among each other when we know?
The real enemy rushes us like buffaloes into a trap.

Gadoshkibos
son of the same
lays at night with his wives.
They ran, hid, but now
they stay put year round.
The whites are crazy.
The children starve on commodity food
and he wonders where the Anishinabe warriors have gone.

Gadoshkibos'
wife, the second,
struggles with her garden

Diane Burns's poems are reprinted with her permission from *Riding the One-Eyed Ford* (Bowling Green, N.Y.: Contact/II Pubns., 1984).

300

ground is good with blood
spilled there and she knows
the whites are crazy
and she handles her hoe like a rifle.
Her sisters in the nations watch the children and know they must wait.

Gadoshkibos
the latest one
reads sociology
at Pomona State
and studies just why
the whites are crazy.
Summertimes he goes back to the blanket
and he wanders the woods and wonders where the warriors have gone.

Big Fun

I don't care if you're married I still love you
I don't care if you're married
After the party's over
I will take you home in my One-Eyed Ford
Way yah hi yo, Way yah hi yo!

Modene!
the roller derby queen!
She's Anishinabe,
that means Human Being!
That's H for hungry!
and B for frijoles!
frybread!
Tortillas!
Watermelon!
Pomona!
Take a sip of this
and a drag of that!
At the rancheria fiesta
It's tit for tat!
Low riders and Levis
go fist in glove!
Give it a little pat
a push or a shove
Move it or lose it!
Take straight or bruise it!
Everyone
has her fun
when the sun

is all done
We're all one
make a run
hide your gun
Hey!
I'm no nun!
'49 in the hills above
         Ventura
Them Okies gotta drum

I'm from Oklahoma
I got no one to call my own
if you will be my honey
I will be your sugar pie, way hi yah,
Way yah hey way yah hi yah!

We're gonna sing all night
bring your blanket
or
be that way then!

Booze 'n' Loozing—Part III

    It's been
    6 months
I go to bars & everyone is so happy
    Everyone buys me club soda
(But it's so boring!)
    It's lonely
& I feel 15 again
      unsure shy   obvious
      unlike the way I've been
I sit straight on the bar stool
  cool as an ice cube (with water inside).

It's not so boring as it is scary
My X-friend Jack Daniels left with my brashness
& left me with
a craving
for license-plate-sized Hershey bars
& Twinkeys & diet root beer.

I don't even take bitters in my eggs
or vanilla extract in anything uncooked.
I know exactly how much money I have
& where I've been spending my time.

At three months
I was so thin
Skin sagged on my face
& my eyes looked far away
But now everything has tightened up
& I've noticed the swelling in my knees is gone.

Old drinking buddies are uncomfortable
but oddly encouraging
We have little to talk about
I'm no longer one of the boys

Now I'm one of the grown-ups.

LOUISE ERDRICH

Louise Erdrich was born in 1954 in Little Falls, Minnesota, and raised in Wahpeton, North Dakota. She is a member of the Turtle Mountain band of the Chippewas. She is best known for her fiction, but like other Indian novelists, she is an excellent poet as well.

Her novels, Love Medicine *(1984),* The Beet Queen *(1986), and* Tracks *(1988), are a cycle portraying the life of the Chippewas, mixed-bloods, and whites in rural North Dakota over a period of five generations. Erdrich has also published two collections of poems,* Jacklight *(1984) and* Baptism of Desire *(1989).*

A Love Medicine

For Lise

Still it is raining lightly
in Wahpeton. The pickup trucks
sizzle beneath the blue neon
bug traps of the dairy bar.

Theresa goes out in green halter and chains
that glitter at her throat.
This dragonfly, my sister,
she belongs more than I
to this night of rising water.

The Red River swells to take the bridge.
She laughs and leaves her man in his Dodge.
He shoves off to search her out.
He wears a long rut in the fog.

And later, at the crest of the flood,
when the pilings are jarred from their sockets
and pitch into the current,
she steps against the fistwork of a man.
She goes down in wet grass
and his boot plants its grin
among the arches of her face.

Louise Erdrich's poems "A Love Medicine," "Family Reunion," "Captivity," "The Strange People," "The Butcher's Wife," and "Here Is a Good Word for Step-and-a-Half Waleski" are reprinted by arrangement with Henry Holt and Company, Inc., from *Jacklight* (© copyright 1984 by Louise Erdrich).

Now she feels her way home in the dark.
The white-violet bulbs of the streetlamps
are seething with insects,
and the trees lean down aching and empty.
The river slaps at the dike works, insistent.

I find her curled up in the roots of a cottonwood.
I find her stretched out in the park, where all night
the animals are turning in their cages.
I find her in a burnt-over ditch, in a field
that is gagging on rain,
sheets of rain sweep up down
to the river held tight against the bridge.

We see that now the moon is leavened and the water,
as deep as it will go,
stops rising. Where we wait for the night to take us
the rain ceases. *Sister, there is nothing
I would not do.*

Family Reunion

Ray's third new car in half as many years.
Full cooler in the trunk, Ray sogging the beer
as I solemnly chauffeur us through the bush
and up the backroads, hardly cowpaths and hub-deep in mud.
All day the sky lowers, clears, lowers again.
Somewhere in the bush near Saint John
there are uncles, a family, one mysterious brother
who stayed on the land when Ray left for the cities.
One week Ray is crocked. We've been through this before.
Even, as a little girl, hands in my dress,
Ah punka, you's my Debby, come and ki me.

Then the road ends in a yard full of dogs.
Them's Indian dogs, Ray says, lookit how they know me.
And they do seem to know him, like I do. His odor—
rank beef of fierce turtle pulled dripping from Metagoshe,
and the inflammable mansmell: hair tonic, ashes, alcohol.
Ray dances an old woman up in his arms.
Fiddles reel in the phonograph and I sink apart
in a corner, start knocking the Blue Ribbons down.
Four generations of people live here.
No one remembers Raymond Twobears.

So what. The walls shiver, the old house caulked with mud
sails back into the middle of Metagoshe.

A three-foot-long snapper is hooked on a troutline,
so mean that we do not dare wrestle him in
but tow him to shore, heavy as an old engine.
Then somehow Ray pries the beak open and shoves
down a cherry bomb. Lights the string tongue.

Headless and clenched in its armor, the snapper
is lugged home in the trunk for tomorrow's soup.
Ray rolls it beneath a bush in the backyard and goes in
to sleep his own head off. Tomorrow I find
that the animal has dragged itself someplace.
I follow torn tracks up a slight hill and over
into a small stream that deepens and widens into a marsh.

Ray finds his way back through the room into his arms.
When the phonograph stops, he slumps hard in his hands
and the boys and their old man fold him into the car
where he curls around his bad heart, hearing how it knocks
and rattles at the bars of his ribs to break out.

Somehow we find our way back. Uncle Ray
sings an old song to the body that pulls him
toward home. The gray fins that his hands have become
screw their bones in the dashboard. His face
has the odd, calm patience of a child who has always
let bad wounds alone, or a creature that has lived
for a long time underwater. And the angels come
lowering their slings and litters.

Captivity

He (my captor) gave me a bisquit, which I put in my pocket, and not dar-
ing to eat it, buried it under a log, fearing he had put something in it to
make me love him.
> —from the narrative of the captivity of Mrs. Mary Rowlandson,
> who was taken prisoner by the Wampanoag when Lancaster,
> Massachusetts, was destroyed, in the year 1676

The stream was swift, and so cold
I thought I would be sliced in two.
But he dragged me from the flood
by the ends of my hair.
I had grown to recognize his face.
I could distinguish it from the others.
There were times I feared I understood

his language, which was not human,
and I knelt to pray for strength.

We were pursued! By God's agents
or pitch devils I did not know.
Only that we must march.
Their guns were loaded with swan shot.
I could not suckle and my child's wail
put them in danger.
He had a woman
with teeth black and glittering.
She fed the child milk of acorns.
The forest closed, the light deepened.

I told myself that I would starve
before I took food from his hands
but I did not starve.
One night
he killed a deer with a young one in her
and gave me to eat of the fawn.
It was so tender,
the bones like the stems of flowers,
that I followed where he took me.
The night was thick. He cut the cord
that bound me to the tree.

After that the birds mocked.
Shadows gaped and roared
and the trees flung down
their sharpened lashes.
He did not notice God's wrath.
God blasted fire from half-buried stumps.
I hid my face in my dress, fearing He would burn us all
but this, too, passed.

Rescued, I see no truth in things.
My husband drives a thick wedge
through the earth, still it shuts
to him year after year.
My child is fed of the first wheat.
I lay myself to sleep
on a Holland-laced pillowbeer.
I lay to sleep.
And in the dark I see myself
as I was outside their circle.

They knelt on deerskins, some with sticks,
and he led his company in the noise

until I could no longer bear
the thought of how I was.
I stripped a branch
and struck the earth,
in time, begging it to open
to admit me
as he was
and feed me honey from the rock.

The Strange People

*The antelope are strange people . . . they are beautiful to look at, and yet
they are tricky. We do not trust them. They appear and disappear; they
are like shadows on the plains. Because of their great beauty, young men
sometimes follow the antelope and are lost forever. Even if those foolish
ones find themselves and return, they are never again right in their
heads.*   —Pretty Shield, Medicine Woman of the Crows,
        transcribed and edited by Frank Linderman (1932)

All night I am the doe, breathing
his name in a frozen field,
the small mist of the word
drifting always before me.

And again he has heard it
and I have gone burning
to meet him, the jacklight
fills my eyes with blue fire;
the heart in my chest
explodes like a hot stone.

Then slung like a sack
in the back of his pickup,
I wipe the death scum
from my mouth, sit up laughing,
and shriek in my speeding grave.

Safely shut in the garage,
when he sharpens his knife
and thinks to have me, like that,
I come toward him,
a lean gray witch,
through the bullets that enter and dissolve.

I sit in his house
drinking coffee till dawn,

and leave as frost reddens on hubcaps,
crawling back into my shadowy body.
All day, asleep in clean grasses,
I dream of the one who could really wound me.

The Butcher's Wife

1

Once, my braids swung heavy as ropes.
Men feared them like the gallows.
Night fell
When I combed them out.
No one could see me in the dark.

Then I stood still
Too long and the braids took root.
I swept, so helpless.
The braids tapped deep and flourished.

A man came by with an ox on his shoulders.
He yoked it to my apron
And pulled me from the ground.
From that time on I wound the braids around my head
So that my arms would be free to tend him.

2

He could lift a grown man by the belt with his teeth.
In a contest, he'd press a whole hog, a side of beef.
He loved his highballs, his herring, and the attentions of women.
He died pounding his chest with no last word for anyone.

The gin vessels in his face broke and darkened. I traced them
Far from that room into Bremen on the Sea.
The narrow streets twisted down to the piers.
And far off, in the black, rocking water, the lights of trawlers
Beckoned, like the heart's uncertain signals,
Faint, and final.

3

Of course I planted a great, full bush of roses on his grave.
Who else would give the butcher roses but his wife?
Each summer, I am reminded of the heart surging from his vest,
Mocking all the high stern angels
By pounding for their spread skirts.

The flowers unfurl, offering themselves,
And I hear his heart pound on the earth like a great fist,
Demanding another round of the best wine in the house.
Another round, he cries, and another round all summer long,
Until the whole damn world reels toward winter drunk.

Here Is a Good Word for Step-and-a-Half Waleski

At first we all wondered what county or town
she had come from. Quite soon it was clear to us all
that was better unquestioned, and better unknown.
Who wanted to hear what had happened or failed
to occur. Why the dry wood had not taken fire.
Much less, why the dogs were unspeakably disturbed

when she ground the cold cinders that littered our walk
with her run-to-ground heels. That Waleski approached
with a swiftness uncommon for one of her age.
Even spiders spun clear of her lengthening shadow.
Her headlong occurrence unnerved even Otto
who wrapped up the pork rinds like they were glass trinkets
and saluted her passage with a good stiff drink.

But mine is a good word for Step-and-a-Half Waleski.
Scavenger, bone picker, lived off our alleys
when all we threw out were the deadliest scrapings
from licked-over pots. And even that hurt.
And for whatever one of us laughed in her face,
at least two prayed in secret, went home half afraid
of the mirror, what possible leavings they'd find there.

But mine is a good word, and even that hurts.
A rhyme-and-a-half for a woman of parts,
because someone must pare the fruit soft to the core
into slivers, must wrap the dead bones in her skirts
and lay these things out on her table, and fit
each oddment to each to resemble a life.

Christ's Twin

He was formed of chicken blood and lightning.
He was what fell out when the jug tipped.
He was waiting at the bottom

of the cliff when the swine plunged over.
He tore out their lungs with a sound like ripping silk.
He hacked the pink carcasses apart, so that the ribs spread
like a terrible butterfly, and there was darkness.
It was he who turned the handle and let the dogs
rush from the basements. He shoved the crust
of the volcano into his roaring mouth.
He showed one empty hand. The other gripped
a crowbar, a monkey wrench, a crop
which was the tail of the ass that bore them to Egypt,
one in each saddlebag, sucking twists
of honeyed goatskin, arguing
already over a woman's breasts.
He understood the prayers that rose
in every language, for he had split the human tongue.
He was not the Devil nor among the Fallen—
it was just that he was clumsy, and curious,
and liked to play with knives. He was the dove
hypnotized by boredom and betrayed by light.
He was the pearl in the mouth, the tangible
emptiness that saints seek at the center of their prayers.
He leaped into a shadow when the massive stone
rolled across the entrance, sealing him with his brother
in the dark as in the beginning.
Only this time he emerged first, bearing the self-
inflicted wound, both brass halos
tacked to the back of his skull.
He raised two crooked fingers; the extra die
tumbled from his lips when he preached
but no one noticed. they were too busy
clawing at the hem of his robe and planning
how to sell him to the world.
They were too busy drinking
at the fountain.
They were drunk.
They would drown for love.

Mary Magdalene

I wash your ankles
with my tears. Unhem
my sweep of hair
and burnish the arch of your foot.
Still your voice cracks
above me.

I cut off my hair and toss it across your pillow.
A dark towel
like the one after sex.
I'm walking out,
my face a dustpan,
my body stiff as a new broom.

I will drive boys
to smash empty bottles on their brows.
I will pull them right out of their skins.
It is the old way that girls
get even with their fathers—
by wrecking their bodies on other men.

FICTION

INDIAN FICTION is like Indian poetry in that the best is a product of the Renaissance begun by Scott Momaday in the late sixties. Momaday's *House Made of Dawn* and James Welch's *Winter in the Blood*, both of which are excerpted below, were the first in a series of excellent Indian novels. Both treat heroes who seem irresponsible—they drink, womanize, and generally appear to drift through life aimlessly. White critics often view them with pity as victims of mainstream American oppression, but anyone knowledgeable about Indian literature would recognize the heroes as modern avatars of the trickster archetype. Abel, the hero of *House Made of Dawn*, and the nameless hero of *Winter in the Blood*, like Trickster, play tricks or are the victim of them, indulge their appetites, and are always on the move.

Welch and Momaday are not the only Indian writers to use tribal myth in their works: most Indian writers expand the traditional boundaries of the novel by working in tribal materials and forms. Leslie Silko's novel *Ceremony* is a modern retelling of Laguna fertility myths similar to the myth of the Holy Grail. Louise Erdrich uses the Chippewa Trickster figure Nanapush in *Love Medicine*, and Misshepeshu, the water monster, in *Tracks*. Gerald Vizenor blends Chippewa myths of Nanapush (whom he calls Nanaboozho) with those of the Chinese trickster Monkey in *Griever: A Monkey King in China*.

While generally adhering to the conventions of narrative realism, Indian novelists—like South American magic realists—often add a dimension to their fiction that strikes white readers as supernatural. Perhaps the most dramatic example of this is the ending of Momaday's latest novel, *Ancient Child*, where the hero turns into a bear.

Novelists depart from the conventions of realism for different reasons. In the case of Indian writers it is generally that they are trying to recreate the sense of reality that their tribal forbears traditionally held. The calen-

dars that Plains tribes such as the Kiowa and the Sioux kept in the eighteenth and nineteenth centuries recorded one event for each year. Often
it would be an important battle with whites or other Indians, but on some
occasions the event would be what whites would consider supernatural—
for example, the Yanktonai Dakota calendar for 1729 records that the
principal event of the year was that a shaman turned himself into a bear. It
is clear from the context that the Indians considered this a natural event,
not miraculous. Since the Enlightenment, European historians have
taken the miraculous out of history. The Indians did not make that distinction as long as they kept their cultures intact. Indian novelists of today
think like other Americans in their daily lives, but recreate the old order
in their fiction.

In this anthology I have included works from among the best and best
known of the Indian fiction writers, Momaday, Welch, Erdrich, and
Vizenor, and two pieces from a newcomer, LeAnne Howe.

HOUSE MADE OF DAWN

By N. Scott Momaday

House Made of Dawn *is Momaday's masterpiece, one of the great American novels of the twentieth century. Primarily it is the story of a young Indian man named Abel, a victim who seems intent on being his own Cain and destroying himself, but it is also the story of Abel's grandfather, Francisco, and of their relationship.*

Francisco's bear hunt is more than a quest for game; it is a rite de passage which establishes him as a man in Tanoan society.[1] Implicit in the narrative is the traditional Indian idea that hunting must involve the consent of the hunted. The hunter and his quarry are not two enemies engaged in a struggle; both are willing participants in a ritual, each playing a necessary part. Although this idea is certainly anthropocentric—bears and buffaloes presumably look at the affair differently—nonetheless, compared to white attitudes towards hunting, it is decidedly civilized. Francisco is not gleeful and bloodthirsty; his attitude is one of religious reverence: " . . . he did not want to break the stillness of the night, for it was holy and profound; it was rest and restoration, the hunter's offering of death and the sad watch of the hunted, waiting somewhere away in the cold darkness and breathing easily of its life, brooding around at last to forgiveness and consent; the silence was essential to them both, and it lay out like a bond between them, ancient and inviolable."

Francisco's Bear Hunt

He was a young man, and he rode out on the buckskin colt to the north and west, leading the hunting horse, across the river and beyond the white cliffs and the plain, beyond the hills and the mesas, the canyons and the caves. And once, where the horses could not go because the face of the rock was almost vertical and unbroken and the ancient handholds were worn away to shadows in the centuries of wind and rain, he climbed among the walls and pinnacles of rock, adhering like a vine to the face of the rock, pressing with no force at all his whole mind and weight upon the sheer ascent, running the roots of his weight into invisible hollows and cracks, and he heard the whistle and moan of the wind among the crags,

---

[1] See also Geary Hobson's "Deer Hunting" in the poetry section above.

Abridged from pages 178–84 in N. Scott Momaday, *House Made of Dawn* (© copyright 1967, 1968 by N. Scott Momaday) with the author's permission.

like ancient voices, and saw the horses far below in the sunlit gorge. And there were the caves. He came suddenly upon a narrow ledge and stood before the mouth of a cave. It was sealed with silver webs, and he brushed them away. He bent to enter and knelt down on the floor. It was dark and cool and close inside, and smelled of damp earth and dead and ancient fires, as if centuries ago the air had entered and stood still behind the web. The dead embers and ashes lay still in a mound upon the floor, and the floor was deep and packed with clay and glazed with the blood of animals. The chiseled dome was low and encrusted with smoke, and the one round wall was a perfect radius of rock and plaster. Here and there were earthen bowls, one very large, chipped and broken only at the mouth, deep and fired within. It was beautiful and thin-shelled and frag- ile-looking, but he struck the nails of his hand against it, and it rang like metal. There was a black metate by the door, the coarse, igneous grain of the shallow bowl forever bleached with meal, and in the ashes of the fire were several ears and cobs of corn, each no bigger than his thumb, charred and brittle, but whole and hard as wood. And there among the things of the dead he listened in the stillness all around and heard only the lowing of the wind . . . and then the plummet and rush of a great swoop- ing bird—out of the corner of his eye he saw the awful shadow which hurtled across the light—and the clatter of wings on the cliff, and the small, thin cry of a rodent. And in the same instant the huge wings heaved with calm, gathering up the dead weight, and rose away.

All afternoon he rode on toward the summit of the blue mountain, and at last he was high among the falls and the steep timbered slopes. The sun fell behind the land above him and the dusk grew up among the trees, and still he went on in the dying light, climbing up to the top of the land. And all afternoon he had seen the tracks of wild animals and heard the motion of the dead leaves and the breaking of branches on either side. Twice he had seen deer, motionless, watching, standing away in easy range, blended with light and shadow, fading away into the leaves and the land. He let them be, but remembered where they were and how they stood, reckoning well and instinctively their notion of fear and flight, their age and weight.

He had seen the tracks of wolves and mountain lions and the deep prints of a half-grown bear, and in the last light he drew up in a small clearing and made his camp. It was a good place, and he was lucky to have come upon it while he still could see. A dead tree had fallen upon a bed of rock; it was clear of the damp earth and the leaves, and the wood made an almost smokeless fire. The timber all around was thick, and it held the light and the sound of the fire within the clearing. He tethered the horses there in the open, as close to the fire as he could, and opened the blanket roll and ate. He slept sitting against the saddle, and kept the fire going and the rifle cocked across his waist.

He awoke startled to the stiffening of the horses. They stood quivering and taut with their heads high and turned around upon the dark and nearest wall of trees. He could see the whites of their eyes and the ears laid back upon the bristling manes and the almost imperceptible shiver and bunch of their haunches to the spine. And at the same time he saw the dark shape sauntering among the trees, and then the others, sitting all around, motionless, the short pointed ears and the soft shining eyes, almost kindly and discreet, the gaze of the gray heads bidding only welcome and wild good will. And he was young and it was the first time he had come among them and he brought the rifle up and made no sound. He swung the sights slowly around from one to another of the still, shadowy shapes, but they made no sign except to cock their heads a notch, sitting still and away in the darkness like a litter of pups, full of shyness and wonder and delight. He was hard on the track of the bear; it was somewhere close by in the night, and it knew of him, had been ahead of him for hours in the afternoon and evening, holding the same methodical pace, unhurried, certain of where it was and where he was and of every step of the way between, keeping always and barely out of sight, almost out of hearing. And it was there now, off in the blackness, standing still and invisible, waiting. And he did not want to break the stillness of the night, for it was holy and profound; it was rest and restoration, the hunter's offering of death and the sad watch of the hunted, waiting somewhere away in the cold darkness and breathing easily of its life, brooding around at last to forgiveness and consent; the silence was essential to them both, and it lay out like a bond between them, ancient and inviolable. He could neither take nor give any advantage of cowardice where no cowardice was, and he laid the rifle down. He spoke low to the horses and soothed them. He drew fresh wood upon the fire and the gray shapes crept away to the edge of the light, and in the morning they were gone.

It was gray before the dawn and there was a thin frost on the leaves, and he saddled up and started out again, slowly, after the track and into the wind. At sunrise he came upon the ridge of the mountain. For hours he followed the ridge, and he could see for miles across the land. It was late in the autumn and clear, and the great shining slopes, green and blue, rose out of the shadows on either side, and the sunlit groves of aspen shone bright with clusters of yellow leaves and thin white lines of bark, and far below in the deep folds of the land he could see the tops of the black pines swaying. At midmorning he was low in a saddle of the ridge, and he came upon a huge outcrop of rock and the track was lost. An ancient watercourse fell away like a flight of stairs to the left, the falls broad and shallow at first, but ever more narrow and deep farther down. He tied the horses and started down the rock on foot, using the rifle to balance himself. He went slowly, quietly down until he came to a deep open funnel in the rock. The ground on either side sloped sharply down to a broad ravine and the edge of the timber beyond, and he saw the scored earth where the bear had left the rock and gone sliding down, and the swath in the brush of the ravine. He thought of going the same way; it would be quick and easy, and he was close to the kill, closing in and growing restless. But he must make no sound of hurry. The bear knew he was coming, knew better than he how close he was, was even now watching him from the wood, waiting, but still he must make no sound of hurry. The walls of the funnel were deep and smooth, and they converged at the bank of the ravine some twenty feet below, and the ravine was filled with sweet clover and paintbrush and sage. He held the rifle out as far as he could reach and let it go; it fell upon a stand of tall sweet clover with scarcely any sound, and the dull stock shone and the long barrel glinted among the curving green and yellow stalks. He let himself down into the funnel, little by little, supported only by the tension of his strength against the walls. The going was hard and slow, and near the end his arms and legs began to shake, but he was young and strong and he dropped from the point of the rock to the sand below and took up the rifle and went on, not hurrying but going only as fast as the bear had gone, going even in the bear's tracks, across the ravine and up the embankment and through the trees, unwary now, sensible only of closing in, going on and looking down at the tracks.

And when at last he looked up, the timber stood around a pool of light, and the bear was standing still and small at the far side of the brake, careless, unheeding. He brought the rifle up, and the bear raised and turned its head and made no sign of fear. It was small and black in the deep shade and dappled with light, its body turned three-quarters away and standing perfectly still, and the flat head and the small black eyes that were fixed upon him hung around upon the shoulder and under the hump of the spine. The bear was young and heavy with tallow, and the underside of the body and the backs of its short, thick legs were tufted with winter hair, longer and lighter than the rest, and dull as dust. His hand tightened on the stock and the rifle bucked and the sharp report rang upon the walls and carried out upon the slopes, and he heard the sudden scattering of birds overhead and saw the darting shadows all around. The bullet slammed into the flesh and jarred the whole black body once, but the head remained motionless and the eyes level upon him. Then, and for one instant only, there was a sad and meaningless haste. The bear turned away and lumbered, though not with fear, not with any hurt, but haste, slightly reflexive, a single step, or two, or three, and it was overcome. It shuddered and looked around again and fell.

The hunt was over, and only then could he hurry; it was over and well done. The wound was small and clean, behind the foreleg and low on the body, where the fur and flesh were thin, and there was no blood at the mouth. He took out his pouch of pollen and made yellow streaks above the bear's eyes. It was almost noon, and he hurried. He disemboweled the bear and laid the flesh open with splints so that the blood should not run into the fur and stain the hide. He ate quickly of the bear's liver, taking it with him, thinking what he must do, remembering now his descent upon the rock and the whole lay of the land, all the angles of his vision from the ridge. He went quickly, a quarter of a mile or more down the ravine, until he came to a place where the horses could keep their footing on the near side of the ridge. The blood of the bear was on him, and the bear's liver was warm and wet in his hand. He came upon the ridge and the colt grew wild in its eyes and blew, pulling away, and its hoofs clattered on the rock and the skin crawled at the roots of its mane. He approached it slowly, talking to it, and took hold of the reins. The hunting horse watched, full of age and indifference, switching its tail. There was no time to lose. He held hard to the reins, turning down the bit in the colt's mouth, and his voice rose a little and was edged. Slowly he brought the bear's flesh up to the flaring nostrils of the colt and smeared the muzzle with it.

And he rode the colt back down the mountain, leading the hunting horse with the bear on its back, and, like the old hunting horse and the young black bear, he and the colt had come of age and were hunters, too. He made camp that night far down in the peneplain and saw the stars and heard the coyotes away by the river. And in the early morning he rode into the town. He was a man then, and smeared with the blood of a bear. He shouted, and the men came out to meet him. They came with rifles, and he gave them strips of the bear's flesh, which they wrapped around the barrels of their guns. And soon the women came with switches, and they spoke to the bear and laid the switches to its hide. The men and women were jubilant and all around, and he rode stone-faced in their midst, looking straight ahead.

WINTER IN THE BLOOD

By James Welch

Winter in the Blood *is the story of a nameless hero. Like Ralph Ellison in* Invisible Man, *Welch chooses not to name his central character, which has the effect of making him an everyman figure of sorts—if he is no one in particular, he is everyone. It is true that we know that the hero is Indian (Blackfoot like Welch), but his story would not be essentially different if he were a white cowboy from rural Montana. In fact, the book most reminiscent of* Winter in the Blood *is not about Indians at all: it is John Hawkes's* The Beetle Leg. *Both are surrealistic stories with a strong element of mystery set in the arid spaces of today's West, although the surrealism in* Winter in the Blood, *which mainly concerns a mysterious airplane man not mentioned in the first chapter, which we have excerpted here, is far less pervasive than it is in the Hawkes book.*

Welch's hero is a common type of hero in modern fiction: the winner as loser. Like Thomas Berger's Rinehart in Vital Parts, *Joan Didion's Maria Wyeth in* Play It as It Lays, *Joanna Davis's Camilla Ryder in* Life Signs, *or Welch's own Grandma's Man, the hero of* Winter in the Blood *seems to be superior to the knaves and fools who surrounded him, but somehow he cannot win for losing. This sort of lovable bumbler who turns out to be his own worst enemy can be traced at least as far back as Fielding and Cervantes, but he seems to be particularly common in today's fiction.*

The title Winter in the Blood *was the suggestion of Welch's editor. Welch's working title was* The Only Good Indian, *a reference, of course, to General Sherman's remark that the only good Indian is a dead one. The hero is a dead Indian; he has been dead spiritually since the death of his father and brother. The title* Winter in the Blood *changes the metaphor but not the meaning. The spiritual coldness that afflicts the hero cannot be cured; it is in his blood. It is also in his blood in the sense that it is in his family—passed down from his grandmother, who was thrown away by the Blackfeet, left to starve and freeze during the terrible Montana winter.*

The central quest in the book is the hero's search for his identity, his roots. He learns the story of his grandmother and learns the identity of his grandfather. Such a reunion with lost kin has been a favorite motif in

This selection from James Welch, *Winter in the Blood,* is reprinted with the author's permission.

literature since Oedipus Rex *and the* Odyssey. *Welch is particularly successful in integrating the theme gracefully into his saga of Montana reservation life, presenting it powerfully without making it obtrusive.*

In the tall weeds of the borrow pit, I took a leak and watched the sorrel mare, her colt beside her, walk through burnt grass to the shady side of the log-and-mud cabin. It was called the Earthboy place, although no one by that name (or any other) had lived in it for twenty years. The roof had fallen in and the mud between the logs had fallen out in chunks, leaving a bare gray skeleton, home only to mice and insects. Tumbleweeds, stark as bone, rocked in a hot wind against the west wall. On the hill behind the cabin, a rectangle of barbed wire held the graves of all the Earthboys, except for a daughter who had married a man from Lodgepole. She could be anywhere, but the Earthboys were gone.

The fence hummed in the sun behind my back as I climbed up to the highway. My right eye was swollen up, but I couldn't remember how or why, just the white man, loose with his wife and buying drinks, his raging tongue a flame above the music and my eyes. She was wild, from Rocky Boy. He was white. He swore at his money, at her breasts, at my hair.

Coming home was not easy anymore. It was never a cinch, but it had become a torture. My throat ached, my bad knee ached and my head ached in the even heat.

The mare and her colt were out of sight behind the cabin. Beyond the graveyard and the prairie hills, the Little Rockies looked black and furry in the heat haze.

Coming home to a mother and an old lady who was my grandmother. And the girl who was thought to be my wife. But she didn't really count. For that matter none of them counted; not one meant anything to me. And for no reason. I felt no hatred, no love, no guilt, no conscience, nothing but a distance that had grown through the years.

It could have been the country, the burnt prairie beneath a blazing sun, the pale green of the Milk River valley, the milky waters of the river, the sagebrush and cottonwoods, the dry, cracked gumbo flats. The country had created a distance as deep as it was empty, and the people accepted and treated each other with distance.

But the distance I felt came not from country or people; it came from within me. I was as distant from myself as a hawk from the moon. And that was why I had no particular feelings toward my mother and grandmother. Or the girl who had come to live with me.

I dropped down on the other side of the highway, slid through the

barbed-wire fence and began the last two miles home. My throat ached
with a terrible thirst.

"She left three days ago, just after you went to town."

"It doesn't matter," I said.

"She took your gun and electric razor."

The room was bright. Although it was early afternoon, the kitchen light
was burning.

"What did you expect me to do? I have your grandmother to look after,
I have no strength, and she is young—Cree!"

"Don't worry," I said.

"At least get your gun back." My mother swept potato peels off the
counter into a paper sack at her feet. "You know she'd sell it for a drink."

The gun, an old .30–30, had once been important to me. Like my father before me, I had killed plenty of deer with it, but I hadn't used it
since the day I killed Buster Cutfinger's dog for no reason except that I
was drunk and it was moving. That was four years ago.

I heard a clicking in the living room. The rocking chair squeaked twice
and was silent.

"How is she?" I asked.

"Hot cereal and pudding—how would you expect her to be?"

"What, no radishes?"

My mother ignored me as she sliced the potatoes into thin wafers.

"Why don't we butcher one of those heifers? She could eat steak for the
rest of her life and then some."

"She'll be gone soon enough without you rushing things. Here, put this
on that eye—it'll draw out the poison." She handed me a slice of potato.

"How's Lame Bull?"

She stopped slicing. "What do you mean by that?"

"How's Lame Bull?"

"He'll be here this evening; you can find out then. Now get me another
bucket of water."

"How's the water?" I asked.

"It'll do. It never rains anymore." She dumped the slices into a pan. "It
never rains around here when you need it."

I thought how warm and flat the water would taste. No rain since mid-
June and the tarred barrels under the eaves of the house were empty. The
cistern would be low and the water silty.

A fly buzzed into the house as I opened the door. The yard was patched
with weeds and foxtail, sagebrush beyond the fence. The earth crumbled
into powder under my feet; beneath the sun which settled into afternoon

heat over the slough, two pintail ducks beat frantically above the cotton-woods and out of sight. As I lowered the bucket into the cistern, a mead-owlark sang from the shade behind the house. The rope was crusty in my hands. Twice I lifted and dropped the bucket, watching the water flow in over the lip until the bucket grew heavy enough to sink.

The girl was no matter. She was a Cree from Havre, scorned by the reservation people. I had brought her home with me three weeks ago. My mother thought we were married and treated her with politeness. My mother was a Catholic and sprinkled holy water in the corners of her house before lightning storms. She drank with the priest from Harlem, a round man with distant eyes, who refused to set foot on the reservation. He never buried Indians in their family graveyards; instead, he made them come to him, to his church, his saints and holy water, his feuding eyes. My mother drank with him in his shingle house beside the yellow plaster church. She thought I had married the girl and tried to welcome her, and the girl sat sullen in the living room across from the old lady, my grandmother, who filled her stone pipe with cuts of tobacco mixed with dried crushed chokecherries. She sat across from the girl, and the girl read movie magazines and imagined that she looked like Raquel Welch.

The old lady imagined that the girl was Cree and enemy and plotted ways to slit her throat. One day the flint striker would do; another day she favored the paring knife she kept hidden in her legging. Day after day, these two sat across from each other until the pile of movie magazines spread halfway across the room and the paring knife grew heavy in the old lady's eyes.

I slid down the riverbank behind the house. After a half-hour search in the heat of the granary, I had found a red and white spoon in my father's toolbox. The treble hook was rusty and the paint on the spoon flecked with rust. I cast across the water just short of the opposite bank. There was almost no current. As I retrieved the lure, three mallards whirred across my line of vision and were gone upriver.

The sugar beet factory up by Chinook had died seven years before. Everybody had thought the factory caused the river to be milky but the water never cleared. The white men from the fish department came in their green trucks and stocked the river with pike. They were enthusiastic and dumped thousands of pike of all sizes into the river. But the river ignored the fish and the fish ignored the river; they refused even to die there. They simply vanished. The white men made tests; they stuck elec-tric rods into the water; they scraped muck from the bottom; they even collected bugs from the fields next to the river; they dumped other kinds of fish in the river. Nothing worked. The fish disappeared. Then the men from the fish department disappeared, and the Indians put away their new fishing poles. But every now and then, a report would trickle down the valley that someone, an irrigator perhaps, had seen an ash-colored swirl suck in a muskrat, and out would come the fishing gear. Nobody ever caught one of these swirls, but it was always worth a try.

I cast the spoon again, this time retrieving faster.

The toolbox had held my father's tools and it was said in those days that he could fix anything made of iron. He overhauled machinery in the fall. It was said that when the leaves turned, First Raise's yard was full of iron; when they fell, the yard was full of leaves. He drank with the white men of Dodson. Not a quiet man, he told them stories and made them laugh. He charged them plenty for fixing their machines. Twenty dollars to kick a baler awake—one dollar for the kick and nineteen for knowing where to kick. He made them laugh until the thirty-below morning ten years ago we found him sleeping in the borrow pit across from Earthboy's place.

He had had dreams. Every fall, before the first cold wind, he dreamed of taking elk in Glacier Park. He planned. He figured out the mileage and the time it would take him to reach the park, and the time it would take to kill an elk and drag it back across the boundary to his waiting pickup. He made a list of food and supplies. He inquired around, trying to find out what the penalty would be if they caught him. He wasn't crafty like Lame Bull or the white men of Dodson, so he had to know the penalty, almost as though the penalty would be the inevitable result of his hunt.

He never got caught because he never made the trip. The dream, the planning and preparation were all part of a ritual—something to be done when the haying was over and the cattle brought down from the hills. In the evening, as he oiled his .30–30, he explained that it was better to shoot a cow elk because the bulls were tough and stringy. He had everything figured out, but he never made the trip.

My lure caught a windfall trunk and the brittle nylon line snapped. A magpie squawked from deep in the woods on the other side of the river.

"Ho, you are fishing, I see. Any good bites?" Lame Bull skittered down the bank amid swirls of dust. He stopped just short of the water.

"I lost my lure," I said.

"You should try bacon," he said, watching my line float limp on the surface. "I know these fish."

It was getting on toward evening. A mosquito lit on Lame Bull's face. I brought in the line and tied it to the reel handle. The calf bawled in the corral. Its mother, an old roan with one wild eye, answered from somewhere in the bend of the horseshoe slough.

"You should try bacon. First you cook it, then dump the grease into the river. First cast, you'll catch a good one."

"Are the fish any good?" I asked.

"Muddy. The flesh is not firm. It's been a poor season." He swatted a cloud of dust from his rump. "I haven't seen such a poor year since the flood. Ask your mother. She'll tell you."

We climbed the bank and started for the house. I remembered the flood. Almost twelve years ago, the whole valley from Chinook on down was under water. We moved up to the agency and stayed in an empty garage. They gave us typhoid shots.

"You, of course, are too young."

"I was almost twenty," I said.

"Your old man tried to ride in from the highway but his horse was shy of water. You were not much more than a baby in Teresa's arms. His horse threw him about halfway in."

"I remember that. I was almost twenty."

"Ho." Lame Bull laughed. "You were not much more than a gleam in your old man's eye."

"His stirrup broke—that's how come the horse threw him. I saw his saddle. It was a weakness in the leather."

"Ho."

"He could outride you any day."

"Ho."

Lame Bull filled the width of the doorframe as he entered the kitchen. He wasn't tall, but broad as a bull from shoulders to butt.

"Ah, Teresa! Your son tells me you are ready to marry me."

"My son tells lies that would make a weasel think twice. He was cut from the same mold as you." Her voice was clear and bitter.

"But why not? We could make music in the sack. We could make those old sheets sing."

"Fool . . . you talk as though my mother had no ears," Teresa said.

Two squeaks came from the living room.

"Old woman! How goes the rocking?" Lame Bull moved past my mother to the living room. "Do you make hay yet?"

The rocking chair squeaked again.

"She has gone to seed," I said. "There is no fertilizer in her bones."

"I seem to find myself surrounded by fools today." Teresa turned on the burner beneath the pan filled with potatoes. "Maybe one of you fools could bring yourself to feed that calf. He'll be bawling all night."

Evening now and the sky had changed to pink reflected off the high western clouds. A pheasant gabbled from a field to the south. A lone cock, he would be stepping from the wild rose along an irrigation ditch to the

sweet alfalfa field, perhaps to graze with other cocks and hens, perhaps
alone. It is difficult to tell what cocks will do when they grow old. They
are like men, full of twists.

The calf was snugged against the fence, its head between the poles,
sucking its mother.

"Hi! Get out of here, you bitch!"

She jumped straight back from the fence, skittered sideways a few feet,
then stood, tensed. Her tongue hung a thread of saliva almost to the
ground and the one wild eye, rimmed white, looked nowhere in
particular.

"Don't you know we're trying to wean this fool?"

I moved slowly toward the calf, backing it into a corner where the horse
shed met the corral fence, talking to it, holding out my hand. Before it
could move I grabbed it by the ear and whirled around so that I could pin
its shoulder against the fence. I slapped a mosquito from my face and the
calf bawled; then it was silent.

Feeling the firmness of its thigh, I remembered how my brother,
Mose, and I used to ride calves, holding them for each other, buckling on
the old chaps we found hanging in the horse shed, then the tense "Turn
him out!" and all hell busted loose. Hour after hour we rode calves until
First Raise caught us.

The calf erupted under my arm, first backing up into the corner, then
lunging forward, throwing me up against the horse shed. A hind hoof
grazed the front of my shirt.

I pitched some hay into the corral, then filled the washtub with slough
water. Tiny bugs darted through the muck. They looked like ladybugs
with long hind legs. A tadpole lay motionless at the bottom of the tub. I
scooped it out and laid it on a flat chunk of manure. It didn't move. I prod-
ded it with a piece of straw. Against the rough texture of the manure it
glistened like a dark teardrop. I returned it to the tub, where it drifted to
the bottom with a slight wriggle of its tail.

The evening was warm and pleasant, the high pink clouds taking on a
purple hint. I chased the cow back up into the bend of the slough. But she
would be back. Her bag was full of milk.

After supper, my mother cleared the table. Lame Bull finished his coffee
and stood up.

"I must remember to get some more mosquito dope." Teresa emptied
the last drops into the palm of her hand. She smeared it on her face and
neck. "If your grandmother wants anything, you see that she gets it." She
rested her hand on Lame Bull's forearm and they walked out the door.

I poured myself another cup of coffee. The sound of the pickup motor surprised me. But maybe they were going after groceries. I went into the living room.

"Old woman, do you want some music?" I leaned on the arms of her rocker, my face not more than six inches from hers.

She looked at my mouth. Her eyes were flat and filmy. From beneath the black scarf, a rim of coarse hair, parted in the middle, framed her gray face.

"Music," I commanded, louder this time.

"Ai, ai," she cackled, nodding her head, rocking just a bit under the weight of my arms.

I switched on the big wooden radio and waited for it to warm up. The glass on the face of the dial was cracked, and the dial itself was missing. A low hum filled the room. Then the music of a thousand violins. The rocking chair squeaked.

"Tobacco," I said.

The old woman looked at me.

I filled her pipe and stuck it between her lips. The kitchen match flared up, revealing the black mole on her upper lip. Three black hairs moved up and down as she sucked the smoke into her mouth.

The chair surrounded by movie magazines was uncomfortable, so I sat on the floor with my back resting against the radio. The violins vibrated through my body. The cover of the *Sports Afield* was missing and the pages were dog-eared, but I thumbed through it, looking for a story I hadn't read. I stopped at an advertisement for a fishing lure that called to fish in their own language. I tore the coupon out. Maybe that was the secret.

I had read all the stories, so I reread the one about three men in Africa who tracked a man-eating lion for four days from the scene of his latest kill—a pregnant black woman. They managed to save the baby, who, they were surprised to learn, would one day be king of the tribe. They tracked the lion's spoor until the fourth day, when they found out that he'd been tracking them all along. They were going in a giant four-day circle. It was very dangerous, said McLeod, a Pepsi dealer from Atlanta, Georgia. They killed the lion that night as he tried to rip a hole in their tent.

I looked at the pictures again. One showed McLeod and Henderson kneeling behind the dead lion; they were surrounded by a group of grinning black men. The third man, Enright, wasn't in the picture.

I looked up. The old lady was watching me. Lame Bull and my mother were gone for three days. When they came back, he was wearing a new pair of boots, the fancy kind with walking heels, and she had on a shim-

mery turquoise dress. They were both sweaty and hung over. Teresa told
me that they had gotten married in Malta.

That night we got drunk around the kitchen table.

Lame Bull had married 360 acres of hay land, all irrigated, leveled, some
of the best land in the valley, as well as a 2000-acre grazing lease. And
he had married a T-Y brand stamped high on the left ribs of every beef on
the place. And, of course, he had married Teresa, my mother. At forty-
seven, he was eight years younger than she, and a success. A prosperous
cattleman.

The next day, Lame Bull and I were up early. He cursed as he swung
the flywheel on the little John Deere. He opened up the petcock on the
gas line, swung the flywheel again, and the motor chugged twice, caught
its rhythm and smoothed out. We hitched the hay wagon behind the tractor and drove slowly past the corral and slough. We followed the footpath
upriver, through patches of wild rose, across a field of sagebrush and
down into a grove of dead white cottonwoods. A deer jumped up from its
willow bed and bounded away, its white tail waving goodbye.

The cabin, log and mud, was tucked away in a bend of the river. A rusty
wire ran from the only window up to the top of the roof. It was connected
to a car aerial, always a mystery to me, as Lame Bull had no electricity.
He gathered up his possessions—a chain saw, a portable radio, two boxes
of clothes, a sheepherder's coat and the high rubber boots he wore when
he irrigated.

"I must remember to get some more tire patches," he said, sticking a
finger through a hole in one of the boots.

We padlocked the cabin, covered the pump with an old piece of tarp
and started back, Lame Bull sniffing the sweet beautiful land that had
been so good to him.

Later, as we drove past the corral, I saw the wild-eyed cow and a small
calf head between the poles. The cow was licking the head. A meadowlark
sang from a post above them. The morning remained cool, the sun shining
from an angle above the horse shed. Behind the sliding door of the shed,
bats would be hanging from the cracks.

Old Bird shuddered, standing with his hindquarters in the dark of the
shed. He lifted his great white head and parted his lips. Even from such a
distance I could see his yellow teeth clenched together as though he were
straining to grin at us. Although he no longer worked, he still preferred
the cool dark of the horse shed to the pasture up behind the slough. Perhaps he still felt important and wished to be consulted when we saddled
up the red horse and Nig on those occasions when it was necessary to ride
through the herd. No matter what season, what weather, he was always

there. Perhaps he felt he had as much right to this place as we had, for even now he was whinnying out a welcome. He was old and had seen most of everything.

Teresa sat on the edge of the concrete cistern.

"Your father won Amos pitching pennies at the fair. He was so drunk he couldn't even see the plates."

"Amos used to follow us out to the highway every morning," I said. "We used to have to throw rocks at him."

"The others drowned because you didn't keep the tub full of water. You boys were like that."

Her fingers, resting on her thighs, were long, the skin stretched over the bone as taut as a drumhead. We could see Lame Bull down by the granary, which doubled as a toolshed. He was sharpening a mower sickle.

"We went to town that day for groceries. I remember we went to the show."

"Yes, and when we came back, all the ducks were drowned. Except Amos. He was perched on the edge of the tub."

"But he never went in. He must have been smarter than the others," I said.

Lame Bull's legs pumped faster. He poured some water on the spinning grindstone.

"He was lucky. One duck can't be smarter than another. They're like Indians."

"Then why didn't he go in with the other ducks?"

"Don't you remember how gray and bitter it was?"

"But the other ducks . . ."

". . . were crazy. You boys were told to keep that tub full." She said this gently, perhaps to ease my guilt, if I still felt any, or perhaps because ducks do not matter. Especially those you win at the fair in Dodson.

We had brought the ducks home in a cardboard box. There were five of them, counting Amos. We dug a hole in the ground big enough for the washtub to fit, and deep enough so that its lip would be even with the ground level. Then we filled the tub to the lip so that the ducks could climb in and out as they chose. But we hadn't counted on the ducks drinking the water and splashing it out as they ruffled their wings. That late afternoon, several days later, the water level had dropped to less than an inch below the rim of the tub. But it was enough. That one inch of galvanized steel could have been the wall of the Grand Canyon to the tiny yellow ducks.

The calf in the corral bawled suddenly.

The day the ducks drowned remained fresh in my mind. The slight

smell of muskrat pelts coming from the shed, the wind blowing my straw
hat away, the wind whipping the glassine window of the shed door; above,
the gray slide of clouds as we stood for what seemed like hours beside the
car glaring at the washtub beyond the fence. And the ducks floating with
their heads deep in the water as though they searched the bottom for
food. And Amos perched on the rim of the tub, looking at them with great
curiosity.

My mother talked on about Amos. Not more than six feet away was the
spot where the ducks had drowned. The weeds grew more abundant
there, as though their spirits had nourished the soil.

"And what happened to Amos?" I said.

"We had him for Christmas. Don't you remember what a handsome
bird he was?"

"But I thought that was the turkey."

"Not at all. A bobcat got that turkey. Don't you remember how your
brother found feathers all the way from the toolshed to the corral?"

"That was a hateful bird!"

"Oh." She laughed. "He used to chase you kids every time you stepped
out the door. We had a baseball bat by the washstand, you remember?
You kids had to take it with you every time you went to the outhouse."

"He never attacked you," I said.

"I should say not! I'd have wrung his damn neck for him."

Lame Bull sat on the wooden frame, the big gray grindstone spinning
faster and faster as his legs pumped. Sparks flew from the sickle.

It was a question I had not wanted to ask: "Who . . . which one of
us . . ."

Teresa read my hesitation. ". . . killed Amos? Who else? You kids had
no stomach for it. You always talked big enough, Lord knows you could
talk up a storm in those days, and your father . . ."

"First Raise killed him?"

"Your father wasn't even around!" Her fine bitter voice rang in the afternoon heat. "But I'll tell you one thing—I've never seen a sorrier sight
when he did come back."

Now I was confused. The turkey was of little importance. I could remember his great wings crashing about my head as he dug his spurs into
my sides, his weight bearing me down to the ground until I cried out. Then
the yelling and the flailing baseball bat and the curses, and finally the
quiet. It was always my father bending over me: "He's all right, Teresa,
he's all right . . ." It was he, I thought, who had killed the turkey. But
now it was my mother who had killed the turkey while First Raise was in
town making the white men laugh. But he always carried me up to the

house and laid me on the bed and sat with me until the burning in my head went away. Now the bobcat killed Amos . . .

"No! The bobcat killed the big turkey," she said, then added quietly, as though Lame Bull might hear over the grinding of steel, as though Bird might hear over the sound of the bawling calf, as though the fish that were never in the river might hear: "I killed Amos."

"Why did he stay away so much?" I said.

"What? Your father?" The question caught her offguard.

"Why would he stay away so much?"

"He didn't. He was around enough. When he was around he got things accomplished."

"But you yourself said he was never around."

"You must have him mixed up with yourself. He always accomplished what he set out to do."

We were sitting on the edge of the cistern. Teresa was rubbing Mazola oil into the surface of a wooden salad bowl. It had been a gift from the priest in Harlem, but she never used it.

"Who do you think built the extra bedroom onto the house?" she said. She rubbed her glistening fingers together. "He was around enough—he was on his way home when they found him, too."

"How do you know that?" But I knew the answer.

"He was pointing toward home. They told me that."

I shook my head.

"What of it?" she demanded.

"Memory fails," I said.

It was always "they" who had found him, yet I had a memory as timeless as the blowing snow that we had found him ourselves, that we had gone searching for him after the third day, or the fourth day, or the fifth, cruising the white level of highway raised between the blue-white of the borrow pits. I could almost remember going into the bar in Dodson and being told that he had left for home the night before; so we must have been searching the borrow pits. How could we have spotted him? Was it a shoe sticking up, or a hand, or just a blue-white lump in the endless skittering whiteness? I had no memory of detail until we dug his grave, yet I was sure we had come upon him first. Winters were always timeless and without detail, but I remembered no other faces, no other voices.

My mother stood and massaged the backs of her thighs. "He was a foolish man," she said.

"Is that why he stayed away?"

"Yes, I believe that was it." She was looking toward the toolshed. Three

freshly sharpened mower sickles leaned against the granary, their tri-
angular teeth glistening like ice in the sun. "You know how it is."

"He wasn't satisfied," I said.

"He accomplished any number of things."

"But none of them satisfied him."

Teresa whirled around, her eyes large and dark with outrage. "And why
not?"

"He wasn't happy . . ."

"Do you suppose he was happy lying in that ditch with his eyes frozen
shut, stinking with beer . . ."

But that was a different figure in the ditch, not First Raise, not the man
who fixed machinery, who planned his hunt with such care that he never
made it. Unlike Teresa, I didn't know the man who froze in the borrow
pit. Maybe that's why I felt nothing until after the funeral.

"He was satisfied," she said. "He was just restless. He could never
settle down."

A sonic boom rattled the shed door, then died in the distance. Teresa
looked up at the sky, her hand over her eyes. The airplane was invisible.
She looked down at me. "Do you blame me?"

I scratched a mosquito bite on the back of my hand and considered.

"He was a wanderer—just like you, just like all these damned Indians." Her voice became confident and bitter again. "You I don't understand. When you went to Tacoma for that second operation, they wanted
you to stay on. You could have become something."

"I don't blame you," I said.

"You're too sensitive. There's nothing wrong with being an Indian. If
you can do the job, what difference does it make?"

"I stayed almost two years."

"Two years!" she said disgustedly. "One would be more like it—and
then you spent all your time up in Seattle, barhopping with those other
derelicts."

"They didn't fix my knee."

"I see: it's supposed to heal by itself. You don't need to do the exercises
they prescribed." She picked up the salad bowl. She was through with
that part of my life. A dandelion parachute had stuck to the rim. "What
about your wife?" She blew the parachute away. "Your grandmother
doesn't like her."

I never expected much from Teresa and I never got it. But neither did
anybody else. Maybe that's why First Raise stayed away so much. Maybe
that's why he stayed in town and made the white men laugh. Despite
their mocking way they respected his ability to fix things; they gave more
than his wife. I wondered why he stuck it out so long. He could have

moved out altogether. The ranch belonged to Teresa, so there was no danger of us starving to death. He probably stayed because of my brother, Mose, and me. We meant something to him, although he would never say it. It was apparent that he enjoyed the way we grew up and learned to do things, drive tractor, ride calves, clean rabbits and pheasants. He would never say it, though, and after Mose got killed, he never showed it. He stayed away more than ever then, a week or two at a time. Sometimes we would go after him; other times he would show up in the yard, looking ruined and fearful. After a time, a month, maybe, of feverish work, he would go off to overhaul a tractor and it would begin again. He never really stayed and he never left altogether. He was always in transit.

Ten years had passed since that winter day his wandering ended, but nothing of any consequence had happened to me. I had had my opportunity, a chance to work in the rehabilitation clinic in Tacoma. They liked me because I was smarter than practically anybody they had ever seen. That's what they said and I believed them. It took a nurse who hated Indians to tell me the truth, that they needed a grant to build another wing and I was to be the first of the male Indians they needed to employ in order to get the grant. She turned out to be my benefactor. So I came home.

"I think your grandmother deserves to be here more than your wife, don't you?"

"She's been here plenty long already," I agreed.

"Your wife wasn't happy here," Teresa said, then added: "She belongs in town."

In the bars, I thought. That's what you mean, but it's not important anymore. Just a girl I picked up and brought home, a fish for dinner, nothing more. Yet it surprised me, those nights alone, when I saw her standing in the moon by the window and I saw the moon on the tops of her breasts and the slight darkness under each rib. The memory was more real than the experience.

Lame Bull had finished his work and was walking toward us. He slapped his gloves against his thigh and looked back at the bank of glistening sickles. He seemed pleased.

"There isn't enough for you here," said my mother. "You would do well to start looking around."

Lame Bull had taken to grinning now that he was a proprietor. All day he grinned as he mowed through the fields of alfalfa and bluejoint. He grinned when he came in to lunch, and in the evening when the little tractor putted into the yard next to the granary, we could see his white teeth through the mosquito netting that hung from his hat brim. He let his whiskers grow so that the spiky hair extended down around his round face. Teresa complained about his sloppy habits, his rough face. She didn't like the way he teased the old lady, and she didn't like his habit of not emptying the dust and chaff in his pants cuffs. He grinned a silent challenge, and the summer nights came alive in the bedroom off the kitchen. Teresa must have liked his music.

We brought in the first crop, Lame Bull mowing alfalfa, snakes, bluejoint, baby rabbits, tangles of barbed wire, sometimes changing sickles four times in a single day. Early next morning he would be down by the granary sharpening the chipped, battered sickles. He insisted on both cutting and baling the hay, so my only job was the monotonous one of raking it into strips for the baler. Around and around I pulled the windrow rake, each circuit shorter than the last as I worked toward the center. I sat on the springy seat of the Farmall, which was fairly new, and watched Lame Bull in the next field. He tinkered endlessly with the baler, setting the tension tighter so that the bales would be more compact, loosening it a turn when they began to break. Occasionally I would see the tractor idling, the regular puffs of black smoke popping from its stack, and Lame Bull's legs sticking out from beneath the baler. He enjoyed being a proprietor and the haying went smoothly until we hired Raymond Long Knife to help stack bales.

Long Knife came from a long line of cowboys. Even his mother, perhaps the best of them all, rode all day, every day, when it came time to round up the cattle for branding. In the makeshift pen, she wrestled calves, castrated them, then threw the balls into the ashes of the branding fire. She made a point of eating the roasted balls while glaring at one man, then another—even her sons, who, like the rest of us, stared at the brown hills until she was done.

Perhaps it was because of this fierce mother that Long Knife had become shrewd in the way dumb men are shrewd. He had learned to give the illusion of work, even to the point of sweating as soon as he put his gloves on, while doing very little. But because he was Belva Long Knife's son and because he always seemed to be hanging around the bar in Dodson, he was in constant demand.

The day we hired him the weather changed. It was one of those rare mid-July days when the wind blows chilly through the cottonwoods and the sky seems to end fifty feet up. The ragged clouds were both a part of and apart from the grayness; streaks of white broke suddenly, allowing sun to filter through for an instant as the clouds closed and drove swiftly north.

Lame Bull of course drove the bull rake, not because he was best at it but because it was the proprietor's job. He wore his down vest and his sweat-stained pearl stetson pulled low over his big head. Although he was thick and squat, half a head shorter than either Teresa or I, he had a long torso; seated on the bull rake, which was mounted on a stripped-down car frame, he looked like a huge man, but he had to slide forward to reach the brake and clutch pedals.

He lowered the rake and charged the first row of bales. The teeth skimmed over the stubble, gathering in the bales; then the proprietor pulled back a lever and the teeth lifted. He swerved around to deliver the bales at our feet. We began to build the stack.

By noon we had the first field cleared. Things went smoothly enough those first two days as we moved from field to field. Long Knife and I built the stacks well, squaring off the corners, locking each layer in place with the next one so that the whole wouldn't lean or worse, collapse. The cloudy weather held steady those days, at times trying to clear up, at other times threatening a downpour. But the weather held and Lame Bull was happy. He gazed lovingly at each stack we left behind us.

The third day there was not a cloud in the sky. We didn't work that morning in order to give the bales a chance to dry out. Although it hadn't rained, the humidity and dew had dampened them just enough so that they might spoil if we tried to stack them right away. After lunch Long Knife and I drove out to the field in the pickup. Lame Bull had broken two teeth on the bull rake and screwed up the hydraulic lift, so he followed us with the tractor and hay wagon. We would have to pick the bales by hand, which meant a long hard afternoon. In the rearview mirror I could see Lame Bull's grinning face, partially hidden behind the tractor's chimney. Long Knife leaned out of the cab window and turned his face to the sky. It was a small round face with a short sharp nose and tiny slanted eyes. They called him Chink because of those eyes. He was a tall man, slender, with just the beginnings of a paunch showing above his belt buckle. On the silver face of the buckle was a picture of a bucking horse and the words: *All-around Cowboy, Wolf Point Stampede, 1954.* The buckle was shiny and worn from scraping against the bars of taverns up and down the valley. He was not called Chink to his face because of the day he almost beat the Hutterite to death with that slashing buckle.

"Jesus, beautiful, ain't it?" he said.

I nodded, but he was still looking out the window. I said, "You bet."

"How much does Lame Bull owe me?"

"Two days—twenty bucks so far."

Long Knife continued to gaze out the window. To the north, just above the horizon, we could see the tail end of the two-day run of clouds.

"Twenty bucks—that ain't much for two days' work, is it?"

I didn't say anything.

"It's enough, though . . . By God, it's enough." He sounded as though he had made a great decision. "How much is he paying you?"

"Same thing—ten bucks a day."

"That sure ain't much." He was still leaning out the window. As he shook his head, his black hair bristled against his short collar.

We crossed the dry irrigation ditch. This was the last field, but the alfalfa grew thickest here and the bales were scarcely ten feet apart. I killed the motor. I could hear Long Knife's hair bristling against his collar as he continued to shake his head. We waited for Lame Bull to catch up.

He stopped the tractor beside the pickup and grinned at us as we climbed out. "You throw 'em up," he said to me. "Raymond will stack 'em—ain't it, Raymond?"

Long Knife looked uncomfortable. I could tell what was coming, but Lame Bull continued to grin. I walked over to a bale beside the wagon and threw it on. I heard Long Knife say something, but the noise of the idling tractor obscured it. I walked around the wagon and threw another bale on. Lame Bull leaned down toward Long Knife: "You what?" I threw another bale on. "You heard me!" I walked behind the wagon to the pickup. I took a drink from the water bag. "You heard me!"

Lame Bull popped the clutch on the tractor. It lurched forward and died. He stepped down and checked the hitch on the wagon. Then he walked to the front of the tractor and kicked the tire. "Remind me to put some more air in this one," he said.

Long Knife kicked one of the big rear tires and nodded. I put the cap on the water bag and hung it on the door handle. Lame Bull had his back to us. He was grinning at the field full of bales. I could tell.

"Look, you give me a ride back to town and I'll buy you a beer," Long Knife said.

I avoided his eyes. I didn't want to be his ally.

Long Knife turned to Lame Bull: "But look at my hands—they're cut and bleeding. Do you want me to get infected?"

Lame Bull refused to look at his hands. "I'll pay your doctor bills when we're through."

"My head is running in circles with this heat."

"I'll pay for your head too."

"We better get started," I said, but no one moved. I sat down on the running board.

"Look at my hands."

I looked at his hands. It was true that they were raw from throwing around the bales. One finger was actually cut.

"You did that last night on one of those movie magazines," I said. "Besides, you should have wore gloves like the rest of us."

Long Knife folded his arms and leaned against the rear fender of the pickup. It was clear that he wasn't going to work anymore, no matter what happened. We were wasting time and I wanted to get the field cleared. It was the last field.

"Listen to me, Lame Bull—let's let him go. You and me'll work twice as hard and when it's done, it's done."

My logic seemed to impress Long Knife. "Listen to him, Lame Bull."

Lame Bull didn't listen. He wasn't listening to anybody. I could tell that, as his eyes swept the field, he was counting bales, converting them into cows and the cows into calves and the calves into cash.

"You can't keep me here against my will. You have to pay me and let me go back to town."

"Listen, Lame Bull—you have to pay him," I said.

"You're damn right," Long Knife said.

"And let him go back to town."

"You tell him, boy."

"He ain't a slave, you know."

There was a pause. I could see the highway from where I sat, but there were no cars. Beyond the highway, the Little Rockies seemed even tinier than their name.

Without turning around, Lame Bull pulled out his sweaty handcarved wallet, took out a bill, crumpled it into a ball and threw it over his head. It landed at our feet.

"That's more like it," Long Knife said, smoothing out the bill. It was a twenty. "You going to give me a ride, boy?"

"I don't have a car."

"You could take the pickup here."

"It isn't mine. It belongs to Teresa," I said.

"But she's your mother." Long Knife was getting desperate.

"She's his wife," I said, looking at Lame Bull's back. "Why don't you ask him for a ride?"

Long Knife thought about this for a minute. He pushed his hat back on his head. "I'll give you two dollars," he said, as though he had just offered Lame Bull a piece of the world. "Two dollars and a beer when we get to town."

The magpie floating light-boned through the afternoon air seemed to stop and jump straight up when Lame Bull's fist landed. Long Knife's head snapped back as he slammed into the pickup, his hat flying clear over the box. It was a sucker punch, straight from the shoulder, with a jump to reach the taller man's nose.

"Jesus Christ almighty!" I said, leaping from the spray of blood.

Lame Bull was not grinning. He picked up Long Knife and threw him in the back of the pickup. "Get in," he said. I retrieved the hat—the sweatband was already wet—and climbed into the cab. Lame Bull had wrapped a blue bandanna around his hand. With shifting gears and whining motor, the pickup shot off across the fields toward the highway.

"You might have to get a tetanus shot for that hand," I said, looking through the back window at Long Knife, his face smeared with blood, his little eyes staring peacefully up at the clear blue sky.

THE TRICKSTER OF LIBERTY

by Gerald Vizenor

Gerald Vizenor, a mixed-blood Anishinaabe (the tribe also known as the Chippewas or the Ojibwas), was born in Minneapolis in 1934. He has taught at the University of Minnesota; the University of California, at Berkeley and at Santa Cruz; and is currently David Burr Chair of Letters at the University of Oklahoma.

Vizenor has five collections of haiku, four collections of essays, and three novels, Darkness in Saint Louis Bearheart *(1978),* Griever: A Monkey King in China *(1987), and* The Trickster of Liberty *(1988).*

"The Last Lecture on the Edge," from The Trickster of Liberty, *takes place on the White Earth Reservation near Beaulieu, Minnesota, a town named after one of Vizenor's forbears. Vizenor is satirizing urban Indians with what he calls "terminal beliefs," ideas that they hold sacred while refusing to grant that anyone else may have a legitimate point of view. The character Coke De Fountain is based on American Indian Movement leaders like Dennis Means, who Vizenor pillories as "Dennis of Wounded Knee" in his essay collection* The People Named the Chippewa.

Vizenor's fiction resembles the work of postmodern writers like Donald Barthelme and Stanley Elkin in its zany humor and bizarre violence.

The Last Lecture on the Edge

Father Mother Browne renounced the priesthood and returned to the baronage, where he became a public mourner and celebrant at funerals on the reservation; he was inspired by the spontaneous paternosters and entreaties at tribal wakes and over the graves. The survivors besought the dead to remember a better past, humor over disease, mythic stories over incurious studies, a woodland renaissance.

Father Mother mourned through the winter, and then on the summer solstice he was moved in a dream to ordain a tavern and sermon center; the Last Lecture was built on a watershed below the scapehouse at the south end of the baronage. The urban mixedbloods who had moved to the reservation were summoned to carve a stone precipice behind the tavern, named the Edge of the White Earth. There, seven modern telephone booths were mounted in a row with double doors, one opened over the precipice.

Those who subscribed to step over the edge were allowed one last call before they dropped into their new names and social identities.

"There ain't no such thing as a last lecture," said the postman, who was troubled over the increased mail service to the baronage. "My wife says something like that, she says, 'These are my last words.' but she never means it."

"The last lecture, one at a time," said Father Mother.

"If you don't mind me saying so," said the postman as he cocked his hat, "you people are a strange lot with those booths, the scapehouse, and now this place."

"Shakespeare said that once."

"Did he now."

"In his last lecture," said Father Mother, "he listed one by one all the strange things he saw around him, once he saw it and named it in a play, that was the end of it, nothing more to say."

"Well, he was on to something there, but he never delivered the mail to this place," said the postman. "If you start something else out here, make it the last letter."

The Last Lecture was a circular cedar structure with a bar and booths on one side and a theater, with tables and chairs, on the other; visitors were invited to present their sermons and last lectures on the theater stage. Mixedblood educators, tribal radicals, writers, painters, a geneticist, a psychotaxidermist, and various pretenders to the tribe took the microphone that summer and told the bold truth; these lost and lonesome mixedbloods practiced their new names, made one last telephone call to their past, and then dropped over the edge into a new wild world.

Marie Gee Hailme was dressed in paisley velvet and black lace when she raised the microphone to deliver her last lecture; her narrow mouth moved in a monotone. More than a hundred tribal people from communities on the reservation crowded into the sermon center to hear the director of urban tribal education, the first to unburden her vanities that season; even the postman was at the bar that night. She mumbled that the tribal values she had introduced in classrooms were amiss and biased.

"My skin is dark," she whispered, "you can see that much, but who, in their right mind, would trust the education of their children to pigmentation?" Marie Gee held the microphone too close to her mouth; her voice hissed in the circular tavern. "Who knows how to grow up like an Indian? Tell me that, and who knows how to teach values that are real Indian?

"I was orphaned and grew up in a church boarding school, so they trusted me, because of their guilt over my dark skin, and put me in charge of developing classroom materials about Indians," she said and lowered the microphone.

"I went all over the state lecturing about Indian values to help white teachers understand how Indian students think and why they drop out of school, but once, right in the middle of a lecture, an Indian student asked me, 'What kind of Indians are you talking about? There aren't no Indians like that out here on our reservation.' I realized that I was describing an invented tribe, my own tribe that acted out my hang-ups, which had nothing to do with being a person stuck in a public school.

"I was telling white teachers that Indians never look you in the eye and Indians never touch. Can you believe that I was teaching that as the basic values and behavior of Indians? Those weren't values, they were my hang-ups, and they had nothing to do with anybody else. My pigmentation and degrees made me an expert on Indians. Would you believe that my dissertation was on Indian values? My hang-ups became the values, and then I compared them to other cultures. White academics loved it, the whole thing made sense to teachers, but it had nothing to do with Indians, because the Indian students never understood what I was saying about the values imposed on them.

"So, I pulled back, turned around last month, and looked at myself and the other Indian teachers, at what we had been doing, and I discovered the obvious, yes, the obvious," she said in the same tone and loosened her padded velvet coat. "We were all mixedbloods, some light and some dark, and married to whites, and most of us had never really lived in reservation communities. Yes, we suffered some in college, but not in the same way as the Indian kids we were trying to reach, the ones we were trying to keep in school when school was the real problem. But there we were, the first generation of Indian education experts, forcing our invented curriculum units, our idea of Indians, on the next generation, forcing Indian kids to accept our biased views.

"That curriculum crap we put together about Indians was just as boring and inaccurate as the white materials we were revising and replacing. We pretended to do this for Indian kids, in their interests, but were we really honest?"

"Never, no, never," a man shouted at the bar.

"I think not. We did it for the money and the power bestowed on us by liberal whites. We should have trashed the schools, not ourselves with the delusions that we were helping Indian students. We were helping ourselves and the schools hold on to their power over children, and all the while we pretended to teach Indian pride. Can you believe that?"

"Pride quit school with me," the man shouted.

"Compromise, the kind that leads to self hatred, is what we were really teaching. I should have listened, the Indian kids knew better, but we used them to do good and get ahead.

"So, here I am giving my last lecture, and tomorrow I'll walk over the Edge of the Earth with a new name and a bus ticket to a crowded place out by the ocean for a new start at my life," she said and tapped her finger on the microphone. "Thanks to Father Mother, I'm through with my ideas about Indian values and education. Too much of that crap could kill an ordinary spirit."

Marie Gee saluted the crowd with the microphone; she bowed to the former priest and then ordered a round of drinks for everyone in the Last Lecture. She was applauded and cheered at the bar; two stout men in a booth raised their straw hats in the seven directions and ordered seven more bottles of beer.

Coke de Fountain waited at the bar in silence; his massive shoulders shuddered when he listened to the educator end her career. He ordered a double gin and then entered his name as a last lecturer. The crowd roared with derision when his name was printed on the board over the noted author Homer Yellow Snow and several other last lecturers scheduled that night.

De Fountain was an urban pantribal radical and dealer in cocaine. His tribal career unfolded in prison, where he studied tribal philosophies and blossomed when he was paroled in braids and a bone choker. He bore a dark cultural frown, posed as a new colonial victim, and learned his racial diatribes in church basements; radical and stoical postures were tied to federal programs. The race to represent the poor started with loose money and ran down to the end with loose power. When the dash was blocked, the radical restored his power over the poor with narcotics; he inspired his urban warriors with cocaine.

Father Mother waved his hands and called attention to the importance of last lectures. "Our next lecturer, the second in line, needs no introduction. You have heard his mixedblood wrath in the cities, you have seen his wild face on television, and some have whispered his name in anger. Now, on our stage, the man who took the most and gave the least back, the mad deacon of the urban word warriors, has agreed to deliver his last lecture on the run."

Coke cleared his throat, a wild rumble, and squeezed loud clicks from the microphone with his scarred hands. The audience hissed and sneered and then waited in silence; bottles, mouths, and hands were cocked.

"Wounded Knee was the beginning in our calendar, the first year of the new warriors," he roared and pounded the microphone in his hand. "We went back and took that place, it was ours, the chapel and the graves, we earned it back, and we did it for the elders, so the elders could be proud again."

"Bullshit," a woman shouted from a booth.

"We always listen to our elders," Coke shouted back and waved one hand in a circle. "We did what the elders wanted us to do, we protected their sacred traditions."

"You did it for the money and blondes," said an elder at the bar. He laughed at the radical and mocked his hand movements. "Money and women, that's why you went to Wounded Knee and that's what will put you back in prison, because you never did anything for anybody."

"Our young people are destroyed in racist schools," he roared, and he sputtered and moved closer with the microphone pressed on his mouth like a rock singer. "Who are you to tell me anything? What have you ever done to save our children?"

"Wounded Knee we will remember," said the elder, "but you, and your mouth, we want to forget, we want to forget what you have done to our memories."

"De Fountain, he's the one who saved our children with drugs, and taught them how to hate," said a tribal woman at a table close to the stage. She turned and shouted to the others, "This man never saved anyone, not even himself. He's evil, he hates himself, he's got no vision, he's a killer of our dreams."

"My conscience is clean. . . ."

"Your conscience is cocaine," the woman screamed.

"I came here to talk about racism and genocide. Genocide!" he barked into the microphone. "What have you ever done but sit on a bar stool and bring disgrace to our sacred mother earth."

"Your mother earth is a blonde," the tribal woman said, and then she moved closer to the radical. "You use women and pretend to love mother earth, but you would rather have a blond woman than live on a reservation. You let a white foster family care for your children while you parade around and hate whites. Why don't you take care of your own kids before you worry so much about mother earth?" The woman stood below him on the aisle with her hands on her hips and chanted, "woman hater, woman hater."

"I don't have to listen to this," he moaned and moved back from the tables, a man in retreat. His power had eroded and now he was alone, cornered in his own lecture by those who had waited in silence on the reservation. "Wounded Knee told the world that we were proud people once again, and we did that for you, we saved our children from the disgrace of white racism."

"Wounded Knee saved you, no one but you and your pack of worthless downtown warriors," said the elder at the bar. "You can't even save your own red ass without a white lawyer, federal money, and now that damn microphone."

"Listen here," he bellowed and aimed the microphone at the old man, "I don't have to give my last lecture here, so pack up your backward ideas and forget it. Down your beer old man and forget it. You've got no pride, there's nothing left in you."

Coke de Fountain dropped the microphone on the floor and the sound rumbled in the tavern. "This is not my last lecture. Never, never," he told Father Mother. "Why should I give my last lecture to those tomahawks?" Coke threw the envelope with his new name at the crowd; he sneered over his shoulder on the way out, slammed the door, and hurried over to the booths at the scapehouse.

Homer Yellow Snow, the spurious tribal author, arrived in a brown limousine minutes behind the radical who withdrew his last lecture. The author told his chauffeur, a muscular blonde, to wait for him on the road below the telephone booths at the Edge of the White Earth.

"Father Mother?" asked Yellow Snow.

"Not me," said the elder at the bar. "He's over there at a table, the one in the white suit and black collar. Would you believe that man was a priest once?"

"Would you believe I was once an Indian?" he asked the elder and then ordered a bottle of white wine to celebrate his wild conversion.

"No, but who asked?"

"No one worth mentioning," the author allowed.

"Yellow Snow, you're here," said Father Mother. He rushed over to the author at the bar. "Please, join us at a table before you begin your lecture."

"Do you have the documents?"

"The whole bundle," responded Father Mother. "Change of names, driver's license, credit cards, voter registration, the new you over the last past."

Patronia retains certain civil records, as several treaties provide, such as birth, death, marriage, and divorce. The Last Lecture expanded these common civil records to include surnames, licenses, legal residences, and other documents demanded by those who deliver their last lectures on the baronage.

Homer Yellow Snow demanded three new names, a recorded tribal death in an auto accident, a wake and burial of his past on the reservation; these were provided at a much higher cost than the usual admissions to the new world.

"So, what's your new name?" asked Marie Gee.

"Not a chance," the author said with a nervous smile. "No one but my chauffeur will ever connect my new names to the past."

"What a pity, we might have pretended," she sighed.

"That's the theme of my lecture."

"Did you prepare your last lecture?" asked Father Mother.

"Yes, but on the way over I read it to my chauffeur and changed my mind," said Yellow Snow. "This time my last lecture will be spontaneous and the prepared speech will become my press release, along with the notice that I was killed tonight in a tragic automobile accident."

"Death kits for the authors," said Marie Gee.

"Pretend Indians," he whispered.

"The late Yellow Snow," announced Father Mother. "We are honored to have one of the best-known tribal authors here to deliver his last lecture."

"Ladies and gentlemen," said the author with the microphone in both hands. He wore turquoise bracelets, a thick silver beltbuckle, and a double beaded necklace. "You are about to hear the last, or rather the first, honest words of Homer Yellow Snow, author, artist, historian, tribal philosopher, and last but not least, a pretend Indian.

"Within the hour, my friends, I will be dead on a reservation road, and the Indian author you thought you knew will step over the edge and become a Greek, an Italian, perhaps a Turk, but no more will I be your Indian."

"Spare me the heartbreak," said a tribal man in a booth with two blondes. "You never were anything to me, white or whatever you pretended to be."

"Let the man talk," said Marie Gee.

"This last lecture actually began several years ago when a mixedblood writer questioned my tribal identity, he challenged an autobiographical essay I had submitted for publication in an anthology," said the author in a sonorous voice. His words were practiced, measured on a line. "You see, my tribal identities were pretentious, my blood recollections were artificial, at best, and this mixedblood writer detected how impossible were my autobiographical experiences. He told the editor of the book to either correct or drop my essay.

"He saw right through my invented tribal childhood, he detected the flaws in my asserted poverty, in my avowed tribal identities, and he was secure enough in his own experiences to challenge me. I should thank him for driving me to this, my last lecture.

"That was the turning point, the beginning of my revisions, double revisions since then, preparations for my last lecture, and now over the edge with my new names. I have Father Mother, this extraordinary man, to thank for an opportunity to start a new life with a proper public confession.

"Save one or two academic skeptics, I had the entire white and tribal worlds believing in me as a writer and historian, and eating out of my hand as a philosopher, especially when I raised foundation support for films and tribal seminars," he said and then paused to consider the audience. The ticktock of the tavern clock measured the silence. Two men in a booth peeled the labels from several beer bottles and rolled the moist paper into wads.

"What other culture could be so easily duped?" asked Homer Yellow Snow. "Listen, all it took was a little dark skin, a descriptive name, turquoise and silver, and that was about it, my friends. With that much, anyone could become an Indian."

"Whites are the real victims," the elder shouted.

"What about white people?" asked Yellow Snow.

"Dupe the whites," the elder answered from the end of the bar. "We duped the whites more than they duped us, we even duped them to think they were duping us."

"Really," mocked the author.

"You duped yourself to pretend you were like us," said a woman in a booth. "You're the white, you're the victim, and that's your problem not ours, so who's the dupe?"

"So there, my tribal friends," he said with hesitation, "you have my story, the adventures of a pretend Indian who published his way to the top with turquoise and a tribal mask, and all of you needed me, white and tribal, to absolve your insecurities and to convince the world that you were more than a lost whisper in a museum, more than a stick figure on birchbark or a faded mark on buffalo hide."

"Yellow Snow, hit the edge," said a disabled man at the bar. He wobbled between the tables with bottles in his hands. "This here is a real skin on your trail, and we got a claim to piss on some of that phoney blood, mister white eyes."

"If you knew who you were, why did you find it so easy to believe in me?" the author asked and then answered, "because you too want to be white, and no matter what you say in public, you trust whites more than you trust Indians, which is to say, you trust pretend Indians more than real ones."

Father Mother handed Homer Yellow Snow his bundle of new names and identities, an invoice for conversion services, and escorted the author through the back door to the booths and the precipice. Yellow Snow telephoned his chauffeur, removed his turquoise, bone choker, beads, and stepped over the edge into the new world with three new names.

The Last Lecture served thirteen tribal pretenders and several hundred mixedbloods in the first few months the tavern was opened. Father Mother provided new names and identities through the baronage for a nominal fee. The cost was so low, and the last lecture such a solace, that some mixedbloods returned several times to unburden their new identities for an even newer name; the last lectures, for some, became an annual ritual. Some mixedbloods, however, belied their own last lectures, balked at the booth and the edge, and returned to their past with dubious resolve and courage.

Coke De Fountain turned his resistence to a new name into a competitive business. The racial freebooter opened the Very Last Plea, a fry bread parlor and tribal desert house, where he provided new descriptive names, cocaine, and membership in the New Breed, a radical urban movement.

Father Mother introduced each last lecturer and listened to their conversions; he endured the returns and repetitions, but one night he interrupted a genetic acarid engineer and delivered his own last lecture.

See See Arachnidan, a mixedblood recluse who had moved back to the reservation, revealed the parasitic testicle ticks that she had bred to attack authoritarian personalities: police officers, court officials, some teachers, and federal agents. "One testick bite causes a rare disease. In an instant, men stutter like rich liberals on the Fourth of July. My testicks are aroused by certain male hormones in groin sweat," she said as the microphone died. She was told to sit down and be silent.

Father Mother stared at the audience for several minutes, and then he delivered his own last lecture. "Listen, I have listened long enough to last lectures of the lost and lonesome. Now it is my time to choose a new name and walk over the edge," he said and placed the microphone on a chair. The audience cheered when he removed his black collar, white coat and trousers. He turned in circles and then walked backward in his shorts and white shoes out the back door of the tavern.

Father Mother was the last lecturer at the Last Lecture; he wrapped himself in a plain brown blanket, entered the telephone booth, and called his mother at the scapehouse. The former priest laughed in the booth and decided to become a woman with a new name in a new wild world.

LOVE MEDICINE

by Louise Erdrich

Love Medicine *is Louise Erdrich's masterpiece, the first of her cycle of books about whites and Indians in North Dakota. She has published three to date,* The Beet Queen *and* Tracks *being the others. In these books Erdrich presents a cast of characters whose venality, grotesqueness, libidinousness, and exuberant humanity remind one of Chaucer's pilgrims.*

"Saint Marie" depicts a young girl, Marie Lazarre, who wants to become a nun, and her mentor, Sister Leopolda. Marie is unaware that she is Leopolda's illegitimate daughter, although she is unaccountably drawn to the nun. In fact, the reader does not learn this either unless s/he reads the third novel in the series, Tracks, *in which it turns out that Leopolda not only is Marie's mother but also has killed Marie's father.*

Later in Love Medicine *we see Marie as an old woman, the grandmother of the character who strongly resembles Erdrich, a medical student with the name Albertine Johnson.*

For more about Erdrich, read her poetry above.

Saint Marie
(1934)

Marie Lazarre

So when I went there, I knew the dark fish must rise. Plumes of radiance had soldered on me. No reservation girl had ever prayed so hard. There was no use in trying to ignore me any longer. I was going up there on the hill with the black robe women. They were not any lighter than me. I was going up there to pray as good as they could. Because I don't have that much Indian blood. And they never thought they'd have a girl from this reservation as a saint they'd have to kneel to. But they'd have me. And I'd be carved in pure gold. With ruby lips. And my toenails would be little pink ocean shells, which they would have to stoop down off their high horse to kiss.

I was ignorant. I was near age fourteen. The length of sky is just about the size of my ignorance. Pure and wide. And it was just that—the pure and wideness of my ignorance—that got me up the hill to Sacred Heart

Convent and brought me back down alive. For maybe Jesus did not take my bait, but them Sisters tried to cram me right down whole.

You ever see a walleye strike so bad the lure is practically out its back end before you reel it in? That is what they done with me. I don't like to make that low comparison, but I have seen a walleye do that once. And it's the same attempt as Sister Leopolda made to get me in her clutch.

I had the mail-order Catholic soul you get in a girl raised out in the bush, whose only thought is getting into town. For Sunday Mass is the only time my father brought his children in except for school, when we were harnessed. Our soul went cheap. We were so anxious to get there we would have walked in on our hands and knees. We just craved going to the store, slinging bottle caps in the dust, making fool eyes at each other. And of course we went to church.

Where they have the convent is on top of the highest hill, so that from its windows the Sisters can be looking into the marrow of the town. Recently a windbreak was planted before the bar "for the purposes of tornado insurance." Don't tell me that. That poplar stand was put up to hide the drinkers as they get the transformation. As they are served into the beast of their burden. While they're drinking, that body comes upon them, and then they stagger or crawl out the bar door, pulling a weight they can't move past the poplars. They don't want no holy witness to their fall.

Anyway, I climbed. That was a long-ago day. There was a road then for wagons that wound in ruts to the top of the hill where they had their buildings of painted brick. Gleaming white. So white the sun glanced off in dazzling display to set forms whirling behind your eyelids. The face of God you could hardly look at. But that day it drizzled, so I could look all I wanted. I saw the homelier side. The cracked whitewash and swallows nesting in the busted ends of eaves. I saw the boards sawed the size of broken windowpanes and the fruit trees, stripped. Only the tough wild rhubarb flourished. Goldenrod rubbed up their walls. It was a poor convent. I didn't see that then but I know that now. Compared to others it was humble, ragtag, out in the middle of no place. It was the end of the world to some. Where the maps stopped. Where God had only half a hand in the creation. Where the Dark One had put in thick bush, liquor, wild dogs, and Indians.

I heard later that the Sacred Heart Convent was a catchall place for nuns that don't get along elsewhere. Nuns that complain too much or lose their mind. I'll always wonder now, after hearing that, where they picked up Sister Leopolda. Perhaps she had scarred someone else, the way she left a mark on me. Perhaps she was just sent around to test her Sisters' faith, here and there, like the spot-checker in a factory. For she was the

definite most-hard trial to anyone's endurance, even when they started
out with veils of wretched love upon their eyes.

I was that girl who thought the black hem of her garment would help
me rise. Veils of love which was only hate petrified by longing—that was
me. I was like those bush Indians who stole the holy black hat of a Jesuit
and swallowed little scraps of it to cure their fevers. But the hat itself carried smallpox and was killing them with belief. Veils of faith! I had this
confidence in Leopolda. She was different. The other Sisters had long ago
gone blank and given up on Satan. He slept for them. They never noticed
his comings and goings. But Leopolda kept track of him and knew his habits, minds he burrowed in, deep spaces where he hid. She knew as much
about him as my grandma, who called him by other names and was not
afraid.

In her class, Sister Leopolda carried a long oak pole for opening high
windows. It had a hook made of iron on one end that could jerk a patch of
your hair out or throttle you by the collar—all from a distance. She used
this deadly hook-pole for catching Satan by surprise. He could have entered without your knowing it—through your lips or your nose or any one
of your seven openings—and gained your mind. But she would see him.
That pole would brain you from behind. And he would gasp, dazzled, and
take the first thing she offered, which was pain.

She had a stringer of children who could only breathe if she said the
word. I was the worst of them. She always said the Dark One wanted me
most of all, and I believed this. I stood out. Evil was a common thing I
trusted. Before sleep sometimes he came and whispered conversation in
the old language of the bush. I listened. He told me things he never told
anyone but Indians. I was privy to both worlds of his knowledge. I listened to him, but I had confidence in Leopolda. She was the only one of
the bunch he even noticed.

There came a day, though, when Leopolda turned the tide with her
hook-pole.

It was a quiet day with everyone working at their desks, when I heard
him. He had sneaked into the closets in the back of the room. He was
scratching around, tasting crumbs in our pockets, stealing buttons, squirt-
ing his dark juice in the linings and the boots. I was the only one who
heard him, and I got bold. I smiled. I glanced back and smiled and looked
up at her sly to see if she had noticed. My heart jumped. For she was
looking straight at me. And she sniffed. She had a big stark bony nose
stuck to the front of her face for smelling out brimstone and evil thoughts.
She had smelled him on me. She stood up. Tall, pale, a blackness leading
into the deeper blackness of the slate wall behind her. Her oak pole had

flown into her grip. She had seen me glance at the closet. Oh, she knew. She knew just where he was. I watched her watch him in her mind's eye. The whole class was watching now. She was staring, sizing, following his scuffle. And all of a sudden she tensed down, posed on her bent kneesprings, cocked her arm back. She threw the oak pole singing over my head, through my braincloud. It cracked through the thin wood door of the back closet, and the heavy pointed hook drove through his heart. I turned. She'd speared her own black rubber overboot where he'd taken refuge in the tip of her darkest toe.

Something howled in my mind. Loss and darkness. I understood. I was to suffer for my smile.

He rose up hard in my heart. I didn't blink when the pole cracked. My skull was tough. I didn't flinch when she shrieked in my ear. I only shrugged at the flowers of hell. He wanted me. More than anything he craved me. But then she did the worst. She did what broke my mind to her. She grabbed me by the collar and dragged me, feet flying, through the room and threw me in the closet with her dead black overboot. And I was there. The only light was a crack beneath the door. I asked the Dark One to enter into me and boost my mind. I asked him to restrain my tears, for they was pushing behind my eyes. But he was afraid to come back there. He was afraid of her sharp pole. And I was afraid of Leopolda's pole for the first time, too. I felt the cold hook in my heart. How it could crack through the door at any minute and drag me out, like a dead fish on a gaff, drop me on the floor like a gutshot squirrel.

I was nothing. I edged back to the wall as far as I could. I breathed the chalk dust. The hem of her full black cloak cut against my cheek. He had left me. Her spear could find me any time. Her keen ears would aim the hook into the beat of my heart.

What was that sound?

It filled the closet, filled it up until it spilled over, but I did not recognize the crying wailing voice as mine until the door cracked open, brightness, and she hoisted me to her camphor-smelling lips.

"He *wants* you," she said. "That's the difference. I give you love."

Love. The black hook. The spear singing through the mind. I saw that she had tracked the Dark One to my heart and flushed him out into the open. So now my heart was an empty nest where she could lurk.

Well, I was weak. I was weak when I let her in, but she got a foothold there. Hard to dislodge as the year passed. Sometimes I felt him—the brush of dim wings—but only rarely did his voice compel. It was between Marie and Leopolda now, and the struggle changed. I began to realize I had been on the wrong track with the fruits of hell. The real way to over-

come Leopolda was this: I'd get to heaven first. And then, when I saw her
coming, I'd shut the gate. She'd be out! That is why, besides the bowing
and the scraping I'd be dealt, I wanted to sit on the altar as a saint.

To this end, I went up on the hill. Sister Leopolda was the consecrated
nun who had sponsored me to come there.

"You're not vain," she said. "You're too honest, looking into the mirror,
for that. You're not smart. You don't have the ambition to get clear. You
have two choices. One, you can marry a no-good Indian, bear his brats,
die like a dog. Or two, you can give yourself to God."

"I'll come up there," I said, "but not because of what you think."

I could have had any damn man on the reservation at the time. And I
could have made him treat me like his own life. I looked good. And I
looked white. But I wanted Sister Leopolda's heart. And here was the
thing: sometimes I wanted her heart in love and admiration. Sometimes.
And sometimes I wanted her heart to roast on a black stick.

She answered the back door where they had instructed me to call. I stood
there with my bundle. She looked me up and down.

"All right," she said finally. "Come in."

She took my hand. Her fingers were like a bundle of broom straws,
so thin and dry, but the strength of them was unnatural. I couldn't have
tugged loose if she was leading me into rooms of white-hot coal. Her
strength was a kind of perverse miracle, for she got it from fasting herself
thin. Because of this hunger practice her lips were a wounded brown and
her skin deadly pale. Her eye sockets were two deep lashless hollows in a
taut skull. I told you about the nose already. It stuck out far and made the
place her eyes moved even deeper, as if she stared out the wrong end of
a gun barrel. She took the bundle from my hands and threw it in the
corner.

"You'll be sleeping behind the stove, child."

It was immense, like a great furnace. There was a small cot close behind it.

"Looks like it could get warm there," I said.

"Hot. It does."

"Do I get a habit?"

I wanted something like the thing she wore. Flowing black cotton. Her
face was strapped in white bandages, and a sharp crest of starched white
cardboard hung over her forehead like a glaring beak. If possible, I
wanted a bigger, longer, whiter beak than hers.

"No," she said, grinning her great skull grin. "You don't get one yet.
Who knows, you might not like us. Or we might not like you."

But she had loved me, or offered me love. And she had tried to hunt the Dark One down. So I had this confidence.

"I'll inherit your keys from you," I said.

She looked at me sharply, and her grin turned strange. She hissed, taking in her breath. Then she turned to the door and took a key from her belt. It was a giant key, and it unlocked the larder where the food was stored.

Inside there was all kinds of good stuff. Things I'd tasted only once or twice in my life. I saw sticks of dried fruit, jars of orange peel, spice like cinnamon. I saw tins of crackers with ships painted on the side. I saw pickles. Jars of herring and the rind of pigs. There was cheese, a big brown block of it from the thick milk of goats. And besides that there was the everyday stuff, in great quantities, the flour and the coffee.

It was the cheese that got to me. When I saw it my stomach hollowed. My tongue dripped. I loved that goat-milk cheese better than anything I'd ever ate. I stared at it. The rich curve in the buttery cloth.

"When you inherit my keys," she said sourly, slamming the door in my face, "you can eat all you want of the priest's cheese."

Then she seemed to consider what she'd done. She looked at me. She took the key from her belt and went back, sliced a hunk off, and put it in my hand.

"If you're good you'll taste this cheese again. When I'm dead and gone," she said.

Then she dragged out the big sack of flour. When I finished that heaven stuff she told me to roll my sleeves up and begin doing God's labor. For a while we worked in silence, mixing up the dough and pounding it out on stone slabs.

"God's work," I said after a while. "If this is God's work, then I've done it all my life."

"Well, you've done it with the Devil in your heart then," she said. "Not God."

"How do you know?" I asked. But I knew she did. And I wished I had not brought up the subject.

"I see right into you like a clear glass," she said. "I always did."

"You don't know it," she continued after a while, "but he's come around here sulking. He's come around here brooding. You brought him in. He knows the smell of me, and he's going to make a last ditch try to get you back. Don't let him." She glared over at me. Her eyes were cold and lighted. "Don't let him touch you. We'll be a long time getting rid of him."

So I was careful. I was careful not to give him an inch. I said a rosary, two rosaries, three, underneath my breath. I said the Creed. I said every

scrap of Latin I knew while we punched the dough with our fists. And
still, I dropped the cup. It rolled under that monstrous iron stove, which
was getting fired up for baking.

And she was on me. She saw he'd entered my distraction.

"Our good cup," she said. "Get it out of there, Marie."

I reached for the poker to snag it out from beneath the stove. But I had
a sinking feel in my stomach as I did this. Sure enough, her long arm
darted past me like a whip. The poker lighted in her hand.

"Reach," she said. "Reach with your arm for that cup. And when your
flesh is hot, remember that the flames you feel are only one fraction of the
heat you will feel in his hellish embrace."

She always did things this way, to teach you lessons. So I wasn't surprised. It was playacting, anyway, because a stove isn't very hot underneath right along the floor. They aren't made that way. Otherwise a wood
floor would burn. So I said yes and got down on my stomach and reached
under. I meant to grab it quick and jump up again, before she could think
up another lesson, but here it happened. Although I groped for the cup,
my hand closed on nothing. That cup was nowhere to be found. I heard
her step toward me, a slow step. I heard the creak of thick shoe leather,
the little *plat* as the folds of her heavy skirts met, a trickle of fine sand
sifting, somewhere, perhaps in the bowels of her, and I was afraid. I tried
to scramble up, but her foot came down lightly behind my ear, and I was
lowered. The foot came down more firmly at the base of my neck, and I
was held.

"You're like I was," she said. "He wants you very much."

"He doesn't want me no more," I said. "He had his fill. I got the cup!"

I heard the valve opening, the hissed intake of breath, and knew that I
should not have spoke.

"You lie," she said. "You're cold. There is a wicked ice forming in your
blood. You don't have a shred of devotion for God. Only wild cold dark
lust. I know it. I know how you feel. I see the beast . . . the beast watches
me out of your eyes sometimes. Cold."

The urgent scrape of metal. It took a moment to know from where. Top
of the stove. Kettle. Lessons. She was steadying herself with the iron
poker. I could feel it like pure certainty, driving into the wood floor. I
would not remind her of pokers. I heard the water as it came, tipped from
the spout, cooling as it fell but still scalding as it struck. I must have
twitched beneath her foot, because she steadied me, and then the poker
nudged up beside my arm as if to guide. "To warm your cold ash heart,"
she said. I felt how patient she would be. The water came. My mind went
dead blank. Again. I could only think the kettle would be cooling slowly in

her hand. I could not stand it. I bit my lip so as not to satisfy her with a
sound. She gave me more reason to keep still.

"I will boil him from your mind if you make a peep," she said, "by filling up your ear."

Any sensible fool would have run back down the hill the minute Leopolda
let them up from under her heel. But I was snared in her black intelli-
gence by then. I could not think straight. I had prayed so hard I think I
broke a cog in my mind. I prayed while her foot squeezed my throat.
While my skin burst. I prayed even when I heard the wind come through,
shrieking in the busted bird nests. I didn't stop when pure light fell, turning slowly behind my eyelids. God's face. Even that did not disrupt my
continued praise. Words came. Words came from nowhere and flooded
my mind.

Now I could pray much better than any one of them. Than all of them
full force. This was proved. I turned to her in a daze when she let me up.
My thoughts were gone, and yet I remember how surprised I was. Tears
glittered in her eyes, deep down, like the sinking reflection in a well.

"It was so hard, Marie," she gasped. Her hands were shaking. The
kettle clattered against the stove. "But I have used all the water up now. I
think he is gone."

"I prayed," I said foolishly. "I prayed very hard."

"Yes," she said. "My dear one, I know."

We sat together quietly because we had no more words. We let the dough
rise and punched it down once. She gave me a bowl of mush, unlocked
the sausage from a special cupboard, and took that in to the Sisters. They
sat down the hall, chewing their sausage, and I could hear them. I could
hear their teeth bite through their bread and meat. I couldn't move. My
shirt was dry but the cloth stuck to my back, and I couldn't think straight.
I was losing the sense to understand how her mind worked. She'd gotten
past me with her poker and I would never be a saint. I despaired. I felt I
had no inside voice, nothing to direct me, no darkness, no Marie. I was
about to throw that cornmeal mush out to the birds and make a run for it,
when the vision rose up blazing in my mind.

I was rippling gold. My breasts were bare and my nipples flashed and
winked. Diamonds tipped them. I could walk through panes of glass. I
could walk through windows. She was at my feet, swallowing the glass
after each step I took. I broke through another and another. The glass she
swallowed ground and cut until her starved insides were only a subtle
dust. She coughed. She coughed a cloud of dust. And then she was only a

black rag that flapped off, snagged in bob wire, hung there for an age, and finally rotted into the breeze.

I saw this, mouth hanging open, gazing off into the flagged boughs of trees.

"Get up!" she cried. "Stop dreaming. It is time to bake."

Two other Sisters had come in with her, wide women with hands like paddles. They were evening and smoothing out the firebox beneath the great jaws of the oven.

"Who is this one?" they asked Leopolda. "Is she yours?"

"She is mine," said Leopolda. "A very good girl."

"What is your name?" one asked me.

"Marie."

"Marie. Star of the Sea."

"She will shine," said Leopolda, "when we have burned off the dark corrosion."

The others laughed, but uncertainly. They were mild and sturdy French, who did not understand Leopolda's twisted jokes, although they muttered respectfully at things she said. I knew they wouldn't believe what she had done with the kettle. There was no question. So I kept quiet.

"*Elle est docile*," they said approvingly as they left to starch the linens.

"Does it pain?" Leopolda asked me as soon as they were out the door.

I did not answer. I felt sick with the hurt.

"Come along," she said.

The building was wholly quiet now. I followed her up the narrow staircase into a hall of little rooms, many doors. Her cell was the quietest, at the very end. Inside, the air smelled stale, as if the door had not been opened for years. There was a crude straw mattress, a tiny bookcase with a picture of Saint Francis hanging over it, a ragged palm, a stool for sitting on, a crucifix. She told me to remove my blouse and sit on the stool. I did so. She took a pot of salve from the bookcase and began to smooth it upon my burns. Her hands made slow, wide circles, stopping the pain. I closed my eyes. I expected to see blackness. Peace. But instead the vision reared up again. My chest was still tipped with diamonds. I was walking through windows. She was chewing up the broken litter I left behind.

"I am going," I said. "Let me go."

But she held me down.

"Don't go," she said quickly. "Don't. We have just begun."

I was weakening. My thoughts were whirling pitifully. The pain had kept me strong, and as it left me I began to forget it; I couldn't hold on. I began to wonder if she'd really scalded me with the kettle. I could not remember. To remember this seemed the most important thing in the

world. But I was losing the memory. The scalding. The pouring. It began
to vanish. I felt like my mind was coming off its hinge, flapping in the
breeze, hanging by the hair of my own pain. I wrenched out of her grip.

"He was always in you," I said. "Even more than in me. He wanted you
even more. And now he's got you. Get thee behind me!"

I shouted that, grabbed my shirt, and ran through the door throwing it
on my body. I got down the stairs and into the kitchen, even, but no matter what I told myself, I couldn't get out the door. It wasn't finished. And
she knew I would not leave. Her quiet step was immediately behind me.

"We must take the bread from the oven now," she said.

She was pretending nothing happened. But for the first time I had gotten through some chink she'd left in her darkness. Touched some doubt.
Her voice was so low and brittle it cracked off at the end of her sentence.

"Help me, Marie," she said slowly.

But I was not going to help her, even though she had calmly buttoned
the back of my shirt up and put the big cloth mittens in my hands for
taking out the loaves. I could have bolted for it then. But I didn't. I knew
that something was nearing completion. Something was about to happen.
My back was a wall of singing flame. I was turning. I watched her take the
long fork in one hand, to tap the loaves. In the other hand she gripped the
black poker to hook the pans.

"Help me," she said again, and I thought, Yes, this is part of it. I put
the mittens on my hands and swung the door open on its hinges. The oven
gaped. She stood back a moment, letting the first blast of heat rush by. I
moved behind her. I could feel the heat at my front and at my back. Before, behind. My skin was turning to beaten gold. It was coming quicker
than I thought. The oven was like the gate of a personal hell. Just big
enough and hot enough for one person, and that was her. One kick and
Leopolda would fly in headfirst. And that would be one-millionth of the
heat she would feel when she finally collapsed in his hellish embrace.

Saints know these numbers.

She bent forward with her fork held out. I kicked her with all my
might. She flew in. But the outstretched poker hit the back wall first, so
she rebounded. The oven was not so deep as I had thought.

There was a moment when I felt a sort of thin, hot disappointment, as
when a fish slips off the line. Only I was the one going to be lost. She was
fearfully silent. She whirled. Her veil had cutting edges. She had the
poker in one hand. In the other she held that long sharp fork she used to
tap the delicate crusts of loaves. Her face turned upside down on her
shoulders. Her face turned blue. But saints are used to miracles. I felt no
trace of fear.

If I was going to be lost, let the diamonds cut! Let her eat ground glass!

"Bitch of Jesus Christ!" I shouted. "Kneel and beg! Lick the floor!"

That was when she stabbed me through the hand with the fork, then took the poker up alongside my head, and knocked me out.

It must have been a half an hour later when I came around. Things were so strange. So strange I can hardly tell it for delight at the remembrance. For when I came around this was actually taking place. I was being worshiped. I had somehow gained the altar of a saint.

I was laying back on the stiff couch in the Mother Superior's office. I looked around me. It was as though my deepest dream had come to life. The Sisters of the convent were kneeling to me. Sister Bonaventure. Sister Dympna. Sister Cecilia Saint-Claire. The two French with hands like paddles. They were down on their knees. Black capes were slung over some of their heads. My name was buzzing up and down the room, like a fat autumn fly lighting on the tips of their tongues between Latin, humming up the heavy blood-dark curtains, circling their little cosseted heads. Marie! Marie! A girl thrown in a closet. Who was afraid of a rubber overboot. Who was half overcome. A girl who came in the back door where they threw their garbage. Marie! Who never found the cup. Who had to eat their cold mush. Marie! Leopolda had her face buried in her knuckles. Saint Marie of the Holy Slops! Saint Marie of the Bread Fork! Saint Marie of the Burnt Back and Scalded Butt!

I broke out and laughed.

They looked up. All holy hell burst loose when they saw I'd woke. I still did not understand what was happening. They were watching, talking, but not to me.

"The marks . . ."

"She has her hand closed."

"*Je ne peux pas voir.*"

I was not stupid enough to ask what they were talking about. I couldn't tell why I was laying in white sheets. I couldn't tell why they were praying to me. But I'll tell you this: it seemed entirely natural. It was me. I lifted up my hand as in my dream. It was completely limp with sacredness.

"Peace be with you."

My arm was dried blood from the wrist down to the elbow. And it hurt. Their faces turned like flat flowers of adoration to follow that hand's movements. I let it swing through the air, imparting a saint's blessing. I had practiced. I knew exactly how to act.

They murmured. I heaved a sigh, and a golden beam of light suddenly broke through the clouded window and flooded down directly on my face. A stroke of perfect luck! They had to be convinced.

Leopolda still knelt in the back of the room. Her knuckles were crammed halfway down her throat. Let me tell you, a saint has senses honed keen as a wolf. I knew that she was over my barrel now. How it happened did not matter. The last thing I remembered was how she flew from the oven and stabbed me. That one thing was most certainly true.

"Come forward, Sister Leopolda." I gestured with my heavenly wound. Oh, it hurt. It bled when I reopened the slight heal. "Kneel beside me," I said.

She kneeled, but her voice box evidently did not work, for her mouth opened, shut, opened, but no sound came out. My throat clenched in noble delight I had read of as befitting a saint. She could not speak. But she was beaten. It was in her eyes. She stared at me now with all the deep hate of the wheel of devilish dust that rolled wild within her emptiness.

"What is it you want to tell me?" I asked. And at last she spoke.

"I have told my Sisters of your passion," she managed to choke out. "How the stigmata . . . the marks of the nails . . . appeared in your palm and you swooned at the holy vision. . . ."

"Yes," I said curiously.

And then, after a moment, I understood.

Leopolda had saved herself with her quick brain. She had witnessed a miracle. She had hid the fork and told this to the others. And of course they believed her, because they never knew how Satan came and went or where he took refuge.

"I saw it from the first," said the large one who put the bread in the oven. "Humility of the spirit. So rare in these girls."

"I saw it too," said the other one with great satisfaction. She sighed quietly. "If only it was me."

Leopolda was kneeling bolt upright, face blazing and twitching, a barely held fountain of blasting poison.

"Christ has marked me," I agreed.

I smiled the saint's smirk into her face. And then I looked at her. That was my mistake.

For I saw her kneeling there. Leopolda with her soul like a rubber overboot. With her face of a starved rat. With the desperate eyes drowning in the deep wells of her wrongness. There would be no one else after me. And I would leave. I saw Leopolda kneeling within the shambles of her love.

My heart had been about to surge from my chest with the blackness of my joyous heat. Now it dropped. I pitied her. I pitied her. Pity twisted in my stomach like that hook-pole was driven through me. I was caught. It was a feeling more terrible than any amount of boiling water and worse than being forked. Still, still, I could not help what I did. I had already smiled in a saint's mealy forgiveness. I heard myself speaking gently.

"Receive the dispensation of my sacred blood," I whispered.

But there was no heart in it. No joy when she bent to touch the floor. No dark leaping. I fell back into the white pillows. Blank dust was whirling through the light shafts. My skin was dust. Dust my lips. Dust the dirty spoons on the ends of my feet.

Rise up! I thought. Rise up and walk! There is no limit to this dust!

LE ANNE HOWE

LeAnne Howe (born 1951) is a Choctaw from Oklahoma. Her family name is Tells and Kills. She majored in English at Oklahoma State University, intending to be a technical writer, but drifted into journalism before becoming a bond salesman, playwright, and short-story writer. She currently lives in Coralville, Iowa.

Howe's publications include Coyote Papers *and* A Stand Up Reader. *Her play,* Big Pow Wow *(written with Roxy Gordon) was produced in Fort Worth.*

Howe's fiction is highly autobiographical. "Moccasins Don't Have High Heels" is based on her experience as a bond salesman. "The Red Wars" is based on her student days.

Moccasins Don't Have High Heels

Dedicated to Bruce Fry, Kirk Davis, Kevin Giddis, and William Tall Mountain. These men have nothing in common and everything in common.

Okay, like it was a day like any other day in the bond business. Everyone had been spitting up blood, eating, or talking to out-of-state buddies when an official from a state agency phoned in and wanted to blow out of 10 million treasuries.

Suddenly I looked around the room and I was alone. Everyone had stepped away.

I picked up the open telephone to our Houston trading desk.

"Edward." (I have changed the names to insure artistic exaggeration.)

"Bid 10 million 8 3/4 Nov. 98s."

"Ed," I continued. "I need a bid."

"98 to the buck, darlin'."

I go back to the client with 97 30/32.

Everyone is still cordial. She wants to do it.

"Ed, I'll sell you 10MM 8 3/4 Nov 98 at 98."

"Hold on, darlin'," he said. "97 28. The market's moving."

I check back with her. There is a screaming and gnashing of teeth, but, she wants to do it.

"Okay, I'll sell 10MM Nov. 8 3/4 at 97 28."

"It's falling, darlin'," he said, "97 26."

I go back to her with 97 24.

A loud scream comes from the phone. Suddenly I'm a mother-fucker. I start to sweat cannonballs. More screaming into my ear and I can just barely make out this low roar, "Yes. Get me out!" More screaming. I put the phone down.

My trader says, "97 22."

I holler. "Do it."

He comes back with, "97 18."

"Do it. Do it. Do it!"

He confirms, "You're done darlin', 97 and a half."

I start screaming. "You got to me, you cocksucker! You got to me, you mother-fucker, cock-sucking pig. . . . "

"Hello, Ma'am. You're done at 97 14."

More shrieking into my receiver.

She says she's sending an Iranian hit squad to our office. She tells me she'll never do business with me again. She says she's putting a curse on our unborn children. She threatens to catch the next plane to Dallas and come into town and rip off my tits.

"Yes. Yes. I am sorry. The market was falling and we were the best bidder on the street. My trader said there is a rumor the Japanese are going to. . . . Hello?

"No way did I get to you. There's no way I'd do that. I am telling the truth. Really. I'll call your assistant with figures. Don't worry about a thing. I'll take care of you. Listen, let me send you some theatre tickets in New York. We've been meaning to get you a couple to your favorite Broadway show. Yes, that's right. Anytime you say. We'll even meet you in New York, too. Whenever you say. Don't worry about a thing. Right, after all it's not our money? Yes, yes, it's gonna be okay." (Click.) "Hello?"

Ah, fuck it. I quit.

Actually I didn't quit. I always said, I was quitting everyday of the week for four and one-half years, but to tell you the truth, I loved it.

After the crash of 1987, our home office eventually consolidated the bond department, and on a cold February morning we shut down the Dallas office and left one by one. Since I was the last one to turn out the lights, I took one final look around.

Lying on top of the desk was a golf putter, the whoopee cushion from a co-worker's operation, a broken telephone cord, an orange nerf ball that had traveled with us from office to office, a political button that said, "If God So loved America, why did he create Democrats?" a couple of plastic handguns and an incredible view of the Dallas skyline. I had brought the guns in, and in mock Harry Kallahan–style, slaughtered my co-workers on a daily basis. They shrugged it off saying, "Aa-a-ah, it's the Tells and Kills in her."

So as a gesture of the passage of time and the memories, I symbolically put the golf putter in my boss's chair, gave the chair a spin, watched it silently go-around-and-around-and-around, just like I imagine the circle in which we live goes. Eventually the chair stood still. I took one last look and walked out the door alone.

That got to me.

For months I had nightmares. Each night I would dream I was back in the bond business, only this time my friends and I sat in grade school desks, all in a row. We are working for, like, this drive-in bank in a shopping center. In my dream our bond trader is in the same room with us watching "I love Lucy."

I am working for minimum wage and sell Indian beads, real estate and, of all things, ice cream to supplement our income to passersby who wander in off the street.

Suddenly a bomb explodes in the trading room. The glass case that holds the Indian beads blows apart. Glass beads blow across the bond room. The ice cream turns to water. We pull a white sheet over the body of our bond trader. We know he's dead. Lady Luck has left us forever. Man, she got to us.

When I left the business this time, I wasn't leaving my job, I was leaving my bond family probably for good. I was getting rid of my high heels and putting on my moccasins. I had to get away. Everything was getting to me, man. You may ask why I stayed with it? Why I did it? The Money. The money got to me.

I took a few months off and a driving tour of Wyoming. Carla, a long time friend, and I did the Wild West trip.

We drove the corduroy roads of the Oregan trail. We saw Fort La'Ramee and sang "Oh Beautiful for Spacious Skies" as we crossed The Great Divide.

The Wyoming lands are lousy with antelope. Their white tails glisten in the sun. They are easy to see but hard to hit unless you're in a Ford Bronco driving forty miles an hour down a mountain road. For the most part there are no cars, no houses, no people, no nuclear power plants. It's an isolationist's dream. Hey, maybe it's a developer's dream. When asked about clear-cutting our national forests, former President Reagan once quipped, "Well, once you've seen one redwood, you've seen 'em all." So I figure maybe big business with the help of the big government will get to them, too.

However there is evidence of humanity in the national forests already. At 9,000 feet elevation we found plastic diet pill dispensers, beer cans. Silver bullets.

Eventually we made our way back to Jackson Hole. It was Old West Days and Alta, a friend of Carla's from Dallas, had flown in for the Old West.

When a band of Shoshoni began dancing a round dance and playing the drum and asking everyone to join in for friendship, Alta got nervous. She said she had been scalped by me in a previous lifetime and Indian drums got to her.

"Le Anne, what are those drums saying? Do they make you want to go to war? Does that sound make you want to start scalping people? Is that drumbeat getting to you the way it's getting to me? How does it feel?"

"Yeah, it's gettin' to me. You're gettin' to me, again, Alta. Maybe you should go inside, Alta, before I reach for my knife and hey, you know what happened last time."

Carla dragged Alta away by coaxing her into another rock shop. Alta looked back to see if I was serious, which I was, but knowing Alta, what she really wanted was more crystals. Crystals talk to Alta and tell her what to do. Who she's been. Who we've been. Where she's going. Where we're going. What's getting to her. What's gettin' to me.

But like, who am I to quibble with success? They say God lives in the Crystal Cathedral. (California, right?)

Actually, when you're Indian, you learn people are always telling you how Indians feel about everything.

"Don't you Indians, like ah-h, see yourselves, ah-h, as just transcending this time, space continuum thing? Yeah, like ah-h, you all practiced this kind of Indian-Zen thing? Right?

"Indian huh? Didn't you used to be white?"

"Indians. Hey you're human too. You don't really feel any different than the rest of us. You put your pants on one leg at a time, Missy, so just stop that nonsense. It's just like, all in your head.

"Indians, I thought you were all dead?"

Priscilla Davis, this really nice white teacher I met while on vacation, told me that she taught on the Pine Ridge Reservation. She said that Indians don't talk much, but that when we say something it's always profound and fraught with meaning.

I just looked at her.

"Oh yeah," she said. "Did you know that Indian women are very jealous of their men?"

I deadpan. "White woman speak truth!"

Don't you get it?

I recently came back from an archaeologist conference in South Dakota on the Ethical Treatment of the Dead and Indians.

I listened to dozens of archaeologists tell us how we felt about the time, space continuum thing. About what diseases got to us.

About how back in the old days, say, one hundred years ago, Indians had small gene pools so we must have practiced incest. But by grinding our skeletons and sawing our skulls apart for analysis they didn't find any evidence of incest. Dr. Jekkell a physical anthropologist who has spent his life dissolving our skeletal remains said that while their facts were inconclusive they were going to keep on looking. Keep on cutting. Keep on trying. Keep on digging us up. He was gonna get to us somehow.

Am I gettin' to you?

I myself like what Edward Galeano said. "Throughout America, from north to south, the dominant culture acknowledges Indians as objects of study, but denies them as subjects of history. Indians have folklore, not culture, they practice superstitions, not religion, they speak dialects, not languages, they make crafts not arts. . . ."

Doesn't it get to you, somehow?

In 1971 in Iowa a road crew unearthed a cemetary. Twenty-six of the bodies were white. They also found one Indian woman and her baby. The whites were placed in new coffins and reburied. The Indian and her baby were boxed up and sent to Iowa City for study.

They got to her, all right. Am I getting to you?

It seems it wasn't enough that the aliens wanted to capture our souls for a once-a-week alien God, they wanted to own our physical bodies. That's why in 1989 Governor Bill Clements of Texas vetoed a bill which would have protected unmarked Indian graves in the Lone Star State. The collectors and grave robbers from Dallas can still get to Indian graves in Texas without being charged with a crime. Ironically Governor Bill told listeners at a state archaeologist meeting that his fantasy profession was to be an archaeologist. But, like ah-h, he went into politics, instead. . . .

He got to us, all right. Am I getting to you?

Does it get to you, somehow?

Probably if I had to think of only one thing Indians represented in our collective histories, it would be that we were the first environmentalists. The first environmental advocates.

We made heap big speeches to Great White Father. "As long as sky blue, grass green and rivers flow."

Hey, that shit didn't fly and the grass ain't green, the sky ain't blue, and the rivers are full of trash. We didn't want to leave this place—this time, space continuum thing to you—but you wanted it. You got it. Now fix it!

Someone said once that lost causes were the only ones worth fighting for, worth dying for. They got to us, all right. But the poisons, man, they're gettin' to you, too.

Am I gettin' to you?
Is it gettin' to you, too?
I will get you, too.
Because, my country (this is my country) tis' of me, tis of thee. First. Last. And Forever.
Am I gettin' to you, somehow?
I will get to you. Somehow.
Because, together,
man, woman, child, all that exists,
Together, we can
GET IT
Together.

THE RED WARS

I can catch all the flies for you, Mama.
I'll go to the flies' nest—Randy Craig, 1977.

Part I

He has long beautiful braids. Clear skin. He does not smoke cigarettes.

A slender man who looks to be about twenty-five. Maybe thirty. He is wearing a navy blue sport coat. Tight-fitting, new 501s. Expensive boots.

I smell him. He is interesting. He is Sioux.

Thunderhawk is not from Oklahoma. He is carrying a leather briefcase with beading on it. I think he must be rich.

He is raising money to help get Dennis Banks out of jail. He is in a hurry.

It is the early 1970s. I am working at the office of the ACLU.

A red-haired woman in the next room is raising money for AIM.

She is telephoning the Oklahoma City liberals. We know it won't take long.

He paces. We stare past each other, never capturing gazes, never out of sight of one another. His scent envelopes me. He touches me with his scent. He seduces me with his scent. I am drunk with his scent. He asks me if I am Indian. I say, Choctaw.

He says, "Of course."

Often, I think of the image of myself that day.

I am young with long straight hair and I do it to myself every day. Many times a day. Alone in the mornings, during my bath, alone at night. I can do it while sitting at my typewriter without moving. It is the image I delight in. The image I remember best. Secretive and silent. A hold over from home. No one guesses what goes on with the timid little receptionist. No one guesses what goes on with Indians when they are alone. The fights, the 49s, unspoken piety, unspoken wild. No one can know just by looking.

Thunderhawk knows of these things and ignores them. He moves closer to my desk. He talks on. He tells me I should join AIM and help build a better tomorrow for Indians.

LeAnne Howe's "The Red Wars" is reprinted with her permission from *A Stand Up Reader* (Into View Press, 1987).

He shows me a map where the new Indian Nation will be established. It will be carved out of a part of New Mexico. All Indians can move there.

He tells me AIM is going to get a seat on the United Nations. He says the seat will be sponsored by Norway.

Thunderhawk whispers about a stash of machine guns and weapons in the desert. He says Indians are going to make the United States take notice. He says Indians will get a separate nation, one way, or the other.

He reminds me of a black and white movie I've just seen on the late show. A drama. An American couple adopts a young boy from Germany after WWII. The boy has been brain-trained by the Nazis and rails at everyone in the movie. It's called, Tomorrow The World.

Thunderhawk tells me I should get involved.

"Come smoke with me, tonight. What are you doing here? Join us. Tomorrow, come with me. I will teach you things."

I tell him I have two babies I must raise. He says they will be taken care of, too.

I tell him I am a student earning credit by working for the ACLU and when I get my degree I will work as a tribal lawyer.

He says, "Of course."

He dismisses me, and alternately goes in and out of the next room. He's checking the redhead's progress.

When it is time to leave, he gives me an address and asks me to change my mind. He touches my hands. I say nothing. He calls me Choctaw, then braces himself and turns away.

At 6 p.m. I call the babysitter. I will be home in time to cook dinner. I put the phone down and smell the back of my hand.

Part II

We meet at a burial for an estranged skull. He is holding a bundle of sage and chanting for the dead in a language I don't understand.

I am reporter for the Dallas Morning News. I am there to see what this is all about.

He is wearing a ribbon shirt and sunglasses. His gray hair is long and braided on the nape of the neck. He is a chain smoker. Someone in the background calls him Chief.

I ask him what tribe is he? He says he is part Dakota and part Navajo. He says he was raised in New York.

I say, "Of course."

He invites me to his home. I am eager to learn why he is called Chief. And, I am hungry to be with Indians: Indians out of costume.

California Red Wing is the Chief of an Indian non-profit corporation. He calls himself a man of medicine. He says he conducts sweats and ceremonies and has learned the prayers from a medicine man who lives on a South Dakota reservation.

California Red Wing says there is another group of Indians in Dallas similar to his not-for-profit group. He says they are fighting him. He tells me they are no good and only in it for the money. He says his group and the Dallas group are always in competition for grant money. He says the Dallas group wants the Texas Sesquicentennial Commission in Austin to proclaim them the only Indian non-profit organization of Texas. California Red Wing says his group will fight over this question until the bitter end.

I tell him I don't understand.

He says things are different in Texas than in Oklahoma. He says they can let you in or keep you out.

I ask who are they?

The telephone interrupts. A woman has been killed in Lake Worth, Texas. Someone is asking California Red Wing to bury her the Indian way. He agrees. He hangs up. He says his heart is heavy. He says the girl was only seventeen and the only black member of his non-profit corporation. He tells me she was part Indian on her mother's side.

I say nothing. I show no emotion. It is a learned thing. I look at California Red Wing. He still wears his sunglasses.

I leave and drive to the nearest bar.

Part III

He is standing at the bar. Short-sleeves rolled up. Flat-top hair. Dark blue shirt, unbuttoned to the third button.

His skin is tanned dark red. His neck-skin is micropitted like the skin of a winesap apple.

His name is Jim or Jack. I will called him Jim-Jack.

We are at a country club in West Columbia, Texas. We are being introduced because he is said to be Indian of some stripe.

He says he builds houses and introduces me to his wife, Betty or Margaret. I will call her BM.

As always the topic turns to what tribe and where from?

We discover we are both from Oklahoma. He says he is Cherokee.

I say, "Naturally."

We talk.

Jim-Jack says he doesn't relate with most Indians. He says he has never asked the government for one thing. He says he's a self-made man.

I say Indians don't get welfare because they are "Indians."

He says most Indians get Indian money. I say they don't. He says his grandparents do. He tells me they live on dirt around the Arkansas River Damn project and that his people want the government to buy, not only the dirt, but, the rocks off the top of the ground. Jim-Jack says he's embarrassed by this. He says his people are trying to gyp the government.

BM giggles and offers to buy me another drink. I say make it a double. BM orders dirty gin martinis.

We drink. Jim-Jack placates me. He says he's for supporting American Indian museums. He wants us to remember our past.

We argue. Jim-Jack says the government should obliterate reservations and set Indians free. Jim-Jack says he wants Indians off the government tit. He says Indians can be proud again if they learn to survive without government assistance.

We order more drinks. I offer to buy his dirty gin. I get loud. I want to fist-fight with Jim-Jack.

I start the uproar by asking Jim-Jack if he's related to BIA boss Ross Swimmer? I ask Jim-Jack if he's a Reagan man?

He answers no to both questions and doesn't understand I am about to smack him in the face with my martini glass.

Rage. Rage. Rage. Indians are not a corporation.

Rage. Rage. Rage. Indians will not die so they can be well thought of. So they can become part of a traveling museum exhibit at SMU.

Rage. Rage. Rage. I will castrate this man, this cultural eunuch with my hands, with my head, with my body. I will emasculate him in the name of Red rights, in the name of Red earth, in the name of my Indian grandmother who is no longer living.

Rage. Rage. Rage. I will smite thine alien-enemy who's tongue is covered with hair.

I am drunk and I realize I have seen too many Cecil B. De Mille movies.

I turn and see the image of my grandmother in the mirror. She is standing at the bar, beside the self-made man holding a martini glass. She is silent and sad. I put the glass down.

INDEX

371